ROME

this fourth edition updated by

NATASHA FOGES

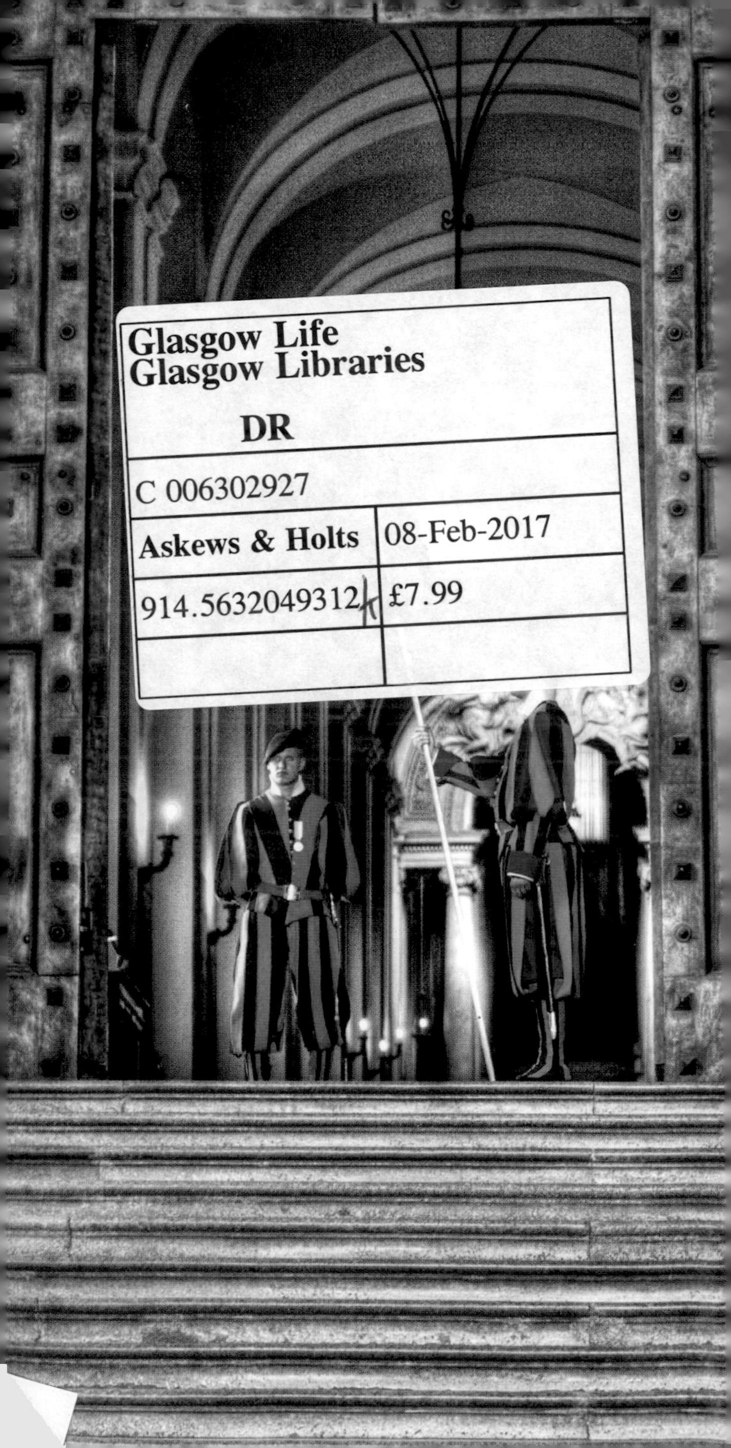

Contents

<< ROME SKYLINE
< SWISS GUARDS AT THE VATICAN

INTRODUCTION TO

ROME

When most people think of Rome they imagine sights and monuments: the Colosseum, Forum, the Vatican and St Peter's. Yet it is much more than an open-air museum: the city has constantly reinvented itself over the years, and with its unpretentious outlook, vibrant people, culture and food it has a modern and irresistible edge. As a historic place, it is special enough, but as a contemporary European capital, it is unique.

TREVI FOUNTAIN

Best places for the perfect Roman pizza

There are loads of great pizzerias in Rome that serve up traditional thin, crispy pizzas with the usual accompaniments of *suppli* and *fiori di zucca*. Most are open evenings only; if you want a lunchtime slice of pizza – *pizza al taglio* – try *Lo Zozzone* (see p.47), *Pizzarium* (see p.155) or *Il Forno di Campo de'Fiori* (see p.57). **THESE ARE OUR OTHER FAVOURITES > Emma p.58 > La Montecarlo p.48 > Li Rioni p.111 > Da Remo p.122**

Rome's eras crowd in on top of one another to a remarkable degree: there are medieval churches atop ancient basilicas and palaces, houses and apartment blocks that incorporate fragments of Roman columns and inscriptions, and roads and piazzas that follow the lines of ancient amphitheatres and stadiums. It's not an easy place to absorb on one visit, and you need to take things slowly, even if you have only a couple of days here. Most of the sights can be approached from a number of directions, and part of the allure of Rome is stumbling across things by accident, gradually piecing the city together, rather than marching around to a timetable. It's best to decide on a few key attractions (check out our ideas in "Best of Rome") and see where your feet take you. Above all, don't be afraid to just wander.

You'd certainly be mad to risk your blood pressure in any kind of vehicle, and the best way of getting around the city centre is to walk. The same goes for the ancient sites, and probably the Vatican and Trastevere quarter too – although for these last two you might want to jump on a bus or a tram going across the river. Keep public transport for longer hops – down to Testaccio, Ostiense or EUR, or to the catacombs and the Via Appia Antica, and of course for trips outside the city: to Ostia Antica, Tivoli or nearby beaches.

ALFRESCO EATING BY THE PANTHEON

However you get around, the atmosphere is like no other city – a monumental, busy capital and yet an appealingly relaxed one, with a centre that has yet to be consumed by chainstores and multinational hotels. Above all, there has perhaps never been a better time to visit. Rome has recently been hauled into the twenty-first century: museums, churches and other buildings that had been "in restoration" as long as anyone can remember have reopened, and some of the city's historic collections have been re-housed. Plus, the city's cultural life has been enhanced, with frequent open-air concerts and a flourishing film festival in October. Transport, too, is being tackled, with the construction of a third metro line, although it may be some time before this is finished.

Whether all this will irrevocably alter the character of the city remains to be seen – the enhanced crowds of visitors, spurred on by the growth of cheap flights in recent years, are certainly having a go. But it's a resilient place, with a character like no other, and for now at least there's definitely no place like Rome.

When to visit

You can enjoy Rome at any time of year. However, you should, if you can, avoid coming in July and especially August, when it can be uncomfortably hot and most Romans are on holiday – indeed in August you may find many of the restaurants recommended in this book closed. May, June and September are the most pleasant months weather-wise – warm but not unbearably so, and not too humid. April and October can be nice too – the city is less crowded, outside Easter, and days can still be warm and sunny. The winter months can be a good time to visit, but bear in mind that the weather is unpredictable and, while you'll find everything pleasantly uncrowded, some attractions will have reduced opening hours.

ROME AT A GLANCE

>>EATING

Food is one of the highlights of any trip to Rome. You won't really eat badly anywhere: there are lots of good choices in the Centro Storico; the **Ghetto** and **Testaccio** have a large number of places serving traditional Roman food, while the densest concentration of restaurants of all kinds can be found in **Trastevere**. There's also an abundance of good, honest **pizzerias**, churning out thin, crispy pizza from wood-fired ovens. Be wary of restaurants adjacent to the major monuments. Note that many places are closed during August.

>>DRINKING

Many Roman bars are traditionally daytime haunts, but there are now also plenty of bars and pubs conducive to an evening's drinking, and the city's old-fashioned wine bars or *enoteche* have also become more popular in recent years. The Milanese tradition of *aperitivi* has taken off in bars throughout the city; many places put on a free buffet at around 6–7pm to attract pre-dinner drinkers. Wherever you are, you can drink late – most places are open until at least 1am – but **Campo de' Fiori** and the **Centro Storico** near Piazza Navona, and the nightlife districts of **Trastevere**, **Testaccio** and **Pigneto** are the liveliest areas in the city centre.

>>SHOPPING

The opening of new flagship stores for the likes of Valentino and Fendi have re-energized Rome's shopping scene in recent years. For designer fashion, head to the streets close to the **Spanish Steps** – Via Condotti, Via Borgognona and Via del Babuino. Nearby **Via del Corso** offers young, affordable fashion; for smarter wares try **Via Cola di Rienzo** in Prati. There are lots of independent boutiques around **Campo de' Fiori** and in **Monti**, and antique shops line **Via dei Coronari**. For foodie souvenirs try the markets on Campo de' Fiori and in **Testaccio**. The Sunday **Porta Portese** flea market is a quintessentially Roman experience.

>>NIGHTLIFE

There's a concentration of clubs in **Ostiense** and **Testaccio**, while **Trastevere**, and the **Centro Storico** from the Jewish Ghetto to the Pantheon, are good for bars, with the odd backstreet club. The **San Lorenzo** and **Pigneto** areas near Termini have plenty of laidback, studenty hangouts, often with live music. More alternative places are run as private clubs – usually known as *centri sociali*, where entry will be free but you may be stung for a membership fee. In summer, Roman nightlife centres on the Tiber, with pop-up venues and food stalls along its banks.

OUR RECOMMENDATIONS FOR WHERE TO EAT, DRINK AND SHOP ARE LISTED AT THE END OF EACH PLACES CHAPTER

Day One in Rome

1 Capitoline Hill > p.62. Rome began here, and the two museums that flank the elegant square are among the city's key sights.

2 Roman Forum > p.68. Some of the most ruined ruins you'll see, but also the most atmospheric.

3 Colosseum > p.66. The most recognizable and perhaps the greatest ancient Roman monument of them all.

Lunch > p.104. Enjoying the good, traditional Roman food at *Valentino*, it's hard to believe you're just a few minutes from the Colosseum.

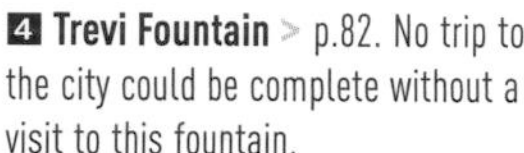

4 Trevi Fountain > p.82. No trip to the city could be complete without a visit to this fountain.

5 Piazza di Spagna > p.78. The Spanish Steps, Keats-Shelley House and the square itself are among the city's most compelling attractions.

6 Ara Pacis > p.82. Enclosed in an impressive purpose-built structure, the amazing frieze here depicts the imperial family during the time of Augustus.

7 Galleria Borghese > p.135. The Bernini sculptures here are the pure essence of Rome (be sure to book in advance).

Dinner > p.132. A meal in lively Trastevere is a must – and you can't go wrong with a slap-up dinner at *La Gensola*.

Ice cream > p.88. *San Crispino* serves arguably the city's best ice cream.

Day Two in Rome

1 St Peter's > p.146. It would be a pity to leave Rome without seeing the city's greatest Baroque attraction.

2 Vatican Museums > p.147. So much more than the Sistine Chapel – this staggering complex of museums is not to be missed.

Lunch > p.155. *Dal Toscano*, a long-established Tuscan restaurant close by the Vatican walls, is a good place to recover from museum fatigue.

3 Piazza Navona > p.40. One of the Centro Storico's loveliest open spaces, and close to the church of San Luigi dei Francesi and Palazzo Altemps.

4 Campo de' Fiori > p.52. Wander through Campo de' Fiori – many people's favourite Roman square – and explore the surrounding streets, full of shops and cafés.

5 The Pantheon > p.34. Rome's most intact ancient sight, and near one of the city's great churches, Santa Maria sopra Minerva.

6 The Ghetto > p.55. Stroll through the crumbling old Jewish quarter, an ancient part of the city centre.

Dinner > p.58. *Piperno* is one of the Ghetto's best restaurants, with fantastic Roman-Jewish cooking served in lovely surroundings.

Ice cream > p.57. *Alberto Pica* is one of the longest running and best of Rome's many *gelaterie*.

1

2

Budget Rome

Rome's piazzas, fountains and other public structures are fantastic, and many of its churches packed with sumptuous art. The big sights can be pricey, though – it's worth timing your visit around the first Sunday of the month, when Rome's state-run museums and monuments are free to all.

1 Santa Maria del Popolo > p.80. Start out at one of the city's most beautiful churches, where two works by Caravaggio can be viewed in their original setting – and for free.

2 Spanish Steps > p.79. All you need is energy to climb to the top and enjoy the views.

3 Trevi Fountain > p.82. The only cost is the coins you decide to chuck in.

Lunch > p.57. *Il Forno di Campo de' Fiori* is renowned for its pizza by the slice.

4 Vittoriano > p.61. Free to clamber up the steps and enjoy the views – though you pay for the lifts to the very top.

5 St Peter's > p.146. There's no entry fee for this or any other Roman church.

6 Vatican Museums > p.147. Free on the last Sunday of the month – perhaps the world's greatest sightseeing bargain.

Dinner > p.155. Head up to *Mondo Arancina* for some of the city's best *arancini* – just €2.50 a pop.

Ice cream > p.154. *Fatamorgana* serves huge portions of delicious ice cream.

Secret Rome

You could spend several days seeing Rome's most obvious sights, and you'd have a wonderful time – mostly with lots of other people. Here are some suggestions for having a great day out in the city, while avoiding the crowds.

1 Piazza dei Cavalieri di Malta > p.113. Peer through the ornate keyhole and you'll be rewarded with a special view – best enjoyed at sunset. Well worth the trek up the Aventine Hill.

2 Rooms of St Ignatius > p.51. Take in the small museum next door to the Gesù; it incorporates the rooms where St Ignatius stayed and a fantastic trompe l'oeil painting by Andrea Pozzo.

3 Galleria Colonna > p.83. Only open on a Saturday morning, and partly because of this an undiscovered treasure among the city's great family palace-galleries.

Lunch > p.89. Tucked away around the corner from the Trevi Fountain, *Colline Emiliane* does delicious Emilian food.

4 Casa de Chirico > p.78. Don't miss this "house" museum, left just as it was when the artist lived and worked here.

5 Santi Quattro Coronati > p.107. The frescoes in the chapel of St Sylvester here are really something special.

6 Museo Storico della Liberazione > p.110. Housed in the wartime headquarters of the Gestapo, this is one of Rome's most moving museums.

Dinner > p.111. Close by San Giovanni, *Charly's Sauciere* is a long-established French food outpost that is little known by tourists.

BEST OF ROME

Museums and galleries

1 Vatican Museums Home to the largest, richest, most diverse and most dazzling collections in the world. > **p.147**

2 Capitoline Museums Two amazing galleries – one displaying Roman sculpture, the other Roman sculpture and Italian art. > **p.62**

3 Galleria Borghese Fabulous Bernini sculpture and one of Rome's best picture galleries, housed in the Borghese family villa. > **p.135**

4 Museo Nazionale Romano You'll find the finest art collection in this museum's two main locations: Palazzo Altemps and Palazzo Massimo. > **p.38 & p.99**

5 Galleria Doria Pamphilj Private art collection that's intimately exhibited. > **p.74**

Viewpoints

1 St Peter's It's worth the climb up the dome to see this classic panorama. > **p.144**

2 Vittoriano Many people's favourite view of Rome, because you can't see the Vittoriano monument itself. > **p.61**

3 Janiculum Hill Of all Rome's hills, this one, to the west of the city centre, gives the fullest panorama of Rome. > **p.129**

4 Spanish Steps Tourist Central, but ignore the crowds – the whole of Rome's centre is spread out before you. > **p.79**

5 Aventine Hill The best views of the Vatican are from the top of Aventine Hill on the other side of the river. > **p.112**

Eating out

1 Roman specialities Sample traditional "poor" cuisine at *Checchino dal 1887*; the oxtail stew is a classic. > **p.122**

2 Eating alfresco Dining outdoors at *Dar Filettaro a Santa Barbara* gives you a great view of the evening *passeggiata*. > p.58

3 Pizza With a thin, crispy base and the freshest of toppings, the pizza at *Da Remo* is irresistible. > p.122

4 Backstreet trattorias Unassuming, tucked-away trattorias can be full of surprises; old-timer *Da Tonino* is a gem. > p.48

5 Fine dining For a blow-the-budget meal, Rome's clutch of Michelin-starred restaurants won't disappoint. Roy Caceres' *Metamorfosi* is our pick. > p.141

Shopping

1 Campo de' Fiori This long-standing fruit and veg market takes place every morning except Sunday; in the surrounding streets you'll find countless independent boutiques. > **p.52**

2 Via del Corso This narrow street, lined with all the mid-range chains, is jam-packed with shoppers at weekends. > **p.74**

3 Via Condotti Lined with eye-wateringly expensive boutiques, this is the main spine of Rome's designer shopping quarter. > **p.78**

4 Via dei Coronari Rome's antiques alley, lined with shops selling everything from Renaissance chests to 1960s Italian coffeepots. > **p.40**

5 Monti Browse Monti's independent boutiques for cool clothes and chic homewares. > **p.101**

Palaces

1 Palazzo Farnese Perhaps the city's most elegant palace, now the French embassy, whose Carracci murals are one of the city's must-sees. > **p.54**

2 Villa Farnesina This Trastevere mansion was home to the banker Agostino Chigi, who employed Raphael to do the decorating. > p.128

3 Palazzo Spada The home of one Cardinal Spada is perhaps best known for its ingenious Borromini trompe l'oeil tunnel. > p.53

4 Palazzo Barberini The Barberini family's palace is one of the most sumptuous in Rome, and it also houses remarkable collections of art. > p.84

5 Palazzo del Quirinale The residence of the Italian president can now be visited on guided tours. > p.86

Churches

1 Santa Maria Maggiore One of the great Roman basilicas, and a treasure trove of art and history. > **p.93**

2 Santa Maria sopra Minerva Rome's only Gothic church is also rich in Renaissance art, fronted by Bernini's endearing Elephant Statue.. > p.34

4 San Pietro in Vincoli A beautifully plain church, home to one of Michelangelo's greatest sculptures. > p.96

3 St Peter's Basilica Italy's largest church is stuffed with masterpieces, most notably Michelangelo's *Pietà* and Bernini's baldacchino. > p.146

5 San Clemente This ancient Roman church is the best place to appreciate the city's multi-layered history. > p.100

Ancient Rome

1 Colosseum The most photographed of Rome's monuments – it has provided the blueprint for virtually all sports stadiums since. > **p.66**

2 The Pantheon An amazing building even in its time, but all the more incredible now, given how completely it has survived. > **p.34**

3 The Roman Forum Political, economic and religious hub of ancient Rome, the Forum is a must see. > **p.60**

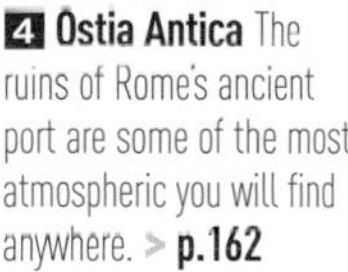

4 Ostia Antica The ruins of Rome's ancient port are some of the most atmospheric you will find anywhere. > **p.162**

5 Domus Aurea Nero's fascinating Golden House has recently reopened after a lengthy restoration. > **p.92**

Baroque Rome

1 Palazzo Barberini Check out Pietro da Cortona's ceiling, gushingly appropriate for the main patrons of the Baroque movement. > **p.84**

2 Santa Maria della Vittoria The daring statue of the *Ecstasy of St Theresa* by Bernini is perhaps the city's most dramatic piece of Baroque art. > **p.86**

3 San Carlo alle Quattro Fontane With four lovely fountains outside, this church is a masterpiece in Baroque design. > **p.85**

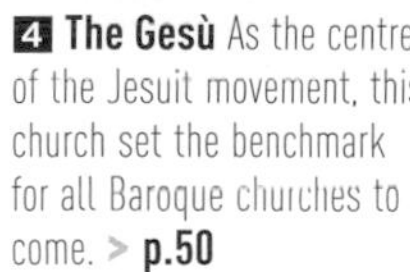

4 The Gesù As the centre of the Jesuit movement, this church set the benchmark for all Baroque churches to come. > **p.50**

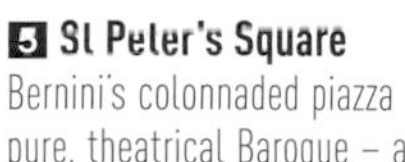

5 St Peter's Square Bernini's colonnaded piazza is pure, theatrical Baroque – as is the church itself. > **p.143**

Outdoor Rome

1 Villa Borghese Rome's largest and most central open space, and by any standards a beautiful and diverse city park. > **p.134**

2 Tivoli Tivoli's two Renaissance gardens are among the region's most compelling sights, and are just 45 minutes from the city centre. > **p.156**

3 Janiculum Hill Some of the best views of the city are from this hill just above Trastevere. > **p.129**

4 Via Appia Antica Though relatively close to the city centre, the Via Appia Antica feels like real countryside and is full of intriguing sights from ancient times. > **p.118**

5 Villa Celimontana Just above the Colosseum, this little park is a good venue for shady picnics. > **p.106**

PLACES

The Centro Storico

The heart of Rome is the Centro Storico ("historic centre"), which makes up most of the triangular knob of land that bulges into a bend in the Tiber. This area, known in ancient Roman times as the Campus Martius, was outside the ancient city centre and mostly given over to barracks and sporting arenas, together with several temples, including the Pantheon. Later it became the heart of the Renaissance city, and nowadays it's the part of the town that is densest in interest, a knot of narrow streets and alleys that hold some of the best of Rome's churches and monuments and its most vivacious street- and nightlife. Whichever direction you wander in there's something to see; indeed its appeal is that even the most aimless ambling leads you past some memorably beautiful and historic spots.

THE PANTHEON

Piazza della Rotonda. Mon–Sat 9.30am–7.30pm, Sun 9am–6pm; free.

MAP PP.36–37, POCKET MAP E15

One of the Centro Storico's busiest sights, the **Pantheon** is the most complete ancient Roman structure in the city, and along with the Colosseum, visually the most impressive. Though originally a temple that formed part of Marcus Agrippa's redesign of the Campus Martius in around 27 BC – hence the inscription – the building was rebuilt by the emperor Hadrian and finished around the year 125 AD. Since consecrated as a church, it's a formidable architectural achievement even now, and inside you get the best impression of the engineering expertise of the time: the diameter is precisely equal to its height (43m), the hole in the centre of the dome – from which shafts of sunlight descend to illuminate the musty interior – a full 9m across. Most impressively, there are no visible arches or vaults to hold the whole thing up; instead they're sunk into the concrete of the walls of the building. It would have been richly decorated, the coffered ceiling heavily stuccoed and the niches filled with the statues of gods. Now, apart from the sheer size of the place, the main object of interest is the tomb of Raphael, between the second and third chapels on the left, with an inscription by the humanist cardinal Pietro Bembo: "Living, great Nature feared he might outvie Her works, and dying, fears herself may die." The same kind of sentiments might well have been reserved for the Pantheon itself.

SANTA MARIA SOPRA MINERVA

Piazza della Minerva 42. Mon–Fri 6.45am–7pm, Sat 6.45am–12.30pm & 3.30–7pm, Sun 8am–12.30pm & 3.30–7pm.

MAP PP.36–37, POCKET MAP E15

THE PANTHEON

Piazza della Minerva is home to the medieval church of **Santa Maria sopra Minerva**, Rome's only Gothic church, and one of the city's art-treasure churches, with the Carafa chapel, in the south transept, home to Filippino Lippi's fresco of the *Assumption*. The children visible in the foreground are portraits of the future Medici popes, Leo X and Clement VII, whose tombs lie either side of the main altar. Look also at the figure of *Christ Bearing the Cross*, just in front, a serene work that Michelangelo completed for the church in 1521. Outside, the diminutive **Elephant Statue** is Bernini's most endearing piece of work: a cheery elephant trumpeting under the weight of the obelisk he carries on his back – a reference to Pope Alexander VII and supposed to illustrate the fact that strength should support wisdom.

SANT'IGNAZIO

Via del Caravita 8a. Jan–July & Sept–Dec Mon–Sat 7.30am–7pm, Sun 9am–7pm; Aug daily 9am–7pm. MAP PP.36–37, POCKET MAP F15

The Jesuit church of **Sant'Ignazio** was dedicated to the founder of the Society of Jesus after his death and canonization. It's worth visiting for its Baroque ceiling by Andrea Pozzo, showing St Ignatius being welcomed into paradise by Christ and the Virgin, a spectacular work that creates the illusion of looking at the sky through open colonnades. Pozzo also painted the ingenious false dome in the crossing (a real dome was planned but was deemed too expensive). Stand on the disc in nave's centre to get the full effect of this trompe l'oeil masterpiece.

PIAZZA DI PIETRA

On the northern side of Piazza Sant'Ignazio lies **Piazza di Pietra**, an attractive open space dominated by the giant Corinthian columns of an ancient Roman temple, built by Antoninus Pius in 145 AD in memory of his father, Hadrian. The hotly contested outdoor tables at *La Caffetteria* (see p.46) allow you to sit and enjoy the view.

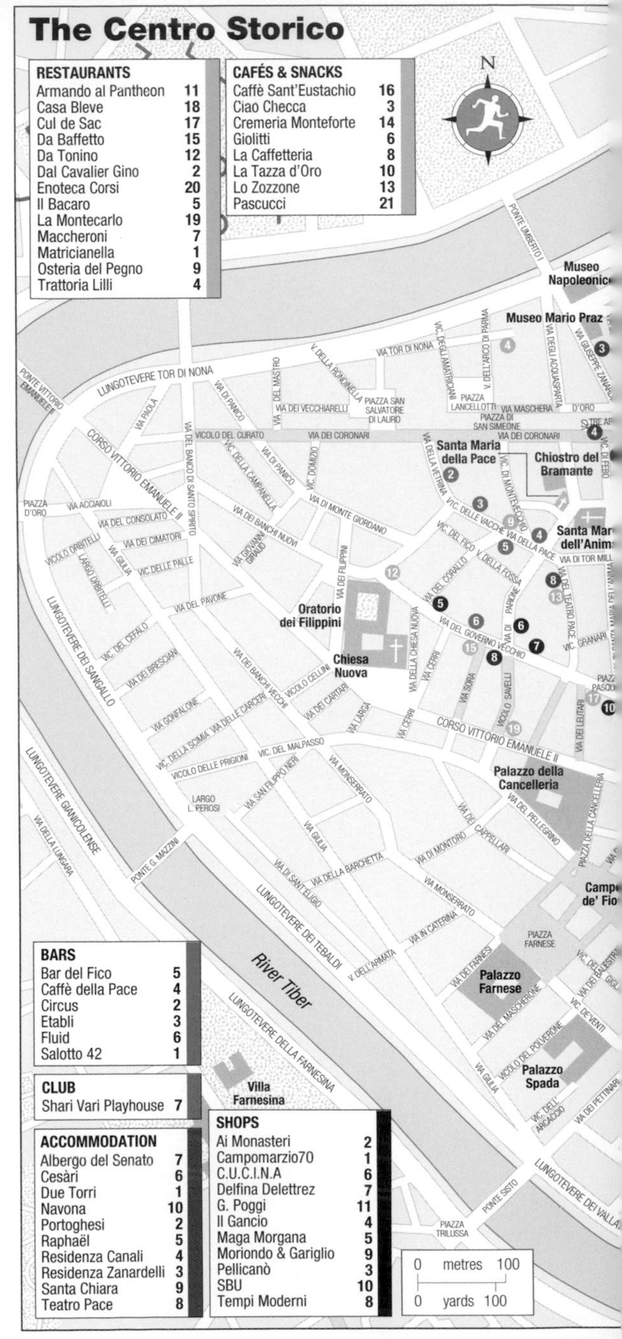
The Centro Storico
RESTAURANTS
Armando al Pantheon 11
Casa Bleve 18
Cul de Sac 17
Da Baffetto 15
Da Tonino 12
Dal Cavalier Gino 2
Enoteca Corsi 20
Il Bacaro 5
La Montecarlo 19
Maccheroni 7
Matricianella 1
Osteria del Pegno 9
Trattoria Lilli 4
CAFÉS & SNACKS
Caffè Sant'Eustachio 16
Ciao Checca 3
Cremeria Monteforte 14
Giolitti 6
La Caffetteria 8
La Tazza d'Oro 10
Lo Zozzone 13
Pascucci 21
N
BARS
Bar del Fico 5
Caffè della Pace 4
Circus 2
Etabli 3
Fluid 6
Salotto 42 1
CLUB
Shari Vari Playhouse 7
ACCOMMODATION
Albergo del Senato 7
Cesàri 6
Due Torri 1
Navona 10
Portoghesi 2
Raphaël 5
Residenza Canali 4
Residenza Zanardelli 3
Santa Chiara 9
Teatro Pace 8
SHOPS
Ai Monasteri 2
Campomarzio70 1
C.U.C.I.N.A 6
Delfina Delettrez 7
G. Poggi 11
Il Gancio 4
Maga Morgana 5
Moriondo & Gariglio 9
Pellicanò 3
SBU 10
Tempi Moderni 8
0 metres 100
0 yards 100
Museo Napoleonico
Museo Mario Praz
Santa Maria della Pace
Chiostro del Bramante
Oratorio dei Filippini
Chiesa Nuova
Palazzo della Cancelleria
Palazzo Farnese
Palazzo Spada
Villa Farnesina
River Tiber
PONTE UMBERTO I
PONTE VITTORIO EMANUELE II
PONTE G. MAZZINI
PONTE SISTO
LUNGOTEVERE TOR DI NONA
LUNGOTEVERE DEI SANGALLO
LUNGOTEVERE GIANICOLENSE
LUNGOTEVERE DEI TEBALDI
LUNGOTEVERE DELLA FARNESINA
CORSO VITTORIO EMANUELE II
VIA DEI CORONARI
VIA GIULIA
VIA DEI BANCHI NUOVI
VIA DEI BANCHI VECCHI
VIA DEL GOVERNO VECCHIO
VIA DI MONTE GIORDANO
VIA DEL PELLEGRINO
VIA MONSERRATO
PIAZZA FARNESE
PIAZZA TRILUSSA
PIAZZA D'ORO
PIAZZA LANCELLOTTI
PIAZZA SAN SALVATORE DI LAURO
PIAZZA DI SAN SIMEONE
LARGO L. PEROSI

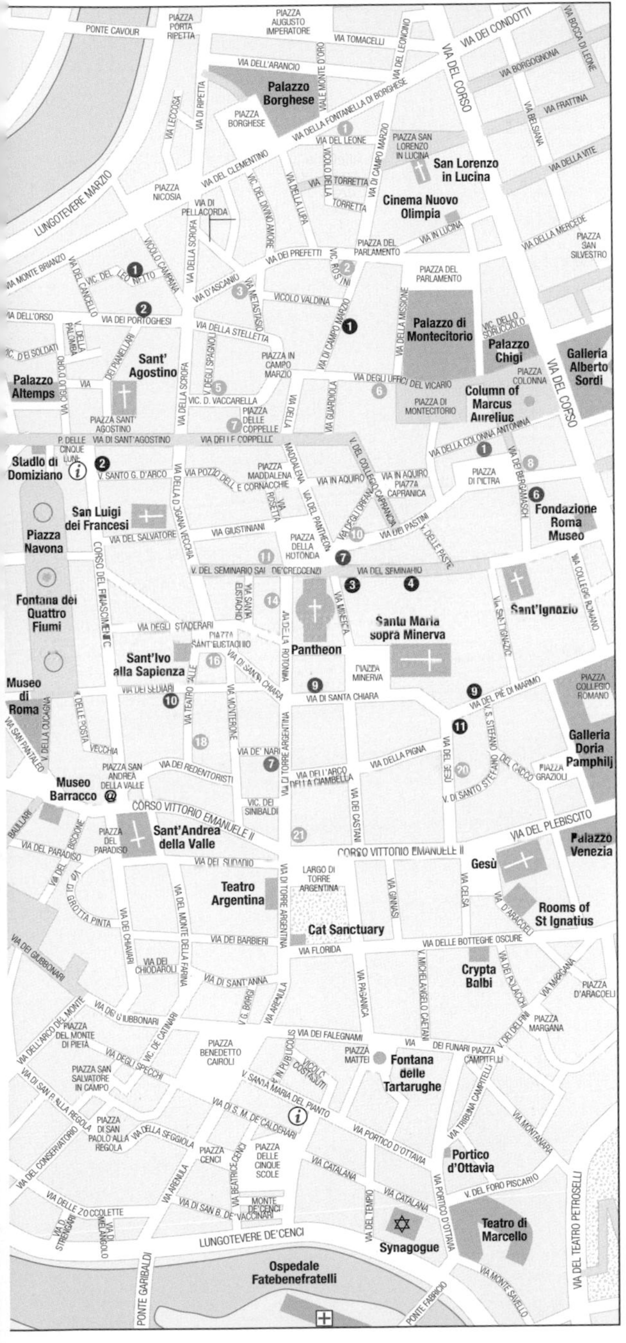
Palazzo Borghese
San Lorenzo in Lucina
Cinema Nuovo Olimpia
Palazzo di Montecitorio
Palazzo Chigi
Galleria Alberto Sordi
Column of Marcus Aurelius
Sant' Agostino
Palazzo Altemps
Stadio di Domiziano
San Luigi dei Francesi
Piazza Navona
Fontana dei Quattro Fiumi
Fondazione Roma Museo
Sant'Ignazio
Santa Maria sopra Minerva
Pantheon
Sant'Ivo alla Sapienza
Museo di Roma
Galleria Doria Pamphilj
Museo Barracco
Sant'Andrea della Valle
Palazzo Venezia
Gesù
Teatro Argentina
Rooms of St Ignatius
Cat Sanctuary
Crypta Balbi
Fontana delle Tartarughe
Portico d'Ottavia
Teatro di Marcello
Synagogue
Ospedale Fatebenefratelli
VIA DEL CORSO
CORSO VITTORIO EMANUELE II
VIA DEL PLEBISCITO
LUNGOTEVERE MARZIO
LUNGOTEVERE DE'CENCI
PONTE CAVOUR
PONTE GARIBALDI
PONTE FABRICIO

PIAZZA DI MONTECITORIO AND PIAZZA COLONNA

MAP PP.36–37, POCKET MAP E14–15

On the northern edge of the Centro Storico, **Piazza Montecitorio** takes its name from the bulky Palazzo di Montecitorio on its northern side, home since 1871 to the lower house of the Italian parliament (open first Sun of each month 10am–6pm; free). Just beyond, **Piazza Colonna**, flanked on its north side by the late sixteenth-century Palazzo Chigi, official residence of the prime minister, hosts the **Column of Marcus Aurelius,** erected 180–190 AD to commemorate military victories in northern Europe, and, like the column of Trajan which inspired it, decorated with scenes from the campaigns.

SANT'AGOSTINO

Piazza di Sant'Agostino. Daily 7.30am–noon & 4–7.30pm. MAP PP.36–37, POCKET MAP D14

The Renaissance facade of the church of **Sant'Agostino** is not much to look at from the outside, but a handful of art treasures might draw you in – this was the church of Rome's creative community in the sixteenth century and as such drew wealthy patrons and well-connected artists. Just inside the door, the serene statue of the *Madonna del Parto*, by Sansovino is traditionally invoked during pregnancy, and is accordingly surrounded by photos of newborn babes and their blissful parents. Further into the church, Raphael's vibrant fresco of *Isaiah* is on the third pillar on the left, beneath which is another work by Sansovino – a craggy *St Anne, Virgin and Child.* But the biggest crowds gather around the first chapel on the left, where the *Madonna di Loreto*, painted in 1605 by Caravaggio, is a characteristic work of what was at the time almost revolutionary realism, scruffy clothes contrasting with the pale, delicate feet and skin of Mary.

PALAZZO ALTEMPS

Piazza di Sant'Apollinare 46 ⓣ06 3996 7700. Tues–Sun 9am–7.45pm. €7, includes Palazzo

PALAZZO ALTEMPS

Massimo, Terme di Diocleziano, Crypta Balbi, valid 3 days; free first Sun of the month. MAP PP.36–37, POCKET MAP D14

Just across the street from the north end of Piazza Navona, the beautifully restored fifteenth-century Palazzo Altemps now houses the cream of the **Museo Nazionale Romano**'s aristocratic collections of Roman statues. Among treasures too many to mention, there are two, almost identical renderings of Apollo the Lyrist, a magnificent statue of Athena taming a serpent, and, just off the far corner of the courtyard, a shameless Dionysus with a satyr and panther. Upstairs, the **Painted Views Room**, so-called for the bucolic scenes on its walls, has a fine statue of Hermes; the Cupboard Room, next door, named for its fresco of a display of wedding gifts against a floral background, has a wonderful statue of a warrior at rest, the *Ludovisi Ares*, restored by Bernini in 1622, and a sensitive portrayal of *Orestes and Electra*, from the first century AD by a sculptor called Menelaus his name is carved at the base of one of the figures. Beyond, one room retains a frieze telling the story of Moses as a cartoon strip, with each scene enacted by nude figures as if on an unfurled tapestry, while in the room itself there is a colossal head of Hera, and – what some consider the highlight of the entire collection – the famous **Ludovisi throne**: an original fifth-century BC Greek work embellished with a delicate relief portraying the birth of Aphrodite. There's also the **Great Room of Galata**, whose huge fireplace, embellished with caryatids and lurking ibex – the symbol of the Altemps family – looks onto the *Suicide of Galatian*, apparently commissioned by Julius Caesar to adorn his Quirinal estate, and an incredible sarcophagus depicting a battle in graphic, almost visceral sculptural detail. Without question, one of Rome's best collections of classical art.

COLUMN OF MARCUS AURELIUS

PALAZZO PRIMOLI

Via Zanardelli 1. MAP PP.36–37, POCKET MAP D14

Around the corner from Palazzo Altemps, the sixteenth-century **Palazzo Primoli** houses two minor museums. The **Museo Mario Praz** (hourly guided tours Thurs & Fri 2.30–7pm, Sat 9am–1.30pm; free; ⓣ06 686 1089), on the top floor, was the home of one Mario Praz, a teacher of English literature, art historian and writer who lived here until his death in 1982. Its nine rooms are stacked to the gills with books, magazines, paintings and ornate furniture; tours of the apartment give you a glimpse of the vanished way of life of an aesthete. On the ground floor, the **Museo Napoleonico** (Tues–Sun 10am–6pm; free; ⓣ06 687 4240, ⓦmuseonapoleonico.it) contains a rather weighty assortment of the personal effects of Napoleon, who lived in Rome in the 1820s.

VIA DEI CORONARI

MAP PP.36–37, POCKET MAP F13–15

Running from the Tiber to the top end of Piazza Navona, this is the fulcrum of Rome's **antiques** trade. Although the prices are as high as you might expect in such a location, there is a huge number of shops (Via dei Coronari itself consists of virtually nothing else), selling a large variety of stuff. A browse makes for one of the city's most absorbing bits of sightseeing.

PIAZZA NAVONA

MAP PP.36–37, POCKET MAP D14–15

The western half of the Centro Storico focuses on **Piazza Navona**, Rome's most famous square. Lined with cafés and restaurants and often thronged with tourists, street artists and pigeons, the best time to come is at night, when the flavour of the place is at its most vibrant, with crowds hanging out around the fountains watching the buskers and street artists or enjoying the scene while nursing a pricey drink at a table outside one of the bars. The square takes its shape from the first-century AD Stadium of Domitian, the principal venue of the athletic events and later chariot races that took place in the Campus Martius, and until the mid-fifteenth century the ruins of the arena were still here, overgrown and disused. It was given a facelift in the mid-seventeenth century by Pope Innocent X, who built most of the grandiose palaces that surround it and commissioned Borromini to redesign the church of **Sant'Agnese in Agone** (Tues–Sat 9.30am–12.30pm & 3.30–7pm, Sun 9am–1pm & 4–8pm) on the piazza's western side. One of three fountains that punctuate Piazza Navona, the **Fontana dei Quattro Fiumi** is a masterpiece by Bernini, built in 1651. Each figure represents one of what were considered at the time to be the four great rivers of the world – the Nile, Danube, Ganges and Plate – though only the horse, symbolizing the Danube, was actually carved by Bernini himself. The fountain is topped with an Egyptian obelisk, brought here by Pope Innocent X from the Circus of Maxentius.

SAN LUIGI DEI FRANCESI

Piazza San Luigi dei Francesi. Mon–Fri 9.30am–1pm & 2.30–6.30pm, Sat 9.30am–12.30pm & 2.30–6.30pm, Sun 11.30am–1pm & 2.30–6.30pm. MAP PP.36–37, POCKET MAP E14

The French national church of **San Luigi dei Francesi** is worth a visit, mainly for the works by Caravaggio it holds. In the last chapel on the left are three paintings: *The Calling of St Matthew*, in which Christ points to Matthew, who is illuminated by a shaft of sunlight; *St Matthew and the Angel*, showing the visit of an angel as the apostle writes

ANTIQUES SHOP ON VIA DEI CORONARI

his Gospel; and *The Martyrdom of St Matthew*. Caravaggio's first public commission, these paintings were rejected at first, partly on grounds of indecorum, and it took considerable reworking by the artist before they were finally accepted. These days they are considered to be among the artist's greatest ever works, especially *The Calling of St Matthew*, which manifests the simple, taut drama, as well as the low-life subject matter, for which Caravaggio became so well known.

PIAZZA NAVONA

STADIO DI DOMIZIANO

Via di Tor Sanguigna 3 ⓣ06 4568 6100, ⓦstadiodomiziano.com. Mon–Fri & Sun 10am–7pm, Sat 10am–8pm. €8. MAP PP.36–37, POCKET MAP D14

Just north of Piazza Navona lie the remains of the **Stadio di Domiziano** (Stadium of Domitian), built in around 86 AD by the emperor as a Roman venue for the Greek athletic games. The underground site holds the well-preserved remains of a small section of the stadium, which once held around 30,000 spectators. If you don't want to pay the steep entrance fee you can get a reasonable view from the balcony at street level.

SANT'IVO ALLA SAPIENZA

Corso del Rinascimento 40. Sun 9am–12.15pm; closed July & Aug. MAP PP.36–37, POCKET MAP E15

Between the Pantheon and Piazza Navona, the Palazzo della Sapienza cradles the church of **Sant'Ivo alla Sapienza** – from the outside at least, one of Rome's most impressive churches, with a playful facade designed by Carlo Borromini. Each of the two small towers is topped with the weird, blancmange-like groupings that are the symbol of the Chigi family and the central cupola spirals helter-skelter fashion to its zenith, crowned with flames that are supposed to represent the sting of the Barberini bee, their family symbol. Inside, too, it's very cleverly designed, impressively light and spacious given the small space the church is squeezed into, rising to the tall parabolic cupola.

SANTA MARIA DELL'ANIMA

Via di Santa Maria dell'Anima 66. Daily 9am–12.45pm & 3–7pm. MAP PP.36–37, POCKET MAP D14

Just off Via dei Coronari, this church takes its name from the statue of the Virgin on its facade, between two pleading souls in purgatory. It's another darkly cosy Roman church, wide and squat and crammed into an impossibly small space. Nowadays it's the German national church in Rome, a richly decorated affair, almost square in shape, with a protruding main sanctuary flanked by Renaissance tombs. The one on the right, a beautiful, rather sad concoction, is that of the last non-Italian pope before John Paul II, the Dutchman Hadrian VI, who died in 1523, while at the far end, above the altar, you can just make out a dark and glowing *Virgin with Saints* by Giulio Romano.

SANTA MARIA DELLA PACE

Via Arco della Pace 5. Mon, Wed, Sat 9am–noon; cloister open Mon–Fri 10am–8pm, Sat & Sun 10am–9pm. MAP PP.36–37, POCKET MAP D14

The church of **Santa Maria della Pace** dates from the late fifteenth century, although its facade and portico were added a couple of hundred years later by Pietro da Cortona. Inside, you can see Raphael's frescoes of various sibyls above the Chigi chapel (first on the right), executed in the early sixteenth century. Opening times are erratic, so if the church is closed, look in on the attached **chiostro del Bramante**, finished in 1504, a beautifully proportioned two-tiered cloister that nowadays holds temporary art exhibitions and a small café where you can grab a coffee and a spot of lunch (entry ticket to exhibition not required).

MUSEO DI ROMA

Piazza San Pantaleo 10 T 060608, W museodiroma.it. Tues–Sun 10am–7pm. €11, free first Sun of month. MAP PP.36–37, POCKET MAP D15

The eighteenth-century Palazzo Braschi is the home of the **Museo di Roma**, which has a permanent collection relating to Rome's history from the Middle Ages to the present day. The large museum is only sporadically interesting; the building is probably the main event, particularly the magnificent Sala Nobile where you go in, the main staircase and some of the renovated rooms. But some of the paintings are absorbing, showing the city during different eras. Frescoes from demolished palaces are highlights.

PIAZZA PASQUINO

MAP PP.36–37, POCKET MAP D15

Just off Piazza Navona, it's easy to miss the battered marble torso of Pasquino, in the corner of the small triangular space of Piazza Pasquino. This is perhaps the best known of Rome's "talking statues" of the Middle Ages and the Renaissance, upon which anonymous comments on the affairs of the day would be attached. These comments had a serious as well as a humorous intent, and gave us the word "pasquinade". The statue is still normally covered with rants, poems and pontifications of all kinds.

VIA DEL GOVERNO VECCHIO

VIA DEL GOVERNO VECCHIO

MAP PP.36–37, POCKET MAP D15

Via del Governo Vecchio leads west from Piazza Pasquino through one of Rome's liveliest quarters, the narrow streets holding some of the city's most vigorous restaurants and bars. A little way down on the left, the delightfully small **Piazza dell'Orologio** is named after the quaint clocktower that is its main feature – part of the Oratorio dei Filippini, designed by Borromini, which is part of the Chiesa Nuova complex (see below).

CHIESA NUOVA

Via del Governo Vecchio 134. Daily 7.30am–noon & 4.30–7.30pm, winter closes 7pm. MAP PP.36–37, POCKET MAP C15

The **Chiesa Nuova** was founded by St Philip Neri, who tended the poor and sick in the streets around here for most of his life, and commissioned this church in 1577. Neri died in 1595 and was canonized in 1622, and this large church, as well as being his last resting-place (he lies in the chapel to the left of the apse), is his principal memorial. Inside, its main features include three paintings by Rubens hung at the high altar, centring on the *Virgin with Angels*, and Pietro da Cortona's ceiling paintings, showing the *Ascension of the Virgin* in the apse and, above the nave, the construction of the church and Neri's famous "vision of fire" of 1544, when a globe of fire entered his mouth and dilated his heart – a physical event which apparently affected his health thereafter.

PALAZZO DELLA CANCELLERIA

Piazza della Cancelleria. MAP PP.36–37, POCKET MAP D15

The grand **Palazzo della Cancelleria** was the seat of the papal government that once ran the city. The Renaissance architect Bramante is thought to have had a hand in its design and it is a well-proportioned edifice, exuding a cool poise quite at odds with the rather grimy nature of its location. You can stroll into the marvellously proportioned, multi-tiered courtyard, off which is **Il Genio di Leonardo da Vinci**, a rather overpriced exhibition dedicated to the great man's many inventions, with large-scale replicas, some of which are interactive (daily 9.30am–7.30pm; €10). **San Lorenzo in Damaso** (daily 7.30am–noon & 4.30–8pm), one of the oldest churches in Rome, also forms part of the complex. It was rebuilt with the palace and has since been greatly restored, most recently at the end of the nineteenth century, and has a painting by Federico Zuccaro, *The Coronation of the Virgin*, over the altar, and a twelfth-century icon of the Virgin Mary in a chapel.

PALAZZO DELLA CANCELLERIA

MUSEO BARRACCO

Corso Vittorio Emanuele II 166 ⓣ060608, ⓦmuseobarracco.it. Tues–Sun: June–Sept 1–7pm, Oct–May 10am–4pm. Free. MAP PP.36–37, POCKET MAP D15

The Piccola Farnesina palace, built by Antonio Sangallo the Younger, holds the **Museo Barracco**, a high-quality collection of ancient sculpture that was donated to the city in 1904 by one Baron Barracco. There are ancient Egyptian pieces, including two sphinxes from the reigns of Hatshepsut and Rameses II, an austere head of an Egyptian priest and a bust of a young Rameses II. Look out for items from the Greek classical period, including a lovely, almost complete figurine of Hercules and a beautiful votive relief dedicated to Apollo. There are also some later Roman pieces, most notably a small figure of Neptune from the first century BC and an odd column-sculpture of a very graphically depicted hermaphrodite. The two charming busts of young Roman boys date from the first century AD.

SANT'ANDREA DELLA VALLE

Piazza Vidoni 6. Daily 7.30am–12.30pm & 4.30–7.30pm. MAP PP.36–37, POCKET MAP E16

The church of **Sant'Andrea della Valle** sports the city's second-tallest dome (after St Peter's) built by Carlo Maderno, and is famous for being the setting for the first scene of Puccini's *Tosca*. Inside, it's one of the most Baroque of Rome's churches and your attention is drawn not only to the dome, decorated with paintings of the *Glory of Paradise* by Giovanni Lanfranco, but also to a marvellous set of frescoes in the apse by his contemporary, Domenichino, illustrating the life of St Andrew. In a side chapel on the right, you may, if you've been in Rome a while, recognize some copies of not only Michelangelo's *Pietà* (the original is in St Peter's), but also of his figures of *Leah* and *Rachel*, from the tomb of his patron, Julius II, in the church of San Pietro in Vincoli (see p.96).

SANT'ANDREA DELLA VALLE

Shops

AI MONASTERI

Corso Rinascimento 72. Mon–Wed, Fri & Sat 10am–1.30pm & 2.30–7pm, Thurs 10am–1pm. MAP PP.36–37, POCKET MAP D14

Cakes, spirits, toiletries and other items, all made by monks.

CAMPOMARZIO70

Via di Campo Marzio 70. Mon noon–8pm, Tues–Sat 10am–8pm, Sun 11am–2pm & 3–7.30pm. MAP PP.36–37, POCKET MAP E14

A posh perfumery with unusual scents by the likes of By Kilian and Roja Dove, as well as Fornasetti scented candles.

C.U.C.I.N.A.

Via dl Parione 31. Mon–Sat 10.30am–7.30pm. MAP PP.36–37, POCKET MAP D15

Longstanding Centro Storico kitchenware shop, selling everything from chocolate moulds to espresso machines.

DELFINA DELETTREZ

Via del Governo Vecchio 67. Mon 3.30–7.30pm, Tues–Sat 10.30am–2pm, & 3–7.30pm. MAP PP.36–37, POCKET MAP D15

Delettrez, a fourth-generation Fendi, lives up to her fashion pedigree with this bijou shop on trendy Via del Governo Vecchio, offering glamorous jewellery with a retro edge.

G. POGGI

Via del Gesù 74/75. Mon–Sat 9am–2pm & 3–7.30pm. MAP PP.36–37, POCKET MAP F15

This long-established store in the heart of the Centro Storico, caters to all your artistic needs, with paper, paint, brushes and more basic stationery items.

IL GANCIO

Via del Seminario 82/83. Daily 10am–7.30pm. MAP PP.36–37, POCKET MAP E15

High-quality leather bags, purses and shoes, all made right here on the premises.

MAGA MORGANA

Via del Governo Vecchio 27. Mon–Sat 10am–8pm. MAP PP.36–37, POCKET MAP C15

The quirky creations by this local label include women's tops, skirts, dresses and hand-knitted jumpers, with a laidback boho feel.

MORIONDO & GARIGLIO

Via Pie di Marmo 21/22. Daily 9am–7.30pm. MAP PP.36–37, POCKET MAP F15

This sumptuous and refined handmade chocolate shop is pricey, but great for exquisitely wrapped gifts.

PELLICANÒ

Via del Seminario 93. Daily 10am–7pm. MAP PP.36–37, POCKET MAP E15

Ezio Pellicano only sells one thing: ties, made by Ezio himself or his wife. You can buy any of the hundreds you see on display, or you can choose from one of the many rolls of material and have your own made up in a couple of days.

MORIONDO & GARIGLIO

SBU

Via di San Pantaleo 68–69. Mon–Sat 10am–7.30pm. MAP PP.36–37, POCKET MAP D15

The bafflingly named Strategic Business Unit offers hip menswear – mainly Italian, with the odd Japanese import – including their popular own-brand jeans. There's a small womenswear section too, plus cool, affordable jewellery.

TEMPI MODERNI

Via del Governo Vecchio 108. Daily 10am–1pm & 3.30–7.30pm. MAP PP.36–37, POCKET MAP D15

Inexpensive costume jewellery, especially Art Nouveau pieces, at reasonable prices, plus a selection of vintage scarves.

Cafés and snacks

CAFFÈ SANT'EUSTACHIO

Piazza Sant'Eustachio. Sun–Thurs 8am–1am, Fri 8.30–1.30am, Sat 8.30–2am. MAP PP.36–37, POCKET MAP E15

Fantastic coffee, as well as coffee-based sweets and cakes.

CAFFÈ SANT'EUSTACHIO

CIAO CHECCA

Piazza di Firenze 25–26. Mon 8.30am–3.30pm & 6.30–10.30pm, Tues 8.30am–3.30pm, Wed–Fri 8.30am–10.30pm, Sat & Sun 9am–10.30pm. MAP PP.36–37, POCKET MAP E14

Finding a quick, healthy meal isn't always easy in Rome. This little takeaway (with a communal table), recognized by the Slow Food movement, is a great lunchtime pit-stop. Tasty dishes such as *pasta alla checca* (with tomatoes, mozzarella and basil; €6.50) are prepared in the open kitchen as you wait; there are gluten-free options too.

CREMERIA MONTEFORTE

Via della Rotonda 22. Tues–Sun 10am–11pm, midnight in summer. MAP PP.36–37, POCKET MAP E15

This award-winning *gelateria* is a tiny treasure right in the shadow of the Pantheon. Their speciality, a Sicilian slush called *cremolato*, comes in ten flavours.

GIOLITTI

Via Uffici del Vicario 40. Daily 7am–1.30am. MAP PP.36–37, POCKET MAP E14

This place is an Italian institution, and had a reputation – now lost – for the country's top ice cream. It's still good, with a choice of seventy flavours.

LA CAFFETTERIA

Piazza di Pietra 65. Daily 7.30am–9pm. MAP PP.36–37, POCKET MAP F14

Bureaucrats flock to this Neapolitan café from the nearby parliament: the pastries are imported from Naples daily, and the espresso is among Rome's best. Good for lunch too.

LA TAZZA D'ORO

Via degli Orfani 84/86. Mon–Sat 7am–8pm, Sun 10.30am–7.30pm. MAP PP.36–37, POCKET MAP E15

This place is well named, since it is by common consent the home of one of Rome's best cups of coffee, and sinfully rich *granita di caffè*, with dollops of whipped cream.

LO ZOZZONE

Via del Teatro Pace 32. Daily 10am–11pm, later in summer. MAP PP.36–37, POCKET MAP D15

This Rome legend, just around the corner from Piazza Navona and with outside seating, serves tasty *pizza bianca*, filled with whatever you want, as well as lots of delicious pizzas and Roman dishes.

PASCUCCI

Via di Torre Argentina 20. Mon–Sat 6am–10pm. MAP PP.36–37, POCKET MAP E16

This café specializes in *frullati* – fresh fruit whipped up with ice and milk. The ultimate Roman refreshment on a hot day.

Restaurants

ARMANDO AL PANTHEON

Salita de' Crescenzi 30 ☎ 06 6880 3034. Mon–Fri 12.30–3pm & 7–11pm, Sat 12.30–3pm. MAP PP.36–37, POCKET MAP E15

Unpretentious surroundings and Roman-style *secondi* (around €18) in this long-standing staple close by the Pantheon.

CASA BLEVE

Via del Teatro Valle 48/49. ☎ 06 686 5970. Mon–Sat 12.30–3pm & 7–11pm. MAP PP.36–37, POCKET MAP E15

Rome's beautiful folk come to enjoy great wine and food in this high-ceilinged, elegant hall in the heart of the Centro Storico. There's a huge wine list, and a refined menu of pasta, meat and fish dishes plus cheese plates and other cold specialities. Not cheap (*primi* around €16), but the food is great and the service ultra-attentive.

CUL DE SAC

Piazza Pasquino 73 ☎ 06 6880 1094. Daily noon–12.30am. MAP PP.36–37, POCKET MAP D15

Busy, long-running wine bar with an excellent wine list, a great city-centre location with outside seating and decent food. A good choice if you don't want a full meal.

DA BAFFETTO

Via del Governo Vecchio 114 ☎ 06 686 1617. Daily noon–3.30pm & 6.30pm–1am. MAP PP.36–37, POCKET MAP D15

Tiny pizzeria that has long been a Rome institution, though it now tends to be swamped by tourists. But it's still good value, and has tables outside in summer.

DA TONINO

Via del Governo Vecchio 18/19 ☎ 06 333 587 0779. Mon–Sat noon–3.30pm & 7–11pm. MAP PP.36–37, POCKET MAP C15

Basic Roman food, delicious and always freshly cooked, at this unmarked Centro Storico favourite. The pasta dishes are around €8; among the *secondi* try the *straccetti* (strips of beef with rocket). The few tables fill up fast, so come early or expect to queue. No credit cards.

MAKING PIZZAS AT DA BAFFETTO

DAL CAVALIER GINO

Vicolo Rosini 4 ⓣ 06 687 3434. Mon–Sat 1–3pm & 8–10.30pm. MAP PP.36–37, POCKET MAP E14

Down a small alley by the parliament building, Gino presides over his constantly bustling restaurant with unhurried authority. The menu is traditionally Roman, and prices on the cheap side – mains for €10–15. No credit cards.

ENOTECA CORSI

Via del Gesù 87/88 ⓣ 06 679 0821.Mon–Wed & Sat noon–3pm, Thurs & Fri noon–3pm & 8–11pm. MAP PP.36–37, POCKET MAP F15

Tucked away between Piazza Venezia and the Pantheon, this is an old-fashioned, inexpensive Roman trattoria and wine shop where you eat what they've cooked that morning.

IL BACARO

Via degli Spagnoli 27 ⓣ 06 687 2554. Mon–Fri 12.30–11pm, Sat & Sun 12.30pm–midnight. MAP PP.36–37, POCKET MAP E14

This cosy little restaurant has a small menu featuring a good and interesting selection of antipasti and *primi*, and main courses for around €20.

LA MONTECARLO

Vicolo Savelli 13 ⓣ 06 686 1877. Tues–Sun noon–1am. MAP PP.36–37, POCKET MAP D15

This hectic pizzeria not far from Piazza Navona is owned by the daughter of the owner of *Da Baffetto* (see p.47) and serves similar crisp, blistered pizza, along with good pasta dishes. Tables outside but be prepared to queue in summer. No credit cards.

MACCHERONI

Piazza delle Coppelle 44 ⓣ 06 6830 7895. Daily 12.30–3pm & 7–11.30pm. MAP PP.36–37, POCKET MAP E14

A friendly restaurant set in the heart of the Centro Storico. Inside is spartan yet comfy, while the outside tables make the most of the pretty street. The basic Italian fare is affordably priced and cheerfully served.

MATRICIANELLA

Via del Leone ⓣ 06 683 2100. Mon–Sat 12.30–3pm & 7.30–11pm. MAP PP.36–37, POCKET MAP E13

This old favourite is one of the best places to try real Roman food, with deep-fried dishes like *filetti di baccalà* and various vegetable *fritti*, classic Roman pasta dishes such as *cacio e pepe* for around €12, and a great wine list.

OSTERIA DEL PEGNO

Vicolo Montevecchio 8 ⓣ 06 6880 7025. Mon, Tues & Thurs–Sun 12.30–3pm & 7.30–10.45pm. MAP PP.36–37, POCKET MAP D14

This bijou restaurant, with a handful of tables outside on an atmospheric alley, serves good-value, classic *cucina romana*, alongside rustic fare such as Ischian rabbit stew, and pizzas cooked in a wood-fired oven.

TRATTORIA LILLI

Via Tor di Nona 73 ⓣ 06 686 1916. Tues–Sat 12.30–3pm & 7.30–11pm, Sun 12.30–3pm. MAP PP.36–37, POCKET MAP D14

One of the city centre's most untouristed trattorias, with a great menu of classic Roman staples, well prepared and served with gritty Roman directness. Starters go for €9–10, mains for €9–12 and litres of house wine for €9.

Bars

BAR DEL FICO

Piazza del Fico 26. Daily 8am–2am.
MAP PP.36–37, POCKET MAP D15

This super little place has a vibrant terrace on which you can sip your (rather expensive) drink and feel at the heart of Rome's urban buzz.

CAFFÈ DELLA PACE

Via della Pace 5. ⓣ 06 686 1216. Mon 3pm–2am, Tues–Sat 9pm–2am. MAP PP.36–37, POCKET MAP D15

The summer bar, with outside tables full of Rome's beautiful people. Quietest during the day, when you can enjoy the nineteenth-century interior – marble, mirrors, mahogany and plants – in peace. Although under threat of closure at the time of writing, its legion of fans have pledged to keep it open.

CIRCUS

Via della Vetrina 15 ⓣ 06 9761 9258. Daily 8am–2am. MAP PP.36–37, POCKET MAP D14

Drop by this cool backstreet bar for its generous *aperitivo* buffet (6.30–9pm; €8), or come for a cocktail late on in the snug back-lit bar. There are dj sets at weekends, and a popular brunch on Sundays.

BAR DEL FICO

ETABLI

Vicolo delle Vacche 9 ⓣ 06 9761 6694, ⓦ etabli.it. Daily 7.30am–2am. MAP PP.36–37, POCKET MAP D14

Lounge-style bar-restaurant in the heart of the Centro Storico's drinking triangle. Comfy sofas, a laidback vibe, live music (Thurs) and dj sets (Fri & Sat).

FLUID

Via del Governo Vecchio 46–47 ⓣ 06 683 2361. Daily 6pm–2am. MAP PP.36–37, POCKET MAP D15

With a cavernous interior, shimmering bar and clubby atmosphere, *Fluid* is a fun place to kick off a night out. Its popular *aperitivo* buffet (€10 including a drink) offers generous helpings.

SALOTTO 42

Piazza di Pietra 42 ⓣ 06 678 5804, ⓦ www.salotto42.it. Daily 10am–2am. MAP PP.36–37, POCKET MAP F14

This dimly lit café (with squishy sofas, a great lunchtime buffet and lots of art and design books to flick through) transforms into a glamorous cocktail bar after dark, with great music, expertly mixed drinks (around €10) and a polished clientele.

Club

SHARI VARI PLAYHOUSE

Via di Torre Argentina 78 ⓣ 06 6880 6936, ⓦ www.sharivari.it. Daily midnight–4am. MAP PP.36–37, POCKET MAP E15

Full of glammed-up Romans, *Shari Vari* is one of the city's newest clubs. Set over different levels and with lots of cosy nooks, it's great for people-watching. Saturday's club tunes draw the crowds, but Tuesday's electronica and Sunday's jazz nights are fun too. Also has an all-day bar with good *aperitivo* buffet.

Campo de' Fiori, the Ghetto and around

This southern slice of Rome's historic core lies between busy Corso Vittorio Emanuele II and the river. It's an appealing area for a wander, with cramped, cobbled streets opening out onto picturesque little piazzas. More of a working quarter than the neighbouring Centro Storico, it is less monumental, with more functional buildings and shops, as evidenced by its main square, Campo de' Fiori, whose fruit-and-veg stalls and down-to-earth bars form a marked contrast to the pavement artists and sleek cafés of Piazza Navona. To the east it merges into the narrow streets and scrabbly Roman ruins of the old Jewish Ghetto, an atmospheric neighbourhood that huddles up close to the city's giant synagogue, while just north of here lies the major traffic intersection and ancient Roman site of Largo di Torre Argentina.

LARGO DI TORRE ARGENTINA

MAP PP.52–53, POCKET MAP E16

The busy traffic hub of **Largo di Torre Argentina** holds the ruins of four Republican-era temples, now home to a thriving colony of cats; down the steps on the southwestern corner you can visit the somewhat pungent **cat sanctuary** (daily noon–6pm; Ⓦromancats.com), which tends to the 250 cats that live in the excavations. On the far side of the square, the Teatro Argentina was, in 1816, the venue for the first performance of Rossini's *Barber of Seville*, not a success at all on the night: Rossini was apparently booed into taking refuge in a nearby pastry shop. Built in 1731, it is today one of the city's most prestigious theatres, and is thought to stand over the spot in Pompey's theatre where Caesar was assassinated.

A PROWLING CAT AT LARGO DI TORRE ARGENTINA

THE GESÙ

Piazza del Gesù. Daily 7.30am–12.30pm & 4–7.45pm. MAP PP.52–53, POCKET MAP F16

The church of the **Gesù** was the first Jesuit church to be built in Rome, and has since served as the model for Jesuit churches everywhere – its wide single-aisled nave and short transepts edging out under a huge dome were ideal

for the large congregations the movement wanted to draw. Today it's still a well-patronized church, notable not only for its size (the glitzy tomb of the order's founder, St Ignatius, is topped by a huge globe of lapis lazuli representing the earth) but also for the staggering richness of its interior. Opposite, the tomb of the Jesuit missionary, St Francis Xavier, holds a reliquary containing the saint's severed arm (the rest of his body is in Goa), while the ceiling's ingenious trompe l'oeil, the *Triumph of the Name of Jesus* by Baciccia, oozes out of its frame in a tangle of writhing bodies, flowing drapery and stucco angels stuck like limpets – the Baroque at its most fervent.

Occupying part of the first floor of the Jesuit headquarters are the **Rooms of St Ignatius** (Mon–Sat 4–6pm, Sun 10am–noon; free), where the saint lived from 1544 until his death in 1556. There are bits and pieces of furniture and memorabilia, but the true draw is the corridor just outside, decorated by Andrea Pozzo in 1680 – a superb exercise in perspective, giving an illusion of a grand hall in what is a relatively small space.

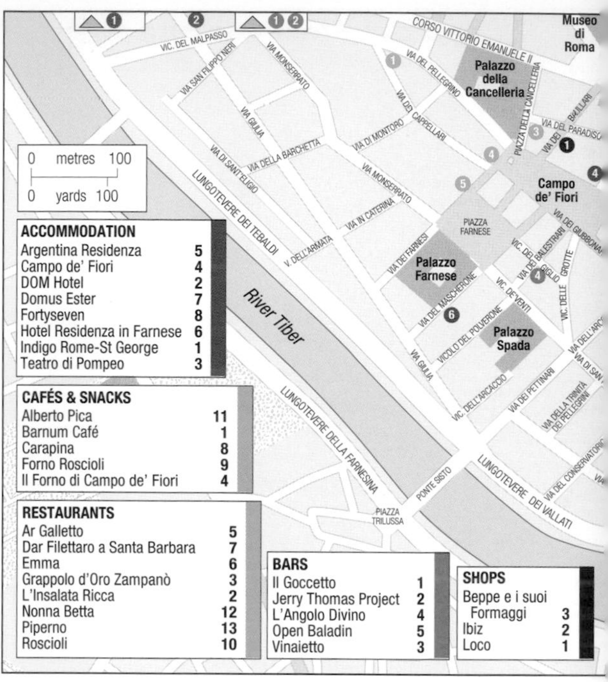

CRYPTA BALBI

Via delle Botteghe Oscure 31 ⓣ 06 3996 7700. Tues–Sun 9am–7.45pm; obligatory tours visit the excavations hourly; 15min. €7, includes Palazzo Massimo, Palazzo Altemps and Terme di Diocleziano, valid 3 days; free first Sun of the month. MAP PP.52–53, POCKET MAP F16

This corner plot is the site of a **Roman theatre**, the remains of which later became incorporated in a number of medieval houses. An above-ground exhibition takes you through the evolution of the site, with lots of English explanation, while tours visit the site proper; try to glean what you can from the various arches, latrines, column bases and supporting walls that make up the cellar of the current building. The real interest is in the close dissection of one city block over two thousand years.

CAMPO DE' FIORI

MAP PP.52–53, POCKET MAP D16

In many ways Rome's most appealing square, **Campo de' Fiori** is home to a lively fruit and vegetable market (Mon–Sat 8am–2pm), flanked by restaurants and cafés, and busy pretty much all day and night; it's one of the best places in town for an early-evening *aperitivo*, but a rough late-night crowd means it's worth avoiding later on, at weekends especially.

No one really knows how the square came by its name, which means "field of flowers", but one theory holds that it was derived from the Roman Campus Martius, which used to cover most of this part of town; another claims it is after Flora, the mistress of Pompey, whose theatre used to stand on what is now the northeast

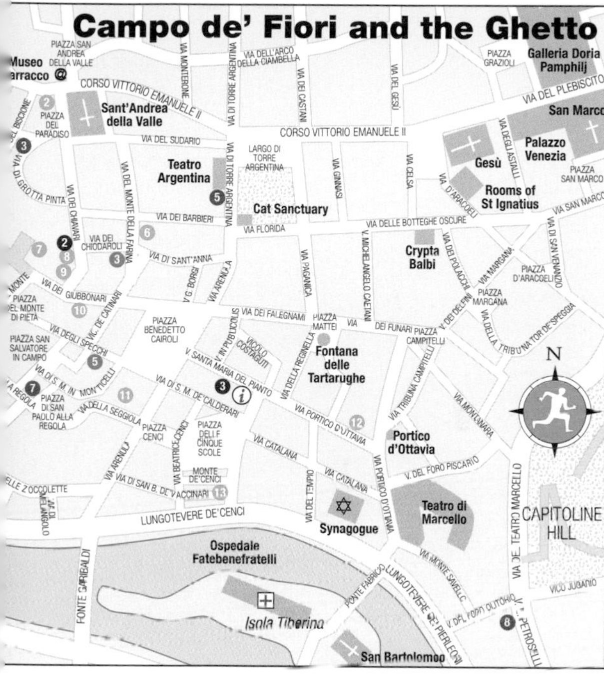

corner of the square – a huge complex by all accounts, which stretched right over to Largo Argentina, and where Julius Caesar was famously stabbed on the Ides of March, 44 BC. Later, Campo de' Fiori was the site of the city's cattle market and public executions, the most notorious of which is commemorated by the statue of a hooded Giordano Bruno in the middle of the square. Bruno was a late sixteenth-century freethinker who was denounced to the Inquisition; when he refused to renounce his philosophical beliefs, he was burned at the stake.

PALAZZO SPADA

Piazza Capo di Ferro 13 ⓣ 06 686 1158, ⓦ galleriaborghese.it. Mon & Wed–Sun 8.30am–7.30pm. €5; free first Sun of month.

MAP PP.52–53, POCKET MAP D16

The Renaissance **Palazzo Spada** houses a **gallery** of paintings collected by Cardinal Bernardino Spada and his brother Virgilio in the seventeenth century. However, the main feature is the building itself: its facade is frilled with stucco adornments, and off the small courtyard is a crafty trompe l'oeil by Borromini – a tunnel whose nine-metre length is multiplied about four times through the architect's tricks with perspective. Inside, the gallery's four rooms aren't spectacularly interesting unless you're a connoisseur of seventeenth- and eighteenth-century Italian painting; of special note, though, are two portraits of Cardinal Bernardino by Guido Reni and Guercino.

PALAZZO FARNESE

Piazza Farnese. Mon, Wed & Fri afternoon visits (45min) in English; €9; book several weeks in advance through ⓦ inventerrome.com. MAP PP.52–53, POCKET MAP D16

Just south of Campo de' Fiori, **Piazza Farnese** is a quite different square, with great fountains spurting out of carved lilies – the Farnese emblem – into marble tubs brought from the Baths of Caracalla, and the sober bulk of the Palazzo Farnese itself. Commissioned in 1514 by Alessandro Farnese – later Pope Paul III – from Antonio di Sangallo the Younger, the building was worked on after the architect's death by Michelangelo, who added the top tier of windows and cornice. It now houses the French Embassy and holds what has been called the greatest of all Baroque ceiling paintings, Annibale Carracci's *Loves of the Gods*, completed in 1603 and splendidly restored in 2015. Centring on the *Marriage of Bacchus and Ariadne*, this is supposed to represent the binding of the Aldobrandini and Farnese families, and is an erotic hotchpotch of cavorting flesh. Carracci did the main plan and the central painting himself, but left the rest to his brother and cousin, Agostino and Ludovico, and various assistants such as Guido Reni and Guercino, who went on to become some of the most sought-after artists of the seventeenth century. It's a fantastic piece of work, perhaps only eclipsed in Rome by the Sistine Chapel itself; sadly, Carracci, disillusioned by the work, and bitter about the relative pittance that he was paid for it, didn't paint much afterwards, and died penniless a few years later.

VIA GIULIA

MAP PP.52–53, POCKET MAP B14–D17

Via Giulia, running parallel to the Tiber, was built by Julius II to connect Ponte Sisto with the Vatican. The street was conceived as the centre of papal Rome, and Julius commissioned Bramante to line it with imposing palaces. Bramante didn't get very far, but the street became a popular

VIA GIULIA

FONTANA DELLE TARTARUGHE

residence for wealthier Roman families, and is still lined with elegant *palazzi*; it makes for a pleasant wander, with features like the playful Fontana del Mascherone to tickle your interest along the way.

VIA PORTICO D'OTTAVIA

MAP PP.52–53, POCKET MAP E17

Cross Via Arenula into the **Ghetto** and the contrast with stately Via Giulia can be felt immediately: this crumbling area of narrow, confusing switchback streets and alleys with a lingering sense of age is one of Rome's most atmospheric. The city's Jewish population stretches as far back as the second century BC, though nowadays a handful of kosher restaurants, butchers and the like are pretty much all that remains to mark this out from any other quarter.

The Ghetto's main artery, **Via Portico d'Ottavia**, leads down to the **Portico d'Ottavia**, a second-century BC gate, rebuilt by Augustus and dedicated to his sister in 23 BC. There's a walkway (summer daily 9am–7pm, winter daily 9am–6pm) through the ancient fish market, leading to the adjacent **Teatro di Marcello** (see p.65).

FONTANA DELLE TARTARUGHE

MAP PP.52–53, POCKET MAP E16

A sheltered enclave between Via Portico d'Ottavia and Via delle Botteghe Oscure, Piazza Mattei might be recognizable from its role as a set in the 1990s film, *The Talented Mr Ripley*. But it's best known as the site of one of the city's most charming fountains, the **Fontana delle Tartarughe**, or Turtle Fountain, a late sixteenth-century creation restored by Bernini, who apparently added the turtles.

THE SYNAGOGUE

Lungotevere Cenci ⓣ 06 6840 0661, ⓦ museoebraico.roma.it. April–Sept Mon–Thurs & Sun 10am–6pm, Fri 10am–4pm; Oct–March Mon–Thurs & Sun 10am–5pm, Fri 9am–2pm; closed Jewish holidays. €11. MAP PP.52–53, POCKET MAP E17

The Ghetto's principal Jewish sight is the huge **Synagogue**, built in 1904. There are hourly guided tours of the building in English, and you should also visit the **Museo Ebraico**, which has a well-presented collection of artefacts relating to Jewish ritual, the history of the Jews in Rome and of course the war years. The interior of the building is impressive, rising to a high, rainbow-hued dome, and the tours (20min) are excellent, giving a good background on the building and the persecution of Rome's Jewish community through history. Hour-long tours of the Ghetto in English are also organized (book through the museum; €8).

ISOLA TIBERINA

MAP PP.52–53, POCKET MAP E17

Almost opposite the Synagogue, the Ponte Fabricio crosses the Tiber to the Isola Tiberina. Built in 62 BC, it's the only classical bridge to remain intact without help from the restorers. The island is a calm respite from the city centre, and is mostly given over to Rome's oldest hospital, that of the **Fatebenefratelli**, founded in 1548 – appropriately, it would seem, as the island was originally home to a third-century BC temple of Aesculapius, the Roman god of healing. The tenth-century church of **San Bartolomeo** (Mon–Sat 9.30am–1.30pm & 3.30–5.30pm, Sun 9.30am–1pm) stands on the temple's original site and is worth a peep inside for its ancient columns, probably rescued from the temple, and an ancient wellhead on the altar steps, carved with figures relating to the founding of the church, including St Bartholomew himself. The saint also features in the painting above the altar, hands tied above his head, on the point of being skinned alive – his famous and gruesome mode of martyrdom.

ISOLA TIBERINA

PIAZZA BOCCA DELLA VERITÀ

MAP PP.52–53, POCKET MAP F18

Piazza Bocca della Verità has as its focus two of the city's better-preserved Roman temples – the Temple of Portunus and the Temple of Hercules Victor, the latter long known as the Tempio Rotondo because of its circular shape. Both date from the end of the second century BC, and are fine examples of republican-era places of worship. You can visit Tempio Rotondo on a guided tour (Italian only; first and third Sun of the month; €5.50; book on ⓣ 06 3996 7700, ⓦ coopculture.it). The feature that gives the square its name, however, is the **Bocca della Verità** (Mouth of Truth), an ancient Roman drain cover in the shape of an enormous face that in medieval times would apparently swallow the hand of anyone who hadn't told the truth. It was particularly popular with husbands anxious to test the fidelity of their wives; now it is one of the city's biggest tour-bus attractions.

The piazza's church, **Santa Maria in Cosmedin** (daily 10am–5pm; crypt €1) is a typically Roman medieval basilica with a huge marble altar and a colourful Cosmati-work mosaic floor – one of the city's finest.

Shops

BEPPE E I SUOI FORMAGGI

Via di Santa Maria del Pianto 9A/11. Mon–Sat 9am–10.30pm. MAP PP.52–53, POCKET MAP E16

This excellent shop is presided over by renowned cheese maker Beppe, and specializes in cheeses from Piemonte and Sardinia. You can also pick up chutneys, jams, chocolates and wine. The attached cheese-centric restaurant is great too.

IBIZ

Via dei Chiavari 39. Mon–Sat 10am–7.30pm. MAP PP.52–53, POCKET MAP D16

Great leather bags, purses and rucksacks in exciting contemporary designs made on the premises.

LOCO

Via dei Baullari 22. Mon 3.30–7.30pm, Tues–Sat 10.30am–7.30pm, Sun 11am–7pm (except Feb, Aug & Sept). MAP PP.52–53, POCKET MAP D16

Pricey, stylish shoes, the like of which you won't find anywhere else.

Cafés and snacks

ALBERTO PICA

Via della Seggiola 12. March–Oct Mon–Sat 8.40am–2pm, Sun 1–11pm; Nov–Feb Mon–Sat 8.40am–1pm. MAP PP.52–53, POCKET MAP E17

Gelato has been in the Pica family for generations, and it shows: this *gelateria* has a great choice of flavours, and the ice cream is sublime.

BARNUM CAFÉ

Via del Pellegrino 87. Mon 9am–midnight, Tues–Sat 9am–2am. MAP PP.52–53, POCKET MAP D15

This friendly circus-themed café with free wi-fi is great for breakfast, coffee or lunch. After dark, it's a relaxing bar with great cocktails and light meals.

CARAPINA

Via dei Chiavari 37. Daily noon–8pm. MAP PP.52–53, POCKET MAP D16

Renowned Florentine *gelateria Carapina* now has a branch in Rome. Top-notch, seasonal ingredients go into making these gourmet ices, with flavours running the gamut from parmesan to whiskey.

FORNO ROSCIOLI

Via dei Chiavari 34. Mon–Sat 6am–8pm. MAP PP.52–53, POCKET MAP D16

Not to be confused with the posher *Roscioli* round the corner (see p.58), this is a top-notch pizza *al taglio* place, with hefty slices costing a few euros. There are also a few hot dishes at lunch (gnocchi in pesto sauce €6), and tasty cakes.

IL FORNO DI CAMPO DE' FIORI

Campo de' Fiori 22. Mon–Sat 7.30am–2.30pm & 4.45–8pm. MAP PP.52–53, POCKET MAP D16

The *pizza bianca* here (just drizzled with olive oil on top) is a Roman legend, and their *pizza rossa* (with a smear of tomato sauce) follows close behind.

ALBERTO PICA

GRAPPOLO D'ORO ZAMPANÒ

Restaurants

AR GALLETTO

Piazza Farnese 104 ⓣ 06 686 1714. Daily 12.30–3pm & 7.30–11pm. MAP PP.52–53, POCKET MAP D16

This popular old-timer has had a chic overhaul, with bottle-lined rooms and coffee-coloured walls, as well as tables outside on one of Rome's stateliest piazzas. The menu offers fairly pricey staples of Roman cuisine and is also strong on fish dishes.

DAR FILETTARO A SANTA BARBARA

Largo dei Librari 88 ⓣ 06 686 4018. Mon–Sat 5.30–11.30pm. MAP PP.52–53, POCKET MAP D16

A fish-and-chip shop without the chips. Paper-covered Formica tables (outdoors in summer), cheap wine, beer and fried cod. A timeless Roman speciality. Service can be offhand.

EMMA

Via del Monte della Farina 28 ⓣ 06 6476 0475, ⓦ emmapizzeria.com. Daily 12.30–3pm & 7–11.30pm. MAP PP.52–53, POCKET MAP E16

This relative newcomer is, for many, central Rome's best pizzeria. More elegant restaurant than simple pizzeria, its organic pizzas (around €12) are unashamedly gourmet.

GRAPPOLO D'ORO ZAMPANÒ

Piazza della Cancelleria 80 ⓣ 06 689 7080. Mon, Tues & Thurs–Sun 12.30–3pm & 7–11.30pm, Wed 7–11.30pm. MAP PP.52–53, POCKET MAP D16

Curiously untouched by the hordes in nearby Campo de' Fiori, this restaurant serves imaginative Roman cuisine in a traditional trattoria atmosphere.

L'INSALATA RICCA

Largo dei Chiavari 85 ⓣ 06 6880 3656, ⓦ insalataricca.it. Daily noon–midnight. MAP PP.52–53, POCKET MAP D15

Over fifty different types of salad, from a simple *Caprese* to the "Exotic" (with pineapple, pine nut and mango). Portions are huge and the ingredients fresh; most salads cost under €10. Lots of outdoor tables too.

NONNA BETTA

Via del Portico d'Ottavia 16 ⓣ 06 6880 6263. Mon & Wed–Sun 11am–11pm. MAP PP.52–53, POCKET MAP E17

The best kosher restaurant in the Ghetto serves all the classes of *cucina Romana*, including fantastic deep-fried artichokes.

PIPERNO

Monte de' Cenci 9 ⓣ 06 6880 6629. Tues–Sat 12.45–2.20pm & 7.45–10.20pm, Sun 12.45–2.20pm. MAP PP.52–53, POCKET MAP E17

Tucked away on a hard-to-find piazza, *Piperno* is one of the area's best Roman-Jewish restaurants. It's not cheap, but it's a lovely space and there's outside seating in the summer. *Antipasti* and *primi* go for around €15, and *secondi* for €15–25.

ROSCIOLI

Via dei Giubbonari 21–22 ⓣ 06 687 5287. Mon–Sat 12.30–4pm & 7pm–midnight; open last three Sats in Dec. MAP PP.52–53, POCKET MAP E16

Is it a deli, a wine bar, or fully

ROSCIOLI

fledged restaurant? Actually it's all three, and you can either just have wine and cheese or go for the full menu, which has great pasta dishes and *secondi* at lunch time and in the evening. It's pricey, and the service can be snooty, but the food is terrific. *Roscioli* also has its own bakery nearby (see p.57).

Bars

IL GOCCETTO

Via dei Banchi Vecchi 14. Mon 6.30pm–midnight, Tues–Sat 11.30–2.30pm & 6.30pm–midnight. MAP PP.52–53, POCKET MAP C15

This family-run wine bar and shop, patronized by devoted regulars, is an atmospheric place for a drink, with wood-clad walls and a cosy feel. There is an extensive menu of wines by the glass and a selection of light appetizers, deli meats and cheeses.

JERRY THOMAS PROJECT

Vicolo Cellini 30 ⊤ 06 9684 5937 or ⊤ 370 114 6287, Ⓦ thejerrythomasproject.it. Tues–Sat 10pm–4am. MAP PP.52–53, POCKET MAP C15

Dedicated to Jerry Thomas, the author of the first guide to cocktail making (published in 1862), this is a hole-in-the-wall speakeasy with a fantastic cocktail menu – a rarity in Rome. Officially you need a password to gain entry, but you might get in without; as space is tight, though, booking is always a good idea. Cash only.

L'ANGOLO DIVINO

Via dei Balestrari 12. Tues–Sat 10.30am–3pm & 5pm–1.30am, Mon & Sun 5pm–1.30am; closed one week in Aug. MAP PP.52–53, POCKET MAP D16

Quite a peaceful haven after lively Campo de' Fiori, this place offers a large selection of wine, and a menu of simple, typical wine-bar food – bread, cheese and cold cuts – as well as pasta dishes such as lasagne with sausage and savoy cabbage (€8.50).

OPEN BALADIN

Via degli Specchi. Daily noon–2am. MAP PP.52–53, POCKET MAP E16

Central Rome's ultimate *birreria*, owned by the Baladin brewing company, has a stark, modern interior and literally hundreds of mainly artisanal Italian beers to choose from, forty of them on tap.

VINAIETTO

Via del Monti della Farina 38. Mon–Sat 10am–3pm & 6–11pm. MAP PP.52–53, POCKET MAP E16

This hole-in-the-wall *enoteca* has just a handful of tables, so most of its regulars drink their wine outside on the cobbles. Though mainly a wine shop, the enthusiastic owners offer a range of wines to drink by the glass – and it's far less expensive than nearby Campo de' Fiori.

Piazza Venezia and the Capitoline Hill

For many people the modern centre of Rome is Piazza Venezia – not so much a square as a road junction, close to both the medieval and Renaissance centre of Rome and the city's ancient ruins, and the best landmarked space in Rome, the great white bulk of the Vittoriano monument marking it out from anywhere else in the city. Behind lie the Piazza del Campidoglio and the Capitoline Hill, one of the first settled of Rome's seven hills.

PALAZZO VENEZIA

Via del Plebiscito 118. Tues–Sun 8.30am–7.30pm. €5. MAP P.61, POCKET MAP F16

Forming the piazza's western side, **Palazzo Venezia**, built for the Venetian Pope Paul II in the mid-fifteenth century, was for a long time the embassy of the Venetian Republic. Mussolini moved in here while in power, occupying the vast Sala del Mappamondo and making his declamatory speeches to the crowds below from the balcony. In 2010, maintenance work on the building's foundations uncovered Mussolini's war bunker; though not yet open to the public, it may be in the future. Most of the rest of the building houses the **Museo Nazionale del Palazzo di Venezia**, with lots of fifteenth-century devotional works from central and northern Italy, some beautifully displayed bronzes and weapons, and ceramic jars from an ancient monastic pharmacy. You can also enjoy views of the palm-filled courtyard from the palace's upper **loggia** – the gardens are some of the prettiest in Rome.

SAN MARCO

Piazza di San Marco 52. Tues–Fri 10am–1pm & 4–6pm, Sat & Sun 10am–1pm & 4–8pm. MAP P.61, POCKET MAP F16

Adjacent to the Palazzo Venezia on its southern side, the church of **San Marco** is one of the oldest basilicas in Rome. Originally founded in 336 AD on the spot where the apostle is said to have lived, it was rebuilt in 833 and added to by various Renaissance and eighteenth-century popes including Pope Paul II. The apse mosaic dates from the ninth century and shows Pope Gregory IV offering his church to Christ above a graceful semicircle of sheep.

PRIESTS WALKING THROUGH PIAZZA VENEZIA

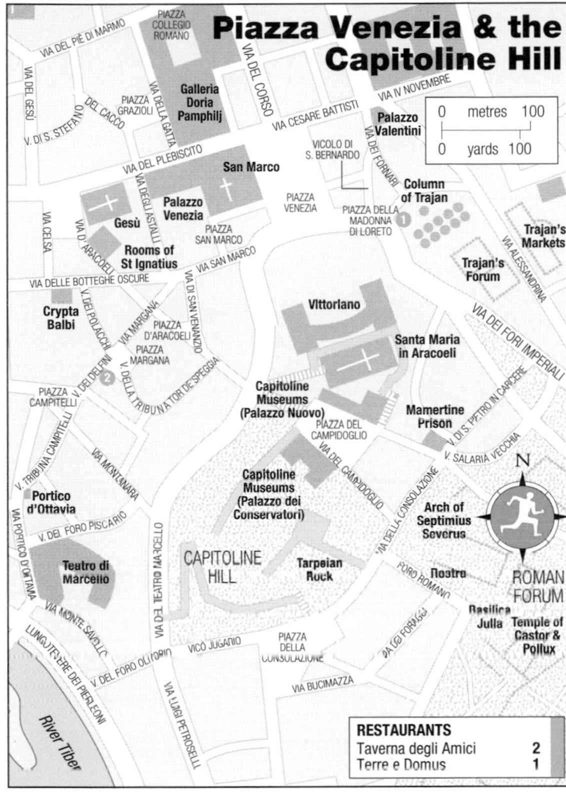

THE VITTORIANO

Daily 9.30am–5.30pm (4.30pm in winter); free. Lifts to terrace: Mon–Thurs 9.30am–6.30pm, Fri–Sun 9.30am–7.30pm; €7. Museum: daily 9.30am–6.30pm; closed first Tues of the month; €5. MAP P.61, POCKET MAP F16–G16

The other buildings on Piazza Venezia pale into insignificance beside the marble monstrosity rearing up across the street– the **Vittorio Emanuele Monument** or **"Vittoriano"**, erected at the turn of the nineteenth century to commemorate Italian Unification. Likened in the past to a typewriter, and, by American GIs, to a wedding cake, there are things to see inside: the large **Museo del Risorgimento** (Ⓦrisorgimento.it), full of busts and weaponry, and the **Complesso del Vittoriano** (Ⓦilvittoriano.com), a space for high-profile temporary exhibitions. But the bigger draws are outside, centring on the tomb of the unknown soldier and an enormous equestrian statue of Vittorio Emanuele II, on a plinth friezed with figures representing the major Italian cities. Clamber up and down the sweeping terraces and take the lifts from behind the monument to the top, which give perhaps the most fabulous views in Rome – partly because it's the one place in Rome from which you can't see the Vittoriano.

PALAZZO VALENTINI

Via IV Novembre 119/A ⓣ 06 32 810, ⓦ palazzovalentini.it. Mon & Wed–Sun 9.30am–6.30pm; visit by guided tour only (1hr 30min). €12. MAP P.61, POCKET MAP G15

Book at least two weeks in advance for a tour of this absorbing attraction: the excavated remains of two **ancient Roman houses** in the depths of a municipal office building, brought to life by technological trickery. Viewed through a glass floor, the excavations offer a glimpse into the lives of a patrician Roman family around the third century, whose lavish home was in the heart of the ancient city. Sound and light effects transform the site, painting the faded walls, embellishing the floor with mosaics and filling the bathing pool with water. The tour ends with a video explaining the story of the nearby Column of Trajan (see p.73).

THE CAPITOLINE HILL

MAP P.61, POCKET MAP F17

The real pity about the Vittoriano is that it obscures the view of the **Capitoline Hill** behind – once, in the days of imperial Rome, the spiritual and political centre of the Roman Empire. Its name derives from its position as the "caput mundi" or "head of the world", and its influence and importance resonates to this day – words like "capitol" and "capital" all derive from here, as does the word "money", which comes from the temple to Juno Moneta that once stood nearby and housed the Roman mint.

THE CAPITOLINE MUSEUMS

Daily 9.30am–7.30pm ⓣ 060608, ⓦ museicapitolini.org. €11.50, €12.50 for joint ticket with Centrale Montemartini (see p.117); valid 7 days. MAP P.61, POCKET MAP F16–F17

If you see no other museums of ancient sculpture in Rome, try to at least see the **Capitoline Museums**, which are perhaps the most venerable of all the city's collections. They're divided into two parts – the Palazzo dei Conservatori and the Palazzo Nuovo – and you should try to see both rather than choosing one. Tickets are valid for a day so you can fit in each museum with a break in between, perhaps for a stroll around the Roman Forum.

The **Palazzo dei Conservatori** is the larger, more varied collection, with some ancient sculpture as well as later pieces and an art gallery. Inside, the centrepiece of the first floor,

THE VITTORIANO

COURTYARD OF THE PALAZZO DEI CONSERVATORI

the Sala degli Orazi e Curiazi, is appropriately decorated with giant, late sixteenth-century frescoes depicting legendary tales from the early days of Rome. Check out the corner room, which contains the so-called *Spinario*, a Roman statue of a boy picking a thorn out of his foot, and, next door, the sacred symbol of Rome, the Etruscan bronze she-wolf nursing the mythic founders of the city. Move on to the airy new wing, where an equestrian statue of Marcus Aurelius, formerly in the square outside, takes centre stage, alongside a giant bronze statue of Constantine – or at least its head, hand and orb – and a rippling bronze of Hercules.

The second-floor *pinacoteca* holds Renaissance paintings from the fourteenth to the late seventeenth centuries – highlights include a couple of portraits by Van Dyck and a *Portrait of a Crossbowman* by Lorenzo Lotto, a pair of paintings by Tintoretto – a *Flagellation* and *Baptism of Christ*, and a fine early work by Ludovico Carracci, *Head of a Boy*. There's also a vast picture by Guercino, depicting the *Burial of St Petronilla* (an early Roman martyr who was the supposed daughter of St Peter), and two paintings by Caravaggio, one a replica of the young *John the Baptist* which hangs in the Palazzo Doria-Pamphilj (see p.34), the other an early work known as *The Fortune-Teller*.

The **Palazzo Nuovo** across the square – also accessible by way of an underpass that holds Roman marble inscriptions – has some of the best of the city's Roman sculpture crammed into half a dozen or so rooms. Among them are the remarkable statue of a *Dying Gaul*, a *Satyr Resting*, the inspiration for Hawthorne's book *The Marble Faun*, and the red marble *Laughing Silenus* – along with busts of Roman emperors and other famous names: a young Augustus, a cruel Caracalla, and the centrepiece, a life-sized portrait of Helena, the mother of Constantine. Also, don't miss the coy *Capitoline Venus*, housed in a room on its own.

THE SHE-WOLF

SANTA MARIA IN ARACOELI

Scala dell'Arcicapitolina 12. Daily: May–Sept 9am–6.30pm; Oct–April 9.30am–5.30pm. MAP P.61, POCKET MAP G16

The church of **Santa Maria in Aracoeli** crowns the highest point on the Capitoline Hill and is built on the ruins of a temple to Juno. Reached by a flight of 124 steps up the steep **Aracoeli staircase**, erected in 1348, or more easily from a side entrance accessible from the Vittoriano or Piazza del Campidoglio, the church is one of Rome's most ancient basilicas, known for its role as keeper of the so-called "Santo Bambino", a small statue of the Christ Child, carved from the wood of a Gethsemane olive tree. The statue is said to have miraculous healing powers and was traditionally called out to the sickbeds of the ill and dying all over the city, its coach commanding instant right of way through the heavy Rome traffic. The Bambino was stolen in 1994, but a copy now stands in its place, in a small chapel to the left of the high altar. Take a look also at the frescoes by Pinturicchio in a chapel on the right, recording the life of San Bernardino.

PIAZZA DEL CAMPIDOGLIO

MAP P.61, POCKET MAP F16–G16

Next door to the Aracoeli staircase, the smoothly rising ramp of the Cordonata leads to **Piazza del Campidoglio**, one of Rome's most perfectly proportioned squares, designed by Michelangelo in the last years of his life for Pope Paul III. Michelangelo died before his plan was completed, but his designs were faithfully executed – balancing the piazza, redesigning the facade of the Palazzo dei Conservatori and projecting an identical building across the way, the Palazzo Nuovo. These buildings are home to the Capitoline Museums (see p.62); the two are angled slightly to focus on Palazzo Senatorio, Rome's town hall. In the centre of the square Michelangelo placed an equestrian statue of Emperor Marcus Aurelius (now a copy), which had previously stood outside San Giovanni in Laterano; early Christians had refrained from melting it down because they believed it to be of Constantine (the first Roman emperor to follow Christianity).

SHE-WOLF AND TARPEIAN ROCK

MAP P.61, POCKET MAP F17

Just off the Piazza del Campidoglio, the statue of Romulus and Remus suckling the **she-wolf** provides one of Rome's most enduring images. Beyond is the **Tarpeian Rock**, from which traitors were thrown in ancient times – and which now gives excellent views over the Forum.

MAMERTINE PRISON

Clivo Argentario 1. Tues, Thurs, Sat & Sun, entry every 30min 9am–noon & 2–4pm. €10. MAP P.61, POCKET MAP G16

Steps lead down from the Tarpeian Rock to little **San Pietro in Carcere** – a low-vaulted church that lies above the ancient **Mamertine Prison** (also known as the Carcer Tullianum), where spies, vanquished soldiers and other enemies of the Roman state were incarcerated, and where St Peter himself was held. It's now part of a multimedia-assisted tour, taking in the depths of the jail, including the column to which St Peter was chained, along with the spring the saint is said to have used to baptize his guards and other prisoners. At the top of the staircase, hollowed out of the stone, is an imprint claimed to be of St Peter's head as he tumbled down the stairs. The tour also takes in further excavations and a film on the saint's life, and finishes with a brief bit of evangelizing in the church.

TEATRO DI MARCELLO

Via del Teatro di Marcello. Daily: summer 9am–7pm, winter 9am–6pm. Free. MAP P.61, POCKET MAP F17

Close to the Capitoline Hill, the **Teatro di Marcello** was begun by Julius Caesar and finished by Augustus. It became a fortified palace in Renaissance times, the property of the powerful Orsini family. Forming the backdrop for summer concerts, it also provides a neat cut-through to the Jewish Ghetto (see p.55) just beyond.

TEATRO DI MARCELLO

Restaurants

TAVERNA DEGLI AMICI

Piazza Margana 36/37 ☎06 6992 0637. Tues–Sun noon–11pm. MAP P.61, POCKET MAP F16

This long-standing place is great for a post-Capitoline Hill lunch, with tables outside on the little square. Lots of Roman classics, at moderate prices – starters for around €12, mains for €15–20.

TERRE E DOMUS

Foro Traiano 82 ☎06 6994 0273. Mon–Sat 8.30am–midnight, Sun 10am–midnight. MAP P.61, POCKET MAP G16

Perfect for lunch after a mooch round the Forum, the menu here centres on local ingredients, offering light meals, pastas and meat and fish *secondi*; pasta and side dish with wine costs €20. Stop by for the evening *aperitivo* buffet (from 6pm) to enjoy the view of Trajan's Column without the crowds.

Ancient Rome

There are remnants of ancient Rome all over the city, but the most famous and concentrated collection of sights – the Forum and Colosseum together with the Palatine Hill – stretches southeast from the Capitoline Hill. You can spend a good half-day, perhaps longer, picking your way through the rubble of what was once the core of the ancient world. The most obvious place to start is the original, Republican-period Forum, the political and commercial heart of the ancient city. You can then visit the later Imperial Forums that lie across Via dei Fori Imperiali before heading up the legendary Palatine Hill, once home to the city's most powerful citizens and now an appealingly tranquil spot. Just beyond the Forum, the Colosseum is Rome's most iconic monument, a beautiful construction seemingly at odds with its violent past.

THE COLOSSEUM

Piazza del Colosseo. Daily 8.30am–1hr before sunset ⓣ 06 3996 7700, ⓦ coopculture.it. €12 joint ticket with the Palatine and Roman Forum. MAP PP.70–71, POCKET MAP G6

The **Colosseum** is perhaps Rome's most awe-inspiring ancient monument: an enormous amphitheatre that, despite the depredations of nearly 2000 years still stands relatively intact. You'll not be alone in appreciating it, and during summer visits can be a chore. But go late in the evening or early morning before the tour buses arrive, and the arena can seem more like the marvel it really is.

THE COLOSSEUM

Originally known as the Flavian Amphitheatre (the name Colosseum is a much later invention), it was begun around 72 AD by Emperor Vespasian, who was anxious to extinguish the memory of Nero, and so chose the site of Nero's Domus Aurea for the stadium. Inside, 60,000 people could be seated, with 10,000 or so standing. The seating was allocated on a strict basis, with the emperor and his attendants

Visiting the Forum, Palatine and Colosseum

A **single ticket** (€12) covers the Colosseum, Forum and Palatine Hill and is valid for two days; you're allowed to visit each attraction once during this time, and the Forum and Palatine Hill count as one site, so have to be visited at the same time. To avoid the inevitable **queues**, buy your ticket online (booking fee of €2 in addition to the ticket price; ⓦ coopculture.it) or at the Forum early in the morning. Holders of the **Archaeologia Card**, **Roma Pass** or **Omnia Card** (see p.185) are allowed to use a different queue. If you book a **tour** you will generally be allowed to skip the queue. There are tours of the Colosseum daily (10.15am–3pm; roughly every 30min–1hr; 45min; €5), as well as daily tours of the underground area, the upper tier and the arena floor (€9) and night tours (mid-April to Oct Mon, Thurs, Fri & Sat; €20), which include a visit to the underground area. Book tours through ⓦ coopculture.it.

For a bite to eat after sightseeing, head to the restaurants around Monti (see p.102) or San Giovanni (see p.111).

occupying the best seats in the house, and the social class of the spectators diminishing nearer the top. There was a labyrinth below that was covered with a wooden floor and punctuated at various places with trap doors and lifts to raise and lower the animals that were to take part in the games. The floor was covered with canvas to make it waterproof and the canvas was covered with several centimetres of sand to absorb blood; in fact, our word "arena" is derived from the Latin word for sand. Once inside, you can wander around most of the ground level, circling the remains of the arena, but you'll get a better view from the lower tier, reached by steep stairways. Here also, in the connecting corridor, is a space for temporary exhibitions, a display of fragments of masonry and a decent bookshop. More stairs lead to the upper tier – even here you are still only about halfway up the original structure – though this and the arena and underground area are visitable only on guided tours (see box above).

THE ARCH OF CONSTANTINE

Via di San Gregorio. MAP PP.70–71 POCKET MAP G6

Just west of the Colosseum, the huge **Arch of Constantine** was placed here in the early decades of the fourth century AD after Constantine had consolidated his power as sole emperor. The arch demonstrates the deterioration of the arts during the late stages of the Roman Empire – most of the sculptural decoration here had to be removed from other monuments, and the builders were probably quite ignorant of the significance of the pieces they borrowed: the round medallions are taken from a temple dedicated to the Emperor Hadrian's lover, Antinous, and show Antinous and Hadrian engaged in a hunt. The other pieces, removed from the Forum of Trajan, show Dacian prisoners captured in Trajan's war there.

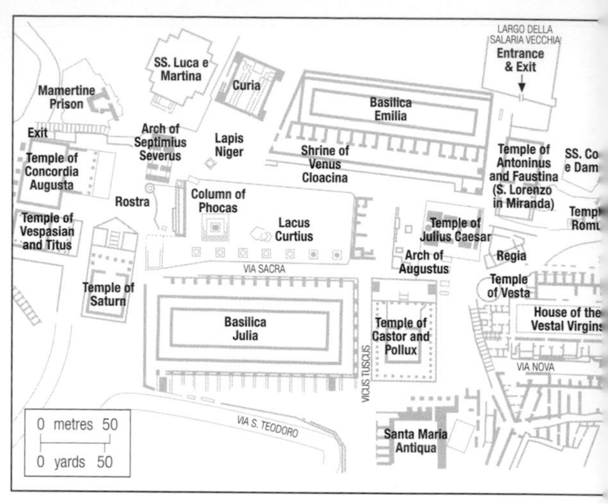

THE ROMAN FORUM

Entrances at Largo della Salaria Vecchia, halfway down Via dei Fori Imperiali; at the Arch of Titus; and on Via di San Gregorio (via the Palatine) 06 3996 7700, coopculture.it. Daily 8.30am–1hr before sunset. €12 joint ticket with Colosseum and Palatine. MAP PP.68–69, POCKET MAP F6–G6

The two or so hectares that make up the **Forum** were once the heart of the Mediterranean world, and although the glories of ancient Rome are hard to glimpse here now, there's a symbolic allure to the place that makes it one of the world's most compelling (not to mention most ruined) sets of ruins anywhere in the world.

Originally an Etruscan burial ground, the Forum was developed in the seventh century BC and expanded over the centuries to incorporate public spaces and temples. Its importance waned after the fourth century, when it became pastureland. Stone and marble relics were taken for use elsewhere in the Middle Ages, and the Forum lay barren until the eighteenth century, when archeologists began excavating.

You need an imagination and a little history to fully appreciate the place, but the public spaces are easy enough to discern, especially the spinal **Via Sacra**, ancient Rome's best-known street, along which victorious emperors and generals would ride in procession to give thanks at the Capitoline's Temple of Juno. A little beyond, the large cube-shaped building is the **Curia** (under restoration at the time of writing), built on the orders of Julius Caesar as part of his programme for expanding the Forum, although what you see now is a third-century AD reconstruction. The Senate met here, and inside three wide stairs rise to the left and right, on which about 300 senators could sit with their folding chairs. In the centre is the speaker's platform, with a porphyry statue of a togaed figure. Nearby, the **Arch of Septimius Severus** was constructed in the early third century AD by his sons Caracalla and Geta to mark their father's victories in what is now Iran. The friezes on it

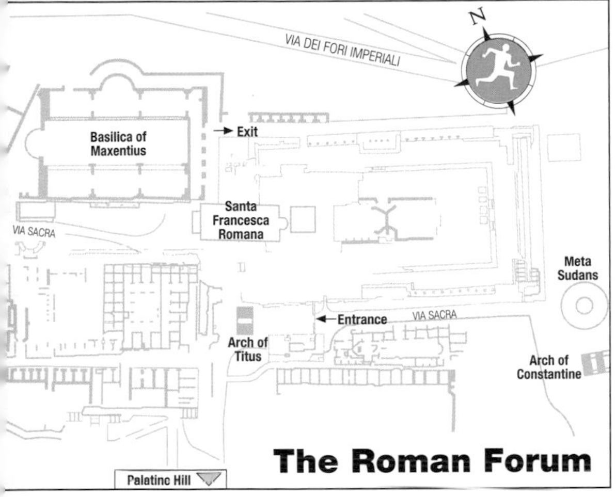

recall Severus and in particular Caracalla, who ruled Rome with undisciplined terror for seven years. To the left of the arch, the low brown wall is the **Rostra,** from which important speeches were made (it was from here that Mark Anthony most likely spoke about Caesar after his death). Left of the Rostra are the long stairs of the **Basilica Julia**, built by Julius Caesar in the 50s BC after he returned from the Gallic wars, and, a bit further along, rails mark the site of the **Lacus Curtius** – the spot where, according to legend, a chasm opened during the earliest days and the soothsayers determined that it would only be closed once Rome had sacrificed its most valuable possession into it. Marcus Curtius, a Roman soldier who declared that Rome's most valuable possession was a loyal citizen, hurled himself and his horse into the void and it duly closed. Further on, to the right, the enormous pile of rubble topped by three graceful Corinthian columns is the **Temple of Castor and Pollux**, dedicated in 484 BC to the divine twins, or Dioscuri, who appeared miraculously to ensure victory for the Romans in a key battle. Beyond here, the **House of the Vestal Virgins** is a second-century AD reconstruction of a building originally built by Nero: four floors of rooms around a central courtyard, still with its pool in the centre and fringed by the statues or inscribed pedestals of the women themselves, with the round Temple of Vesta at the near end.

Almost opposite, a shady walkway to the left leads up to the **Basilica of Maxentius** – in terms of size and ingenuity, probably the Forum's most impressive remains. Begun by Maxentius, it was continued by his co-emperor and rival, Constantine, after he had defeated Maxentius at the Battle of Ponte Milvio in 312 AD. Back on the Via Sacra, the hill climbs more steeply to the **Arch of Titus**, built by Titus' brother, Domitian, after the emperor's death in 81 AD to commemorate his triumphant return after victories in Judea in 70 AD.

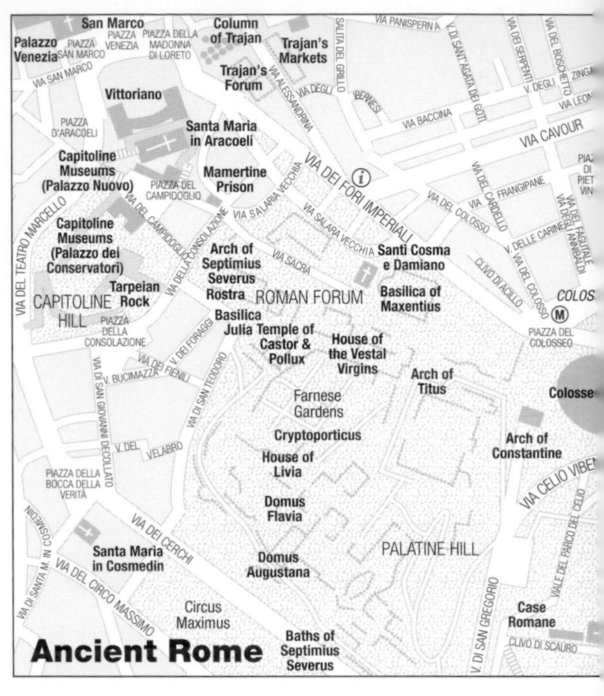

THE PALATINE HILL

Entrance at Via di San Gregorio 30 or through the Roman Forum ☎ 06 3996 7700, Ⓦ coopculture.it. Daily 8.30am–1hr before sunset. €12 joint ticket with Colosseum and Roman Forum. MAP PP.70–71, POCKET MAP G7

Rising above the Roman Forum, the **Palatine** is supposedly where the city of Rome was founded, and is home to some of its most ancient remnants. In a way it's a more pleasant site to tour than the Forum, a good place to have a picnic and relax after the rigours of the ruins below. In the days of the Republic, the Palatine was the most desirable address in Rome (the word "palace" is derived from Palatine), and the big names continued to colonize it during the Imperial era, trying to outdo each other with ever larger and more magnificent dwellings.

Following the main path up from the Forum, the **Domus Flavia** was one of the most splendid residences, although it's now almost completely ruined. To the left, the top level of the gargantuan **Domus Augustana** spreads to the far brink of the hill – not the home of Augustus as its name suggests, but the private house of any emperor. You can look down from here on its vast central courtyard with fountains and wander to the brink of the deep trench of the Stadium, on the far side of which the ruins of the **Baths of Septimius Severus** cling to the side of the hill, the terrace giving good views over the Colosseum and the churches of the Celian Hill opposite. Nearby, the **Museo Palatino** contains a vast assortment of statuary, pottery, terracotta antefixes and architectural fragments. If you walk in the opposite direction from the Domus Flavia, you get to the **Cryptoporticus** (currently closed), a long passage built by Nero to link his Domus Aurea with the Palatine, and decorated along part of its length with well-preserved Roman stucco-work. A left turn leads to the **Casa di Livia**, whose recently restored frescoed rooms can be visited on guided tours (daily at 12.45pm; 1hr; €4; book on ⓣ06 3996 7700). The tour also takes in the **Casa di Augusto** west of here, which holds beautiful frescoes in striking shades of blue, red and ochre, dating back to 30 BC and considered to be among the most magnificent examples of Roman wall paintings anywhere. Further south, steps take you to the **Farnese Gardens**, among the first botanical gardens in Europe, laid out in the mid-sixteenth century and now a tidily planted, shady retreat from the exposed heat of the ruins. The terrace at the opposite end looks down on the excavations of an Iron Age village that perhaps marks the real centre of Rome's ancient beginnings.

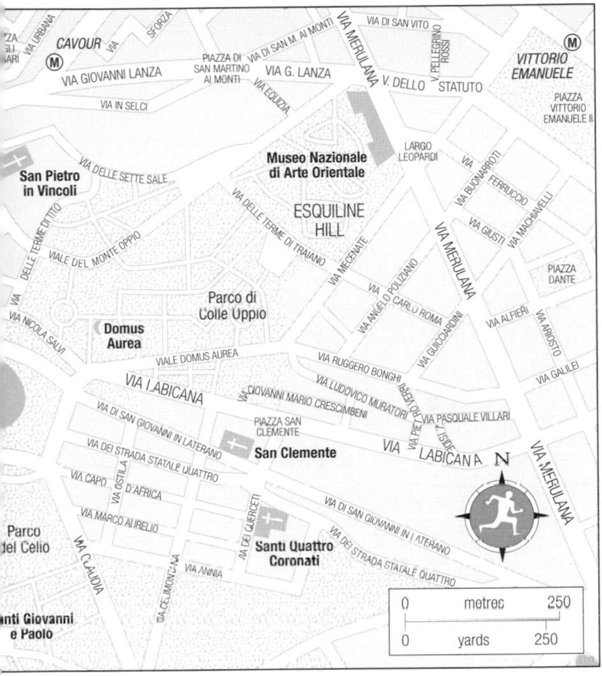

CIRCUS MAXIMUS

MAP PP.70–71, POCKET MAP F7

The southern side of the Palatine Hill drops down to **Circus Maximus**, a long green expanse that was the ancient city's main venue for chariot races. At one time this arena had a capacity of up to 400,000 spectators, and it still retains something of its original purpose as an occasional venue for festivals and concerts, though archeological authorities refused permission for chariot-racing scenes to be filmed here during the recent remake of *Ben Hur*.

IMPERIAL FORUMS

MAP PP.70–71, POCKET MAP F5

The original Roman Forum was the centre of republican-era Rome but the rise of the empire, and Rome's increased importance as a world power, led to the extensions of the **Imperial Forums** nearby. Julius Caesar began the expansion in around 50 BC, and work was continued after his assassination by his nephew and successor Augustus, and later by the Flavian emperors – Vespasian, Nerva and finally Trajan. With the exception of Trajan's markets, access to the area isn't possible, though from mid-April to October, sound and light shows offer grandstand views of the illuminated forums of Augustus and Caesar (W viaggioneifori.it).

TRAJAN'S MARKETS

Via IV Novembre 94 W www.mercatiditraiano.it. Tues–Sun 9am–7pm. €9.50. MAP PP.70–71, POCKET MAP F5

Trajan's Markets encompass a perfectly preserved crescent of ancients shops and arcades. The museum starts with the airy Great Hall; beyond is the Great Hemicycle section, with displays of important finds from the various forums, as well as the Via Biberatica, an ancient street lined with the

TRAJAN'S MARKETS

THE COLUMN OF TRAJAN

well-preserved remains of shops and bars. Outside, the **Forum of Trajan** holds the **Column of Trajan**, erected to celebrate the emperor's victories in Dacia and covered top to bottom with reliefs commemorating the highlights of the campaign.

SANTI COSMA E DAMIANO

Via dei Fori Imperiali 1. Daily 9am–1pm & 3–7pm. €1 donation for presepio. MAP PP.70–71, POCKET MAP F6

Across the road from the Forum of Augustus, the vestibule of the church of **Santi Cosma e Damiano** was originally created from the Temple of Romulus in the Forum, which you can look down into from the nave of the church. Turn around, and you'll see the mosaics in the apse, showing the naturalistic figures of the two saints being presented to Christ by St Peter and St Paul, flanked by St Felix on the left and St Theodore on the right. Outside, the cloister is wonderfully peaceful compared to the busy roads around. For a €1 donation you can also visit the massive eighteenth-century Neapolitan **presepio** or Christmas crib (Fri–Sun 10am–1pm & 3–6pm; closed Aug), displayed in a room in the corner, a huge piece of work with literally hundreds of figures spread among the ruins of ancient Rome.

The Tridente, Trevi and Quirinale

The northern part of Rome's city centre is sometimes known as the Tridente, due to the shape of the roads leading down from the apex of Piazza del Popolo – Via del Corso in the centre, Via di Ripetta on the left and Via del Babuino on the right. This was historically the artistic quarter of the capital, to which artists and Grand Tourists would flock, in search of the colourful, exotic city. At the top of the Spanish Steps you can turn left for the Pincio and Villa Borghese, or right for Via Sistina and the Quirinale district, which holds some of the city's most compelling sights, including the enormous Palazzo Barberini, home of some of the best of Rome's art. West of here is the Trevi Fountain, one of the city's most iconic and popular sights.

VIA DEL CORSO

MAP PP.76–77, POCKET MAP F13–15

Running north–south from Piazza del Popolo to Piazza Venezia, **Via del Corso** divides the city centre in two: the western side gives onto the dense streets of the Centro Storico and to the east, the swish shopping streets that converge on Piazza di Spagna. Named after the races that used to take place along here during Renaissance times, it is also Rome's main shopping street.

GALLERIA DORIA PAMPHILJ

Via del Corso 305. Daily 9am–7pm; €12, including audio guide in English; ☎ 06 679 7323, ⓦ www.doriapamphilj.it. MAP PP.76–77, POCKET MAP F15

The **Palazzo Doria Pamphilj** is among the city's finest Rococo palaces; the Doria-Pamphilj have long been one of Rome's most illustrious families, and still own the building and live in part of it. They were prodigious collectors of art, and, inside, the **Galleria Doria Pamphilj** constitutes one of Rome's best late Renaissance art collections, its paintings mounted in the style of the time, crammed in floor-to-ceiling, around the main courtyard. There are many highlights: a rare Italian work by Bruegel the Elder, a highly realistic portrait of an old man, the fabulously ugly *Moneylenders and their Clients* by Quentin Metsys, and a Hans Memling *Deposition*, as well as several paintings by Caravaggio – the magnificent *Rest on the Flight into Egypt*, *John the Baptist* and *Repentant Magdalene*. Look out, too, for the gallery's most famous works: a badly cracked bust of Innocent X by Bernini, which the sculptor apparently replaced in a week with the more famous version down the hall, and Velázquez's famous painting of the same man in the same room.

VIA DEL CORSO AT SUNSET

All in all, it is a marvellous collection of work, displayed in a wonderfully appropriate setting. Hourly guided tours take in the **private apartments**, some of which were lived in until recently, hence the family photos dotted around the place. Highlights include the Venice-themed Saletta Verde, with lagoon green furnishings, and the sunken, frescoed Bath of Diana on the ground floor.

FONDAZIONE ROMA MUSEO

Via del Corso 320 ⓣ06 2276 1260, ⓦfondazioneromamuseo.it. Tues–Sun 11am–8pm. Tickets from €10. MAP PP.76–77, POCKET MAP F14/15

Run by a cultural foundation, the **Fondazione Roma Museo** is a major exhibition space offering a dose of culture on shop-heavy Via del Corso. Its high-profile international shows are always worth a look.

SAN LORENZO IN LUCINA

Piazza di San Lorenzo in Lucina. Daily 8am–8pm. MAP PP.76–77, POCKET MAP E13

The church of **San Lorenzo in Lucina**, with its ancient campanile and columned portico, originally dates from the fifth century but was rebuilt in the twelfth. Inside, a section of the griddle on which St Lawrence was roasted (see p.100) lies in the first chapel on the right. A little further down is the tomb of the French painter Nicolas Poussin by his compatriot Chateaubriand; Poussin spent much of his life in Rome and died here in 1665.

CASA DI GOETHE

Via del Corso 18 ⓣ06 3265 0412, ⓦcasadigoethe.it; Tues–Sun 10am–6pm. €5. MAP PP.76–77, POCKET MAP E3

A short way down Via del Corso from Piazza del Popolo, the **Casa di Goethe** is a small and genuinely engaging museum, housed in the home the writer occupied for two years when travelling in Italy. He wrote much of his classic travelogue *Italian Journey* here – indeed, each room is decorated with a quote from the book – and the house has been restored as a modern exhibition space and holds books, letters, prints and drawings, plus a reconstruction of Goethe's study in Weimar. Among the objects on display are Piranesi prints of public spaces in Rome, watercolours by Goethe himself, a 1982 Warhol portrait of Goethe, and drawings by the German artist **Tischbein**, with whom he shared the premises.

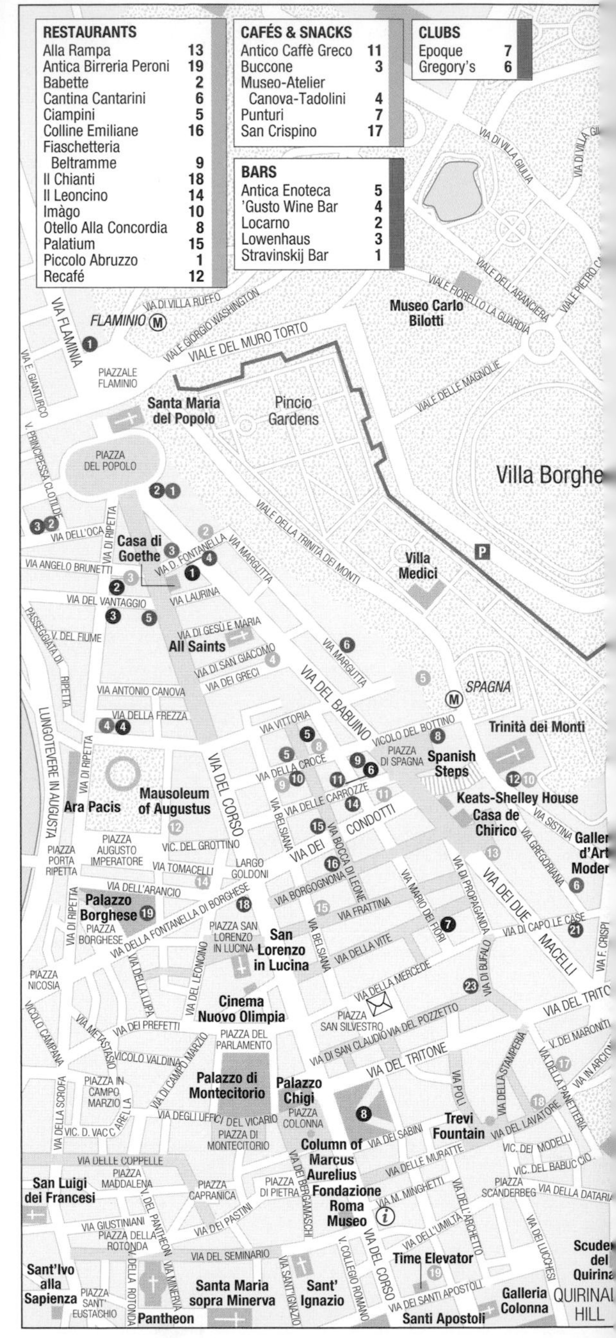
RESTAURANTS
Alla Rampa 13
Antica Birreria Peroni 19
Babette 2
Cantina Cantarini 6
Ciampini 5
Colline Emiliane 16
Fiaschetteria Beltramme 9
Il Chianti 18
Il Leoncino 14
Imàgo 10
Otello Alla Concordia 8
Palatium 15
Piccolo Abruzzo 1
Recafé 12
CAFÉS & SNACKS
Antico Caffè Greco 11
Buccone 3
Museo-Atelier Canova-Tadolini 4
Punturi 7
San Crispino 17
BARS
Antica Enoteca 5
'Gusto Wine Bar 4
Locarno 2
Lowenhaus 3
Stravinskij Bar 1
CLUBS
Epoque 7
Gregory's 6
FLAMINIO
VIA FLAMINIA
VIA DI VILLA RUFFO
VIALE GIORGIO WASHINGTON
VIALE DEL MURO TORTO
PIAZZALE FLAMINIO
VIA E. GIANTURCO
V. PRINCIPESSA CLOTILDE
Santa Maria del Popolo
Pincio Gardens
PIAZZA DEL POPOLO
Museo Carlo Bilotti
VIA DI VILLA GIULIA
VIALE FIORELLO LA GUARDIA
VIALE DELL'ARANCIERA
VIALE DELLE MAGNOLIE
Villa Borghese
VIALE DELLA TRINITÀ DEI MONTI
Villa Medici
VIA DELL'OCA
VIA DI RIPETTA
Casa di Goethe
VIA D. FONTANELLA
VIA MARGUTTA
VIA ANGELO BRUNETTI
VIA DEL VANTAGGIO
VIA LAURINA
PASSEGGIATA DI RIPETTA
V. DEL FIUME
VIA DI GESÙ E MARIA
All Saints
VIA DI SAN GIACOMO
VIA DEI GRECI
VIA DEL BABUINO
SPAGNA
VIA ANTONIO CANOVA
VIA DELLA FREZZA
LUNGOTEVERE IN AUGUSTA
VIA VITTORIA
VICOLO DEL BOTTINO
PIAZZA DI SPAGNA
Spanish Steps
Trinità dei Monti
VIA DELLA CROCE
VIA DELLE CARROZZE
Keats-Shelley House
Ara Pacis
Mausoleum of Augustus
VIA DEL CORSO
VIA BELSIANA
VIA DEI CONDOTTI
VIA BOCCA DI LEONE
Casa de Chirico
VIA SISTINA
VIA GREGORIANA
Galleria d'Arte Moderna
PIAZZA AUGUSTO IMPERATORE
PIAZZA PORTA RIPETTA
VIC. DEL GROTTINO
VIA TOMACELLI
LARGO GOLDONI
VIA BORGOGNONA
VIA MARIO DE' FIORI
VIA DI PROPAGANDA
VIA DEI DUE MACELLI
VIA DELL'ARANCIO
Palazzo Borghese
PIAZZA BORGHESE
VIA DELLA FONTANELLA DI BORGHESE
VIA FRATTINA
PIAZZA SAN LORENZO IN LUCINA
San Lorenzo in Lucina
VIA DELLA VITE
VIA DI CAPO LE CASE
PIAZZA NICOSIA
VIA DELLA LUPA
VIA DEL LEONCINO
VIA DELLA MERCEDE
VIA DI BUFALO
VIA DEL TRITONE
VICOLO CAMPANA
VIA METASTASIO
VIA DEI PREFETTI
Cinema Nuovo Olimpia
PIAZZA SAN SILVESTRO
VIA DEL POZZETTO
PIAZZA DEL PARLAMENTO
VIA DI SAN CLAUDIO
V. DEI MARONITI
VICOLO VALDINA
VIA DI CAMPO MARZIO
PIAZZA IN CAMPO MARZIO
Palazzo di Montecitorio
Palazzo Chigi
VIA POLI
VIA DELLA STAMPERIA
VIA DELLA PANETTERIA
VIA DELLA SCROFA
VIA DEGLI UFFICI DEL VICARIO
PIAZZA COLONNA
Trevi Fountain
VIA DEL LAVATORE
VIC. D. VACCARELLA
PIAZZA DI MONTECITORIO
Column of Marcus Aurelius
VIA DEI SABINI
VIC. DEI MODELLI
VIA DELLE COPPELLE
VIA DELLE MURATTE
VIC. DEL BABUCCIO
San Luigi dei Francesi
PIAZZA MADDALENA
PIAZZA CAPRANICA
PIAZZA DI PIETRA
VIA DEI BERGAMASCHI
Fondazione Roma Museo
VIA M. MINGHETTI
PIAZZA SCANDERBEG
VIA DELLA DATARIA
VIA GIUSTINIANI
PIAZZA DELLA ROTONDA
V. DEL PANTHEON
VIA DEI PASTINI
VIA DELL'UMILTÀ
VIA DELL'ARCHETTO
VIA DEI LUCCHESI
VIA DEL SEMINARIO
V. COLLEGIO ROMANO
Time Elevator
Scuderie del Quirinale
Sant'Ivo alla Sapienza
PIAZZA SANT' EUSTACHIO
VIA DELLA ROTONDA
VIA MINERVA
Pantheon
Santa Maria sopra Minerva
VIA SANT'IGNAZIO
Sant' Ignazio
VIA DEI SANTI APOSTOLI
Santi Apostoli
Galleria Colonna
QUIRINAL HILL

The Tridente, Trevi & Quirinale

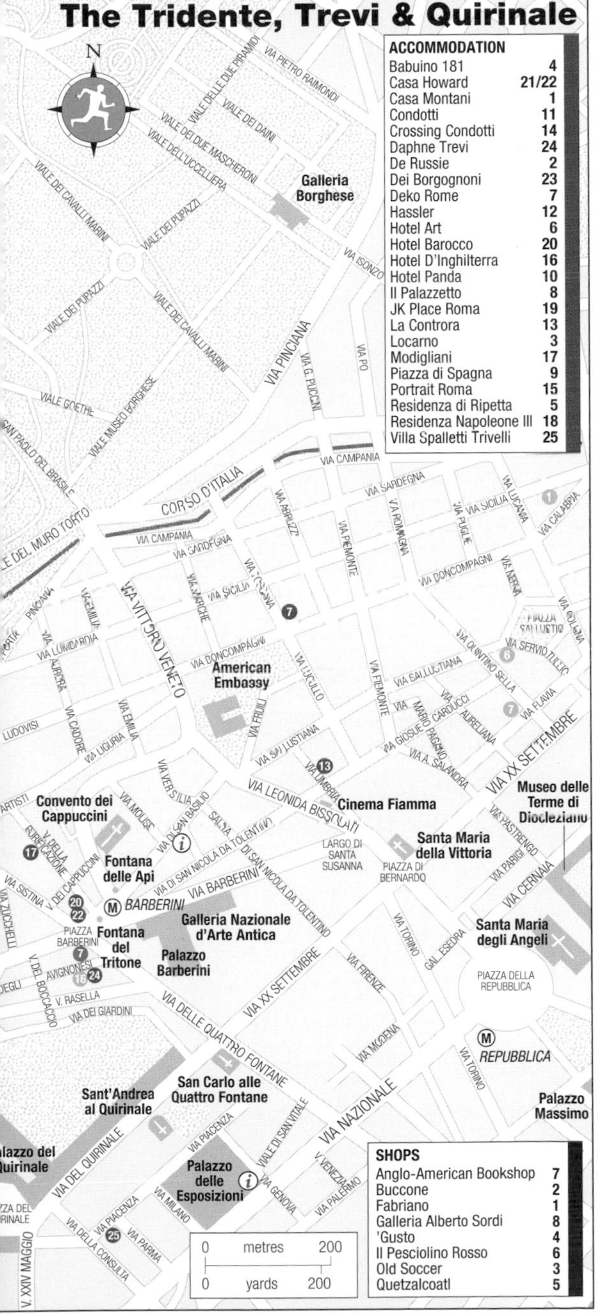

ACCOMMODATION	
Babuino 181	4
Casa Howard	21/22
Casa Montani	1
Condotti	11
Crossing Condotti	14
Daphne Trevi	24
De Russie	2
Dei Borgognoni	23
Deko Rome	7
Hassler	12
Hotel Art	6
Hotel Barocco	20
Hotel D'Inghilterra	16
Hotel Panda	10
Il Palazzetto	8
JK Place Roma	19
La Controra	13
Locarno	3
Modigliani	17
Piazza di Spagna	9
Portrait Roma	15
Residenza di Ripetta	5
Residenza Napoleone III	18
Villa Spalletti Trivelli	25

SHOPS	
Anglo-American Bookshop	7
Buccone	2
Fabriano	1
Galleria Alberto Sordi	8
'Gusto	4
Il Pesciolino Rosso	6
Old Soccer	3
Quetzalcoatl	5

PIAZZA DI SPAGNA

MAP PP.76–77, POCKET MAP F3

Piazza di Spagna underlines the area's international credentials, taking its name from the Spanish Embassy that has been standing here since the seventeenth century. It's a long, thin straggle of a square, almost entirely enclosed by buildings and centring on the distinctive boat-shaped Fontana della Barcaccia, the last work of Bernini's father, which remembers the great flood of Christmas Day 1598, when a barge from the Tiber was washed up on the slopes of Pincio Hill close by. The square itself is fringed by high-end clothes and jewellery shops and normally thronged with tourists, but for all that it is one of the city's most appealing open spaces and a fitting prelude to a spot of designer shopping on **Via Condotti** and nearby **Via Borgognona**.

KEATS-SHELLEY HOUSE

Piazza di Spagna 26 Ⓦ www.keats-shelley-house.org. Mon–Sat 10am–1pm & 2–6pm. €5. MAP PP.76–77, POCKET MAP F3

The English poet John Keats lived and died in a house on Piazza di Spagna in 1821, and it now serves as the **Keats-Shelley House**, an archive of English-language literary and historical works and a museum of manuscripts and mementoes relating to the Keats circle of the early nineteenth century – namely Keats himself, Shelley and Mary Shelley, and Byron (who at one time lived across the square). Keats came to Rome to recover his health but spent months in pain here before he finally died, at the age of just 25, confined to the house with his artist friend Joseph Severn. Among many bits of manuscript, letters and the like, you can see the poet's death mask, stored in the room where he died.

CASA DE CHIRICO

Piazza di Spagna 31 Ⓣ 06 679 6546, Ⓦ www.fondazionedechirico.org. Tues–Sat & 1st Sun of the month 9am–1pm, 1hr tours, only by appointment at 10am, 11am & noon. €7. MAP PP.76–77, POCKET MAP F3

Almost next door to the Keats-Shelley House, the fourth-floor **Casa de Chirico** was the home of the Greek-Italian artist Giorgio de Chirico for thirty years until his death in 1978. It's now a small

KEATS-SHELLEY HOUSE

museum that gives a glimpse into how De Chirico lived, and has a great many of his paintings on display: works from his classic surrealist period, and portraits of himself and his wife, who modelled for him. Upstairs, in keeping with the untouched nature of the house, De Chirico's bedroom is left with his books and rather uncomfortable looking single bed, while down the hall, the artist's studio, lit by a skylight in the terrace above, has his brushes and canvases.

SPANISH STEPS

MAP PP.76–77, POCKET MAP F3

The **Spanish Steps** sweep down in a cascade of balustrades and balconies, the hangout of young hopefuls waiting to be chosen as artists' models during the nineteenth century, and nowadays not much changed in their role as a venue for international posing and flirting late into the summer nights. The Steps, like the square, could in fact just as easily be known as the "French Steps" because of the French church of Trinità dei Monti they lead up to, and because it was largely a French initiative to build them. After a few decades of haggling over the plans, they were finally laid in 1725, to a design by Francesco de Sanctis, and they now form one of the city's most distinctive and deliberately showy attractions.

TRINITÀ DEI MONTI

Piazza della Trinità dei Monti. Tues, Wed & Fri–Sun 6.30am–8pm, Thurs 6.30am–noon.

MAP PP.76–77, POCKET MAP F3

Crowning the Spanish Steps, **Trinità dei Monti** is a largely sixteenth-century church designed by Carlo Maderno and paid for by the French. Its rose-coloured Baroque facade overlooks the rest of Rome from its hilltop site, and it's worth clambering up just for the views. While here you may as well pop your head around the door for a couple of impressive works by Daniele da Volterra, notably a soft, beautifully composed fresco of the *Assumption* in the third chapel on the right, whose array of finely realized figures includes a portrait of his teacher Michelangelo, and a superb, ingeniously composed *Deposition* across the nave. The French Baroque painter, Poussin, considered the latter – which was probably painted from a series of cartoons by Michelangelo (he's the greybeard on the right) – as the world's third greatest painting (Raphael's *Transfiguration* was, he thought, the best).

VILLA MEDICI

Viale della Trinità dei Monti 1 ⓣ 06 6761 311, ⓦ villamedici.it. Guided tours of the villa and gardens Tues–Sun: April, May, Sept & Oct 10am, 11am, noon (in English), 2pm, 3pm, 4.30pm & 6pm; June–Aug 10am, 11am, noon (in English), 3pm, 4.30pm & 6pm; Nov–March 10am, 11am, noon (in English), 2.30pm & 4pm; tours last 1hr 30min. €12. MAP PP.76–77, POCKET MAP F3

Walking north from the top of the Spanish Steps, you reach the sixteenth-century **Villa Medici**, home to the French Academy. Tours take in a couple of the villa's frescoed rooms, but the formal **gardens** are the real draw; you can visit the little Studiolo on the far side of the gardens, frescoed by Jacopo Zucchi in the mid-sixteenth century, and the Gipsoteca just beyond, full of casts of classical sculpture, while the views from the villa's terrace are among the best in Rome. The academy puts on exhibitions and concerts throughout the year; check the website.

THE PINCIO GARDENS

MAP PP.76–77, POCKET MAP E2

The terrace and gardens of the **Pincio**, a short walk from the top of the Spanish Steps, were laid out by Valadier in the early nineteenth century. Fringed with dilapidated busts of classical and Italian heroes, they give fine views over the roofs, domes and TV antennae of central Rome, right across to St Peter's and the Janiculum Hill. The view is the main event here, but there are also plenty of shady benches if you fancy a break, and the quirky nineteenth-century water clock at the back is worth a look. You can also hire bikes, rollerblades and odd little four-wheel carriages for getting around the gardens and the adjacent Villa Borghese (see p.134).

SANTA MARIA DEL POPOLO

Piazza del Popolo. Mon–Thurs & Sun 7.30am–12.30pm & 4–7pm, Fri & Sat 7.30am–7pm. MAP PP.76–77, POCKET MAP E2

Santa Maria del Popolo holds some of the best Renaissance art of any Roman church, with frescoes by Pinturicchio in the first chapel of the south aisle, and fine sculpture and mosaics in the Raphael-designed Chigi chapel (second on the left). Designed for the banker

VIEW FROM PINCIO GARDENS

Agostino Chigi in 1516, the chapel was not finished until the seventeenth century and most of the work was undertaken by other artists: Michelangelo's protégé, Sebastiano del Piombo, was responsible for the altarpiece, and two of the sculptures in the corner niches, of Daniel and Habakkuk, are by Bernini. The church's star attractions are the two pictures by Caravaggio in the left-hand chapel of the north transept: the *Conversion of St Paul* and the *Crucifixion of St Peter*, whose realism was considered extremely risqué in their time.

PIAZZA DEL POPOLO

MAP PP.76–77, POCKET MAP E2

The oval-shaped expanse of **Piazza del Popolo** is a dignified meeting of roads laid out in 1538 by Pope Paul III to make an impressive entrance to the city; it owes its present symmetry to Valadier, who added the central fountain in 1814. The monumental Porta del Popolo went up in 1655 and was the work of Bernini; the Chigi family symbol of his patron, Alexander VII – a heap of hills surmounted by a star – can clearly be seen above the main gateway. During summer, the steps around the obelisk and fountain, and the cafés on either side of the square, are popular hangouts. But the square's real attraction is the unbroken view it gives all the way back down Via del Corso to the central columns of the Vittoriano. If you get to choose your first view of the centre of Rome, make it this one.

PIAZZA DEL POPOLO

VIA DEL BABUINO

MAP PP.76–77, POCKET MAP E3–F3

Leading south from Piazza del Popolo to the Piazza di Spagna, **Via del Babuino** and the narrow **Via Margutta** – where the film-maker Federico Fellini once lived – was, in the 1960s, the core of a thriving art community and home to the city's best galleries and a fair number of its artists. High rents forced out all but the most successful, and the neighbourhood now supports a prosperous trade in antiques and designer fashions. Via del Babuino – literally "Street of the Baboon" – derives its name from the statue of Silenus that reclines outside the Tadolini studio about halfway down on the right. In ancient times the wall behind was a focus for satirical graffiti, although it is now coated with graffiti-proof paint. Inside the studio, the **Museo-Atelier Canova-Tadolini** (see p.88) is a café-restaurant, but a highly original one, littered with the sculptural work of four generations of the Tadolini family.

ARA PACIS

Lungotevere in Augusta ⓣ 060608, ⓦ arapacis.it. Daily 9.30am–7.30pm. €10.50, exhibitions extra. MAP PP.76–77, POCKET MAP E3

Forming the central core of the largely modern square of Piazza Augusto Imperatore, just off Via del Corso, the massive Mausoleum of Augustus is the burial place of the emperor and his family (closed for long-term restoration). On the far side of the square, the **Ara Pacis Augustae** or "Altar of Augustan Peace" is now enclosed in a purpose-built structure designed by the New York-based architect Richard Meier. A marble block enclosed by sculpted walls, the altar was built in 13 BC, probably to celebrate Augustus' victory over Spain and Gaul and the peace it heralded. Much of it had been dug up piecemeal over the years, but the bulk was uncovered in the middle of the last century. It is a superb example of imperial Roman sculpture, with a frieze on one side depicting the imperial family at the height of its power. It shows Augustus, his great general Marcus Agrippa and Augustus' wife Livia, followed by a victory procession containing her son (and Augustus' eventual successor) Tiberius and niece Antonia and her husband, Drusus, among others, while on the opposite side, the veiled figure is believed to be Julia, Augustus' daughter. A separate exhibition space attracts high-profile international shows.

GALLERIA D'ARTE MODERNA DI ROMA

Via Francesco Crispi 24 ⓣ 06 060608, ⓦ galleriaartemodernaroma.it. Tues–Sun 10am–6.30pm. €7.50. MAP PP.76–77, POCKET MAP F4

Not to be confused with Rome's main modern art museum (see p.138), the **Galleria d'Arte Moderna di Roma** is a much smaller affair – only about 150 works are on display at any one time. Rotating pieces from the museum's 3000-strong collection of nineteenth- and twentieth-century paintings, drawings and sculptures include works by prominent Italian artists such as Giacomo Manzù and Giacomo Balla.

TREVI FOUNTAIN

MAP PP.76–77, POCKET MAP G14

One of Rome's more surprising sights, the **Trevi Fountain** is a huge, Baroque gush of water over statues and rocks

ARA PACIS

TREVI FOUNTAIN

built onto the backside of a Renaissance palace. There was a Trevi fountain, designed by Alberti, around the corner in Via dei Crociferi, a smaller, more modest affair by all accounts, but Urban VIII decided to upgrade it in line with his other grandiose schemes of the time and employed Bernini, among others, to design an alternative nearby. Work didn't begin until 1732, when Niccolò Salvi won a competition held by Clement XII to design the fountain, and even then it took thirty years to finish the project. It's now, of course, the place you come to chuck in a coin if you want to guarantee your return to Rome, though you might remember Anita Ekberg throwing herself into it in *La Dolce Vita* (you're not encouraged to do the same).

In 2015 the fountain underwent a €2.2 million **restoration** – the most comprehensive in its history – funded by the Italian fashion house Fendi.

TIME ELEVATOR

Via dei Santissimi Apostoli 20 ⓣ06 6992 1823; ⓦtime-elevator.it. Daily 10.30am–7.30pm; shows every 45min–1hr. €12, 5–12 years €9. MAP PP.76–77, POCKET MAP F15

Flight-simulator seats and headphones (English audio available) set the stage for a 45min virtual tour of three thousand years of Roman history; one way of priming the kids for the sights they will be seeing.

GALLERIA COLONNA

Piazza dei Santissimi Apostoli 66 ⓣ06 670 43611, ⓦgalleriacolonna.it. Sat 9am–1.15pm, closed Aug. €12; free guided tours in English at noon. MAP PP.76–77, POCKET MAP G15

The **Galleria Colonna** is well worth a visit if you can time it right, not least for its chandelier-decked Great Hall, which glorifies the achievements of the nobleman Marcantonio Colonna – notably his great victory against the Turks at the Battle of Lepanto in 1589. Of the paintings, highlights include two lascivious depictions of Venus and Cupid, facing each other across the room, by Bronzino and Ghirlandaio, a group of landscapes by Dughet (Poussin's brother-in-law), Carracci's early and unusually spontaneous *Bean Eater*, a *Portrait of a Venetian Gentleman*, caught in supremely confident pose by Veronese, and a Tintoretto portrait of an old man. A newly opened wing holds seventeenth-century tapestries and other masterpieces.

SANTI APOSTOLI

Piazza dei Santi Apostoli 51. Daily 7am–noon & 4–7pm. MAP PP.76–77, POCKET MAP G15

The back of Palazzo Colonna is taken up by **Santi Apostoli**, a sixth-century basilica encased in an eighteenth-century shell. This Franciscan church was once part of the Colonna estate, and its airy interior is still looked after by the friars, who pad silently around while you take in its clash of Byzantine, Renaissance and Baroque styles. The north aisle contains the Italian sculptor Canova's first work in Rome, the grand tomb of Clement XIV above the door to the sacristry. But the church's statue-encrusted portico is its most impressive feature, commissioned by Pope Julius II, who lived in the palace next door.

PIAZZA BARBERINI

MAP PP.76–77, POCKET MAP F4–G4

At the top of the busy shopping street of Via del Tritone, Piazza Barberini is centred around Bernini's **Fontana del Tritone**, whose god of the sea gushes a high jet of water from a conch shell. Traditionally, this was the Barberini family's quarter of the city, and works by Bernini in their honour – they were the sculptor's greatest patrons – are thick on the ground here. He finished the Tritone fountain in 1644, before going on to design the **Fontana delle Api** (Fountain of the Bees) – a scallop shell studded with bees, the symbol of the Barberinis – across the road at the bottom end of Via Veneto.

CONVENTO DEI CAPPUCCINI

Via Veneto 27 ⓣ 06 8880 3695, ⓦ www.cappucciniviaveneto.it. Daily 9am–7pm; ticket office closes 30min earlier. €8.50. MAP PP.76–77, POCKET MAP G3

The church of **Santa Maria della Concezione**, another Barberini-sponsored creation,

FONTANA DEL TRITONE IN PIAZZA BARBERINI

holds the **Convento dei Cappuccini**, now an eight-room **museum** exploring the lives of the Capuchin friars. The star exhibit is Caravaggio's *St Francis in Meditation*; other rooms focus on daily objects that offer a glimpse into the friars' lives, from medicine-making apparatus to a collection of watches they wore as a reminder of their own mortality. What most visitors come to see, however, is the **crypt**, seen at the end of the museum. Erected in the mid-eighteenth century, it holds the bones of 3700 monks and paupers, painstakingly assembled into works of art, and fashioned into chandeliers, shelves and door frames. One of the more macabre and bizarre sights of Rome.

VIA VENETO

MAP PP.76–77, POCKET MAP G3

The pricey bars and restaurants lining Via Veneto were once the haunt of Rome's beautiful people, made famous by Fellini's 1960 film *La Dolce Vita*. But they left a long time ago, and the street, despite being home to some of Rome's fanciest hotels, has never quite recovered the cachet it had in the Sixties and Seventies. Nonetheless, its pretty tree-lined aspect, pavement cafés, swanky stores and uniformed hotel bellmen lend it an upmarket European air that is unlike anywhere else in Rome.

PALAZZO BARBERINI

Via delle Quattro Fontane 13. ☎ 06 482 4184. Tues–Sun 8.30am–7pm. €7, or €9 including Palazzo Corsini, valid three days; free first Sun of the month; apartment tours (first Sat of the month 11am; €6) need to be booked in advance on ☎ 06 3996 7700. MAP PP.76–77. POCKET MAP G4

The Palazzo Barberini is home to the **Galleria Nazionale d'Arte Antica** – a rich patchwork of mainly Italian art from the early Renaissance to the late Baroque period. It's a splendid collection, highlighted by works by Titian, El Greco and Caravaggio. But perhaps the most impressive feature of the gallery is the building itself, worked on by Bernini, Borromini and Maderno. The first-floor Gran Salone is dominated by Pietro da Cortona's manic fresco of *The Triumph of Divine Providence*, an exuberant Baroque work which almost crawls down the walls to meet you. Of the paintings, be sure to see Caravaggio's *Judith Beheading Holofernes*; Fra' Filippo Lippi's *Madonna and Child*; and Raphael's *Fornarina* – a painting of the daughter of a Trasteveran baker thought to have been his mistress (Raphael's name appears clearly on the woman's bracelet). Look out also for Bronzino's rendering of the marvellously erect *Stefano Colonna* and a portrait of *Henry VIII* by Hans Holbein.

SAN CARLO ALLE QUATTRO FONTANE

Via del Quirinale 23. Mon–Fri 10am–1pm & 3–6pm, Sat & Sun 10am–1pm. MAP PP.76–77. POCKET MAP G4

The church of **San Carlo alle Quattro Fontane** – next door to the four fountains that give it its name – was Borromini's first real design commission. In it he displays all the ingenuity he later became known for, cramming the church elegantly into a tiny and awkwardly shaped site that apparently covers roughly the same surface area as one of the main piers of St Peter's.

SANT'ANDREA AL QUIRINALE

Via del Quirinale 29. Tues–Sat 8.30am–noon & 2.30–6pm, Sun 9am–noon & 2.30–6pm. MAP PP.76–77. POCKET MAP G4

A flamboyant building that Bernini planned as a kind of flat oval shape to fit into its wide but shallow site. Like San Carlo, it's ingenious inside, its wide, elliptical nave cleverly made into a grand space despite its small size. For €2 you can visit the sacristy, with its artful frescoes, where cherubs pull aside painted drapery to let in light from mock windows, and the rooms of St Stanislaus Kostka, where the Polish saint lived (and died) in 1568. Paintings by Andrea Pozzo illustrate the saint's life and culminate in a chapel that focuses on a rather lifelike painted statue of Stanislaus on his deathbed.

PALAZZO BARBERINI

PALAZZO DEL QUIRINALE

Piazza del Quirinale ⓣ06 3996 7557, ⓦpalazzo.quirinale.it. Visit by obligatory guided tour Tues, Wed, Fri, Sat & Sun 9.30am–4pm; book at least a week in advance. 1hr 20min tour €1.50, 2hr 30min tour €10. MAP PP.76–77, POCKET MAP F4

The sixteenth-century **Palazzo del Quirinale** was the official summer residence of the popes until Unification, when it became the royal palace. It's now the home of Italy's president. The main feature of the piazza outside is the huge statue of the Dioscuri, aka Castor and Pollux: 5m-tall Roman copies of classical Greek statues, brought here by Pope Sixtus V in the early sixteenth century. Two **tours** visit the palace's interior. The first (1hr 20min) starts with a fragment of Melozzo da Forlì's fifteenth-century fresco of Christ, painted for the apse of Santi Apostoli, and takes in the sumptuous rooms of the *piano nobile*, including the Hall of Mirrors and Hall of Tapestries; the second (2hr 20min) goes on to see the palace's porcelain collection, a museum of carriages and the gardens.

SCUDERIE DEL QUIRINALE

Via XXIV Maggio 16 ⓣ06 3996 7500, ⓦscuderiequirinale.it. Exhibitions around €12. MAP PP.76–77, POCKET MAP F4

Set in the old papal stables and strikingly remodelled in the 1990s, this is one of Rome's biggest and best art spaces, putting on prestigious international exhibitions.

VIA XX SETTEMBRE

MAP PP.76–77, POCKET MAP G4–H3

Via XX Settembre spears out to the Aurelian Wall from Via del Quirinale and was the route by which troops entered the city on September 20, 1870 – the place where they breached the wall is marked with a column. It's not Rome's most appealing thoroughfare, flanked by national government offices. However, halfway down, the Fontana dell'Acqua Felice is worth a look: it focuses on a massive, bearded figure of Moses playfully fronted by four basking lions, and marks the end of the Acqua Felice aqueduct.

PALAZZO DEL QUIRINALE

SANTA MARIA DELLA VITTORIA

Via XX Settembre 17. Daily 8.30am–noon & 3.30–6pm. MAP PP.76–77, POCKET MAP G3

Santa Maria della Vittoria's best-known feature is Bernini's sculpture the *Ecstasy of St Theresa of Avila*, the centrepiece of the sepulchral chapel of Cardinal Cornaro. St Theresa is one of the Catholic Church's most enduring mystics, and the sculpture records the moment when, in 1537, she had a vision of an angel piercing her heart with a dart. It's very Baroque in the most populist sense – not only is the event quite literally staged, but St Theresa's ecstasy verges on the worldly as she lies back in groaning submission beneath a mass of dishevelled garments and drapery. The Cornaro cardinals are depicted murmuring and nudging each other as they watch the spectacle from theatre boxes.

Shops

ANGLO-AMERICAN BOOKSHOP

Via della Vite 102. Mon 3.30–7.30pm, Tues–Sat 10.30am–7.30pm; open later on Mon and closes earlier on Sat in summer. MAP PP.76–77, POCKET MAP F13

One of the best selections of new English books in Rome, especially for history.

BUCCONE

Via di Ripetta 19. Mon–Fri 9am–9.30pm, Sat 9am–11.30pm, Sun 11am–6pm. MAP PP.76–77, POCKET MAP E3

The centre's best wine shop, this is an atmospheric enoteca with a large selection of wines, spirits and especially grappa.

FABRIANO

Via del Babuino 173. Daily 10am–8pm. MAP PP.76–77, POCKET MAP E3

Tridente branch of this chain, specializing in lovely stationery in rainbow colours, plus a range of wallets and bags.

GALLERIA ALBERTO SORDI

Via del Corso. Mon–Fri 8.30am–9pm, Sat 8.30am –9pm, Sun 9.30am–9pm. MAP PP.76–77, POCKET MAP F14

This nineteenth-century shopping arcade is home to some great shops and provides a cool escape from the Via del Corso crowds on hot days.

'GUSTO

Piazza Augusto Imperatore 7. Daily 10.30am–8pm. MAP PP.76–77, POCKET MAP E3

Everything for the aspirant gourmet: wines, decanters, glasses and all the top-of-the-line kitchen gadgets you could ever hope to find. Also a large selection of cookbooks in English.

IL PESCIOLINO ROSSO

Via Bocca di Leone 49. Daily 10.30am–2.30pm & 3.30–7.30pm. MAP PP.76–77, POCKET MAP E3

'GUSTO

This tiny shop is packed with beautiful toys, mostly of the tasteful wooden variety. Great for unusual gifts.

OLD SOCCER

Via di Ripetta 30. Daily 10am–7.30pm. MAP PP.76–77, POCKET MAP E3

Old-fashioned Italian football shirts – ironically enough, made in England. Great presents for football-mad friends.

QUETZALCOATL

Via delle Carrozze 26. Daily 10am–7.30pm. MAP PP.76–77, POCKET MAP E3

Chocolates here are presented as if they were art; once you taste them, you'll probably feel that they are. Gift boxes of all sizes available.

Cafés and snacks

ANTICO CAFFÈ GRECO

Via Condotti 86. Daily 9am–9pm. MAP PP.76–77, POCKET MAP F3

Founded in 1760, and patronized by Casanova, Byron, Goethe and Stendhal, this café is a bit of a tourist joint these days, but its *granita di caffè* is still a hit on a hot day.

BUCCONE

Via di Ripetta 19. Mon–Fri 9am–9.30pm, Sat 9am–11.30pm, Sun 11am–6pm. MAP PP.76–77, POCKET MAP E13

One of the best places for lunch in the Piazza del Popolo area, with tables laid out amid its bottle-lined shelves, and a daily changing menu. Salads or cold meat platters as well as a few hot daily specials go for €9–14.

MUSEO-ATELIER CANOVA-TADOLINI

Via del Babuino 150a. Mon–Sat 8am–11.30pm, Sun 10am–11.30pm. MAP PP.76–77, POCKET MAP E3

It's a bit odd eating surrounded by this café-cum-museum's sculptures – and it's not cheap – but this is one of the few places to sit down along this busy street, serving sandwiches, salads and pasta dishes.

PUNTURI

Via Flavia 48. Mon–Fri 8am–8pm, Sat 8am–8pm. MAP PP.76–77, POCKET MAP H3

A historic *gastronomia*, with superb pizza by the slice and a handful of hot dishes – lasagne, *arancini* – at lunch time.

SAN CRISPINO

Via della Panetteria 42. Mon–Thurs & Sun noon–12.30am, Fri & Sat noon–1.30am, closed Tues in winter. MAP PP.76–77, POCKET MAP G14

Considered by many to be the best ice cream in Rome. Wonderful flavours – all natural – other *gelato* you've known can't compete.

SAN CRISPINO

Restaurants

ALLA RAMPA

Piazza Mignanelli 18 ☎ 06 678 2621. Daily noon–11pm. MAP PP.76–77, POCKET MAP G13

Touristy, but with perhaps the best antipasti buffet in town – a snip at €11. The dining room, a mocked-up piazza, is pretty kitsch but the outside terrace, just off Piazza di Spagna, is large and undeniably appealing.

ANTICA BIRRERIA PERONI

Via San Marcello 19 ☎ 06 679 5310. Mon–Sat noon–midnight. MAP PP.76–77, POCKET MAP F15

Wood-panelled and featuring photos of old Rome and an original Art Nouveau frieze, this no-frills trattoria has been feeding hungry Romans for over a century. Great atmosphere, and hearty portions at low prices (ravioli with ricotta and spinach €7.50).

BABETTE

Via Margutta 1–3 ☎ 06 321 1559. Mon 7–10.30pm, Tues–Sun 1–3pm & 7–10.30pm; closed Aug. MAP PP.76–77, POCKET MAP E2

The name comes from the Danish foodie film, *Babette's Feast*, but food here is Italian rather than Danish, with a popular lunch buffet at weekends (€28), good-value dinners and a lovely courtyard.

CANTINA CANTARINI

Piazza Sallustio 12 ☎ 06 474 3341. Mon–Sat 12.30–3.30pm & 7.30–11pm. MAP PP.76–77, POCKET MAP H3

Very simple, very popular restaurant serving rustic food from both the Marche region and Rome (meat Mon–Thurs, fish Thurs at dinner to Sat). Excellent value.

ANTICA BIRRERIA PERONI

CIAMPINI

Viale Trinità dei Monti ☎ 06 678 5678. Daily 12.30–3.30pm & 7–11pm. MAP PP.76–77, POCKET MAP F3

The best branch of this city-wide chain, with great views from its garden terrace, where you watch the resident turtles in the fountain while choosing from a good selection of pasta dishes – and meat and fish mains from the grill – chicken, swordfish and the like.

COLLINE EMILIANE

Via degli Avignonesi 22 ☎ 06 481 7538. Tues–Sat 12.45–2.45pm & 7.30–10.45pm, Sun 12.45–2.45pm. MAP PP.76–77, POCKET MAP G4

Just down from Piazza Barberini, on a quiet backstreet not far from the Trevi Fountain, this cosy family-run restaurant serves excellent Emilian food at moderate prices (mains around €17).

FIASCHETTERIA BELTRAMME

Via della Croce 39 ☎ 06 6979 7200. Daily noon–11pm. MAP PP.76–77, POCKET MAP E3

Originally this place sold only wine, by the *fiasco* (flask). A few blocks from the Spanish Steps, it is now a full-blown restaurant and just about always packed. But if you want authentic Roman food and atmosphere at affordable prices – around €12 for a *primo*, €15 for a *secondo* – then this is the place. Service can be a bit slow. Bookings taken for dinner only.

IL CHIANTI

Via del Lavatore 81/82a ☎ 06 678 7550. Daily 12.30–3.30pm & 7–11.30pm. MAP PP.76–77, POCKET MAP G14

Just metres from the Trevi Fountain, this Tuscan specialist is a find in a part of town not generally known for its good-value food and drink. Good spreads of Tuscan cheese and cold meats, a selection of meat dishes and the usual pasta dishes and pizzas. You can sit outside in summer if you can bear the travelling musicians who congregate to entertain the tourists.

IL LEONCINO

Via del Leoncino 28 ☎ 06 686 7757. Mon, Tues & Thurs–Sun 1–2.30pm & 7pm–midnight. MAP PP.76–77, POCKET MAP E13

Cheap, hectic and genuine pizzeria – one of the very best for lovers of crispy Roman-style pizza, baked in a wooden oven.

IMÀGO

Hotel Hassler, Piazza Trinità dei Monti 6 ☎ 06 6993 4726. Daily 7–10.30pm. MAP PP.76–77, POCKET MAP F3

With panoramic views of Rome's skyline at every turn (book a window table), Michelin-starred *Imàgo* is a romantic spot for a special-occasion meal. If you're hungry, opt for chef Francesco Apreda's tasting menu, featuring ten courses of modern Italian cuisine for €140 per person. Men are required to wear a jacket.

OTELLO ALLA CONCORDIA

Via della Croce 81 ☎ 06 679 1178. Mon–Sat 12.15–3pm & 7–11pm, open Sun 12.15–3pm mid-Sept to May. MAP PP.76–77, POCKET MAP E3

This place used to be one of Fellini's favourites – he lived just a few blocks away on Via Margutta – and it remains an elegant yet affordable choice in the heart of Rome. A complete offering of Roman and Italian dishes, but ask for *spaghetti Otello* for a taste of tradition – a delicious combination of fresh tomatoes and basil with garlic.

RECAFÉ

PALATIUM

Via Frattina 94 ☎ 06 6920 2132. Daily 8am–11pm. MAP PP.76–77, POCKET MAP F13

Smart and sleek, this Spanish Steps-area wine bar-cum-restaurant celebrates the wine and food of the Lazio region around Rome, with a short menu of local specialities and a long list of Lazio wines. Dishes like *tonnarelli cacio e pepe* or mains like rabbit or sausage from the hills to the north and south of the city go for €13–18.

PICCOLO ABRUZZO

Via Sicilia 237 ☎ 06 4282 0176. Daily 12.30–3pm & 6.30pm–12.30am. MAP PP.76–77, POCKET MAP H2

A five-minute stroll up the unprepossessing Via Sicilia from Via Veneto, this is a great alternative to the glitzy, mob-run places on the *Dolce Vita* street. No menu, just a seemingly endless parade of Abruzzese and other goodies plonked on your table at regular intervals – all for around €35 a head. Be sure to come hungry.

RECAFÉ

Piazza Augusto Imperatore 9 ☎ 06 6813 4730. Mon 12.15–3.30pm & 7.30pm–midnight, Tues–Sun 12.15–midnight. MAP PP.76–77, POCKET MAP E13

The entrance on Via del Corso is a Neapolitan café, while on the Piazza Augusta Imperatore side you can enjoy proper Neapolitan pizzas, good pasta and salad dishes and excellent grilled *secondi* for moderate prices – €13 or so for a *primo*, €13–23 for a *secondo*. The ambience is chic and the large outside terrace always has a buzz about it.

Bars

ANTICA ENOTECA

Via della Croce 76b. Daily noon–1am. MAP PP.76–77, POCKET MAP E3

An old Spanish Steps-area wine bar with a cosy interior and a selection of hot and cold dishes, including soups and attractive desserts. Intriguing trompe l'oeil decorations inside, majolica-topped tables outside.

'GUSTO WINE BAR

Via della Frezza 16 ⓣ 06 322 6273. Daily noon–2am. MAP PP.76–77, POCKET MAP E3

This stylish modern bar is part of the *'Gusto* empire (see p.87), and serves drinks, sandwiches and tapas to Rome's chattering classes. Access to the bar is around the corner from the main entrance.

LOCARNO

Via della Penna 22 ⓣ 06 361 0041. Daily 7am–1am. MAP PP.76–77, POCKET MAP E2

The decadent atmosphere graced with hip cocktail-sippers and a clubby back room with cosy fireplace make this Rome's most egalitarian hotel bar. It's frequented by literati, artists, near-paupers, fashionistas and ordinary folk. Warm weather adds a roof terrace to the mix.

LOWENHAUS

Via della Fontanella 16. Daily 10.30am–2am MAP PP.76–77, POCKET MAP E2

Just off Piazza del Popolo, this bar serves big German beers and sausage and other snacks in an authentic *bierkeller*-style space. Full meals too, and outside seating.

STRAVINSKIJ BAR

Hotel de Russie, Via del Babuino 9 ⓣ 06 3288 8874. Daily 9am–1am. MAP PP.76–77, POCKET MAP E2

STRAVINSKIJ BAR

On a warm evening, there's no better place in Rome for a cocktail than this bar's lovely courtyard. The *Hotel de Russie*'s well-heeled guests rub shoulders with sharp-suited business folk and assorted models and starlets, sipping the bar's creative cocktails (try the Clarita, with tequila, pink grapefruit, honey and lavender bitter).

Clubs

EPOQUE

Just off Piazza Barberini ⓣ 351 195 8110, ⓦ clubepoque.com. Fri & Sat noon–3pm & 8pm–4am. Entry €15–20. MAP PP.76–77, POCKET MAP F4

A bar/restaurant/club, Epoque lays on weekend burlesque shows followed by vintage-flavoured dj sets that mix 50s, 60s, 80s and 90s tunes.

GREGORY'S

Via Gregoriana 54d ⓣ 06 679 6386, ⓦ www.gregorysjazz.com. Tues–Sun 8pm–2am; concerts start around 10pm. MAP PP.76–77, POCKET MAP G13

Just up the Spanish Steps and to the right, this elegant nightspot pulls in the crowds with its live jazz, improvised by Roman and international musicians.

The Esquiline, Monti and Termini

Monti is named after the two hills it encompasses: the Esquiline, the city's highest and largest, once ancient Rome's most fashionable residential quarter; and the Viminale, the smallest – home to the Interior Ministry and little else. In recent years Monti has become increasingly gentrified, its cobbled streets lined with cosy bars and restaurants and arty boutiques. It is also home to key sights like Nero's Domus Aurea and the basilica of Santa Maria Maggiore, and is close to Termini station, the focal point of a down-at-heel area that holds much of the city's budget accommodation. Nearby, studenty San Lorenzo and hip Pigneto are nightlife hubs, full of bars and restaurants.

DOMUS AUREA

Viale della Domus Aurea 1 ⓣ 06 3996 7700, ⓦ coopculture.it. Sat & Sun 9am–5pm; last entry 3.45pm; entry by prebooked guided tour only, limited to groups of 25 people; visits last 1hr 15min; check the website for changes to opening hours. €12. MAP PP.94–95, POCKET MAP H6

Currently undergoing a decade-long, €39-million restoration, the **Domus Aurea**, or "Golden House", was a vast undertaking built on the Oppian Hill after the fire of 64 AD (allegedly started by Nero) devastated two-thirds of ancient Rome, conveniently clearing the way for Nero's villa complex. Scholars reckon the villa and its surrounding parkland extended for a square kilometre or more to the slopes of the Palatine, Esquiline and Celian hills.

Among countless excesses, it is thought the facade was coated in solid gold, one of the dining rooms was rigged up to shower flower petals and scent on guests, and that Nero erected a huge statue of himself as a sun god, so big that 24 elephants were needed to put the base in place. Nero died four years after the palace's completion, and Vespasian tore much of it down in disgust, draining its lake and building the Colosseum on top. Later, Trajan built his baths on top of the rest of the complex, and it was pretty much forgotten until its wall paintings were discovered by Renaissance artists, including Raphael and Pinturicchio, who descended ladders into what they at first believed was some kind of mystical cave.

Engaging **tours** take you through a series of chilly rooms and corridors (dress warmly, even in summer), several of which are decorated in the so-called Third Pompeiian style, with garlands of flowers, fruit, vines and foliage. Highlights are the **Room of the Gilded Vault**, its original ceiling dotted with holes made by the Renaissance painter-explorers, and the **Octagonal Room**, with a hole in the middle of its domed ceiling and a stepped artificial waterfall.

SANTA MARIA MAGGIORE

Piazza di Santa Maria Maggiore. Daily: basilica 7am–6.45pm; museum 9.30am–6.30pm; loggia and apostolic palace 9am–6.30pm. Basilica free, museum €3, loggia and apostolic palace €3. MAP PP.94–95, POCKET MAP H5

One of the city's four patriarchal basilicas, **Santa Maria Maggiore** includes one of Rome's best-preserved Byzantine interiors. It was originally built during the fifth century after the Virgin Mary appeared to Pope Liberius in a dream on the night of August 4, 352 AD. She told him to erect a church in her honour on the Esquiline Hill – the exact spot would be marked the next morning by newly fallen snow outlining the plan of the church. Despite it being the height of summer, Liberius duly found the miraculous blueprint and the event is commemorated every year on August 5, when at midday Mass white rose petals are showered on the congregation from the ceiling, and at night the fire department operates an artificial snow machine in the piazza in front of the church.

Inside, the **basilica** is fringed on both sides with well-kept mosaics, most of which date from the time of Pope Sixtus III and recount incidents from the Old Testament. The chapel in the right transept holds the elaborate tomb of Sixtus V – another, less famous Sistine chapel, decorated with frescoes and stucco reliefs showing events from his reign. Outside is the tomb of the Bernini family; opposite, the Pauline chapel is home to the tombs of the Borghese pope, Paul V, and his immediate predecessor Clement VIII, as well as that of Pauline Bonaparte, Napoleon's sister. Between the two chapels, the *confessio* contains a kneeling statue of Pope Pius IX, and, beneath it, a reliquary that is said to contain fragments of the crib of Christ. It's the mosaics of the arch that really dazzle, a vivid representation of scenes from the life of Christ. The **museum** underneath the basilica sports what is, even by Roman standards, a wide variety of relics, while the **loggia** above the main entrance has some magnificent mosaics showing Christ among various saints, sitting above four scenes that tell the story of the miracle of the snow. Off the loggia, the "**Room of the Popes**", part of the **apostolic palace**, holds various devotional items; don't miss Bernini's splendid staircase next door.

The Esquiline, Monti & Termini

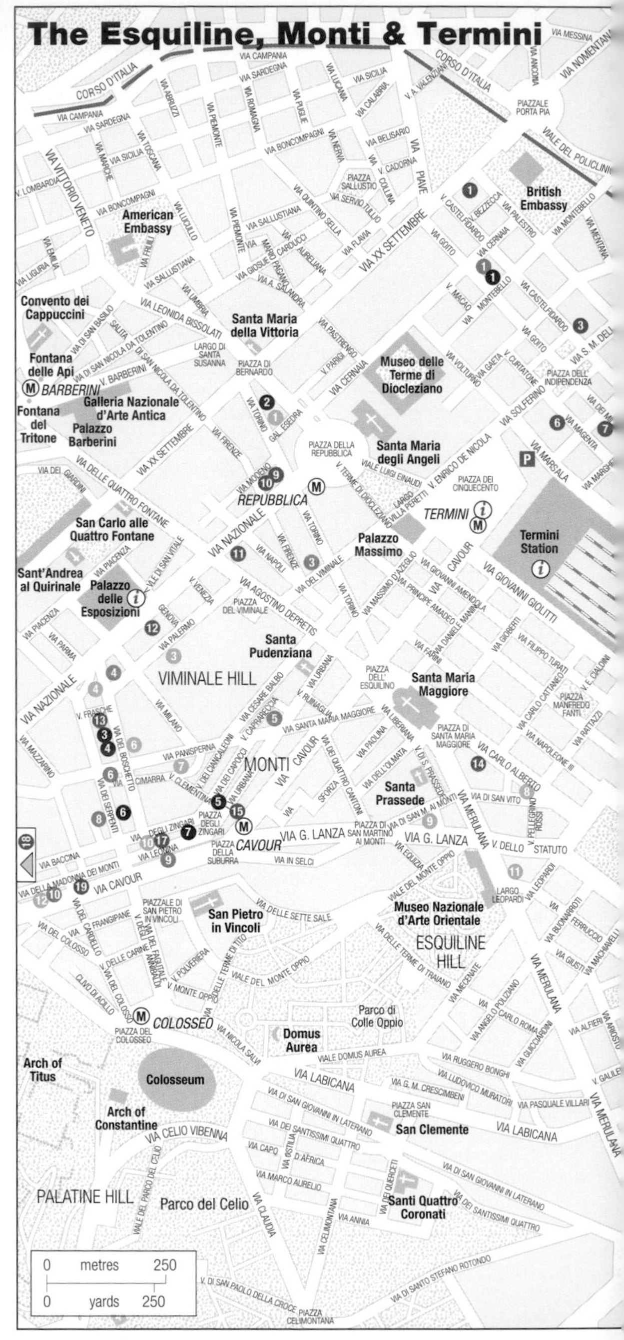

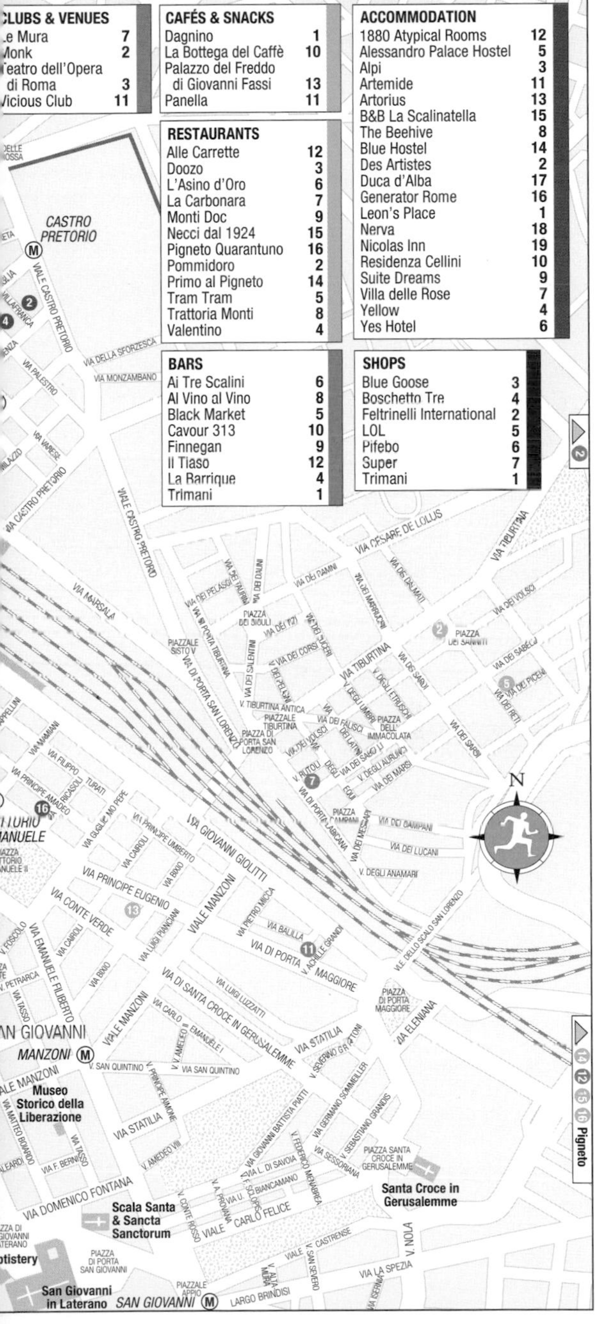
CLUBS & VENUES
Le Mura 7
Monk 2
Teatro dell'Opera di Roma 3
Vicious Club 11
CAFÉS & SNACKS
Dagnino 1
La Bottega del Caffè 10
Palazzo del Freddo di Giovanni Fassi 13
Panella 11
ACCOMMODATION
1880 Atypical Rooms 12
Alessandro Palace Hostel 5
Alpi 3
Artemide 11
Artorius 13
B&B La Scalinatella 15
The Beehive 8
Blue Hostel 14
Des Artistes 2
Duca d'Alba 17
Generator Rome 16
Leon's Place 1
Nerva 18
Nicolas Inn 19
Residenza Cellini 10
Suite Dreams 9
Villa delle Rose 7
Yellow 4
Yes Hotel 6
RESTAURANTS
Alle Carrette 12
Doozo 3
L'Asino d'Oro 6
La Carbonara 7
Monti Doc 9
Necci dal 1924 15
Pigneto Quarantuno 16
Pommidoro 2
Primo al Pigneto 14
Tram Tram 5
Trattoria Monti 8
Valentino 4
BARS
Ai Tre Scalini 6
Al Vino al Vino 8
Black Market 5
Cavour 313 10
Finnegan 9
Il Tiaso 12
La Barrique 4
Trimani 1
SHOPS
Blue Goose 3
Boschetto Tre 4
Feltrinelli International 2
LOL 5
Pifebo 6
Super 7
Trimani 1
CASTRO PRETORIO
VIALE CASTRO PRETORIO
VIA DELLA SFORZESCA
VIA MONZAMBANO
VIA PALESTRO
VIA MARSALA
VIA CESARE DE LOLLIS
VIA TIBURTINA
VIA DEI VOLSCI
PIAZZA DEI SANNITI
PIAZZA DEI SICULI
PIAZZALE SISTO V
VIA DI PORTA SAN LORENZO
PIAZZA DI PORTA SAN LORENZO
PIAZZALE TIBURTINA
PIAZZA DELL' IMMACOLATA
VIA DEI SARDI
PIAZZA CAMPANI
VIA DEI CAMPANI
VIA DEI LUCANI
V. DEGLI ANAMARI
VIA GIOVANNI GIOLITTI
VIA PRINCIPE EUGENIO
VIA CONTE VERDE
VIALE MANZONI
VIA EMANUELE FILIBERTO
VIA DI PORTA MAGGIORE
PIAZZA DI PORTA MAGGIORE
VLE. DELLO SCALO SAN LORENZO
VIA ELENIANA
VIA DI SANTA CROCE IN GERUSALEMME
VIA STATILIA
MANZONI
V. SAN QUINTINO
Museo Storico della Liberazione
PIAZZA SANTA CROCE IN GERUSALEMME
Santa Croce in Gerusalemme
VIA DOMENICO FONTANA
Scala Santa & Sancta Sanctorum
VIALE CARLO FELICE
VIALE CASTRENSE
PIAZZA DI PORTA SAN GIOVANNI
San Giovanni in Laterano
SAN GIOVANNI
LARGO BRINDISI
VIA LA SPEZIA
V. NOLA
Pigneto

SANTA PUDENZIANA MOSAIC

SANTA PUDENZIANA

Via Urbana 160. Daily 8.30am–noon & 3–6pm. MAP PP.94–95, POCKET MAP H5

This church was for many years believed to have been built on the site where St Peter lived and worshipped and once housed two relics: the chair that St Peter used as his throne and the table at which he said Mass, though both have long gone – to the Vatican and the Lateran Palace respectively. It still has one feature of ancient origin – its superb fifth-century apse **mosaics**, fluid and beautiful works centring on a golden enthroned Christ surrounded by the apostles.

SAN PIETRO IN VINCOLI

Piazza di San Pietro in Vincoli 4a. Daily 8am–12.30pm & 3–7pm; closes 6pm Oct–March. MAP PP.94–95, POCKET MAP G5

San Pietro in Vincoli is one of Rome's most delightfully plain churches. It was built to house an important relic, the two sets of chains (*vincoli*) that bound St Peter when imprisoned in Jerusalem and held him in the Mammertine Prison, which miraculously fused together when they were brought into contact with each other. The chains can still be seen in the *confessio* beneath the high altar, but most people come for the tomb of Pope Julius II at the far end of the southern aisle. The aisle occupied Michelangelo on and off for much of his career and was the cause of many a dispute with Julius and his successors. He reluctantly gave it up to paint the Sistine Chapel – the only statues that he managed to complete are the *Moses*, *Leah* and *Rachel*, which remain here, and two *Dying Slaves*, which are now in the Louvre, Paris. The figures are among the artist's most captivating works, especially *Moses*: because of a medieval mistranslation of scripture, he is depicted with satyr's horns instead of the "radiance of the Lord" that Exodus tells us shone around his head. Nonetheless this powerful statue is so lifelike that Michelangelo is alleged to have struck its knee with his hammer and shouted "Speak, damn you!"

SANTA PRASSEDE

Via di Santa Prassede 9a. Mon–Sat 7am–noon & 3–6pm, Sun 7.30am–12.30pm & 3–6pm. MAP PP.94–95, POCKET MAP H5

The ninth-century church of **Santa Prassede** occupies an ancient site where it's claimed St Prassede harboured Christians on the run from the Roman persecutions. She apparently collected the blood and remains of the martyrs and placed them in a well where she herself was later buried; a red porphyry disc in the floor of the nave marks the spot. The Byzantine mosaics are the most striking feature, particularly those in the chapel of St Zeno, which make it glitter like a jewel-encrusted box.

MUSEO NAZIONALE D'ARTE ORIENTALE

Via Merulana 248 ⊙ 06 469 748. Tues, Wed & Fri 9am–2pm, Thurs, Sat & Sun 9am–7.30pm. €6. MAP PP.94–95, POCKET MAP H5

Housed in the imposing Palazzo Brancaccio, the **Museo Nazionale d'Arte Orientale** is a first-rate collection of oriental art. Italy's connection with the Far East goes back to Marco Polo in the thirteenth century, and the quality of this collection of Islamic, Chinese, Indian and Southeast Asian art reflects this long relationship. Highlights include finds dating back to 1500 BC from a necropolis in Pakistan; architectural fragments, art works and jewellery from Tibet, Nepal and Pakistan; a solid collection from China, with predictable Buddhas and vases alongside curiosities such as a large Wei-dynasty Buddha with two boddhisatvas.

PIAZZA VITTORIO EMANUELE II

MAP PP.94–95, POCKET MAP J5

Piazza Vittorio Emanuele II lies at the centre of a district that became known as the "quartiere piemontese" when the government located many of its major ministries here after Unification. The arcades of the square, certainly, recall central Turin, but it's more recently become the immigrant quarter of Rome, with a heavy concentration of African, Asian and Middle Eastern shops and restaurants. You'll hear a dozen different languages spoken as you pass through, although the morning **market** that used to take place here has moved a few blocks east to Via Giolitti, between Via Ricasoli and Via Lamarmora. Raucous and usually crammed with locals, this is a good place to shop for a picnic.

PIAZZA DELLA REPUBBLICA

MAP PP.94–95, POCKET MAP H4

Typical of Rome's nineteenth-century regeneration, **Piazza della Repubblica** is a dignified semicircle of buildings that used to be rather dilapidated but is now – with the help of the very stylish *Hotel Exedra* – once again resurgent. The traffic roars ceaselessly around the centrepiece of the Fontana delle Naiadi, with its languishing nymphs and sea monsters. The piazza's shape follows the outline of the Baths of Diocletian, the remains of which lie across the piazza (see p.98).

FONTANA DELLE NAIADI, PIAZZA DELLA REPUBBLICA

SANTA MARIA DEGLI ANGELI

Piazza della Repubblica. Daily 7am–6.30pm. MAP PP.94–95, POCKET MAP H4

The basilica of **Santa Maria degli Angeli** was built on the ruins of the Baths of Diocletian. Designed by Michelangelo in 1563, a year before his death, it gives a good impression of the size and grandeur of the baths complex: the crescent shape of the facade remains from the original caldarium, the large transept was once the tepidarium, and eight of its huge pink-granite pillars are originals from the baths. Luigi Vanvitelli rearranged the interior in 1749, by and large imitating Michelangelo's designs. The meridian that strikes diagonally across the floor in the south transept, flanked by representations of the twelve signs of the zodiac, was until 1846 the regulator of time for Romans (now a cannon shot is fired daily at noon from the Janiculum Hill).

PALAZZO DELLE ESPOSIZIONI

Via Nazionale 194 ⓣ06 3996 7500, ⓦwww.palazzoesposizioni.it. Tues–Thurs & Sun 10am–8pm, Fri & Sat 10am–10.30pm. Approx €12. MAP PP.94–95, POCKET MAP G4

Via Nazionale connects Piazza Venezia and the town centre of with the area around Stazione Termini and the eastern districts beyond. A focus for development after Unification, its overbearing buildings are now occupied by hotels and bland, mid-range shops. It's worth strolling down as far as the imposing **Palazzo delle Esposizioni**, though, a cultural centre that hosts large-scale exhibitions and events, and also houses a cinema, bookshop, café and restaurant.

TERME DI DIOCLEZIANO

Viale Enrico De Nicola 79 ⓣ06 3996 7700. Tues–Sun 9am–7.30pm. €7 joint ticket includes Palazzo Altemps, Palazzo Massimo & Crypta Balbi, valid 3 days; free first Sun of the month. MAP PP.94–95, POCKET MAP H3

Behind the church of Santa Maria degli Angeli, the huge halls and courtyards of the **Baths of Diocletian** have been renovated and they now hold what is probably the least interesting part of the Museo Nazionale Romano – the **Museo delle Terme di Diocleziano**, the best bit of which is the large cloister of the church whose sides are crammed with statuary, funerary monuments and fragments from all over Rome. The galleries that wrap around the cloister hold a reasonable collection of pre-Roman and Roman finds: terracotta statues,

PALAZZO DELLE ESPOSIZIONI

PALAZZO MASSIMO ALLE TERME

armour and weapons found in Roman tombs.

PALAZZO MASSIMO ALLE TERME

Largo di Villa Peretti 1 ⓣ 06 3996 7700. Tues–Sun 9am–7.45pm. €7 joint ticket includes Palazzo Altemps, Terme di Diocleziano & Crypta Balbi, valid 3 days; free first Sun of the month. MAP PP.94–95, POCKET MAP I14

The snazzily restored Palazzo Massimo is home to one of the two principal parts of the **Museo Nazionale Romano** (the other is in the Palazzo Altemps) – a superb collection of Greek and Roman antiquities, second only to the Vatican's. As one of the great museums of Rome, there are too many highlights to do it justice here, and there is something worth seeing on every floor. Start at the **basement**, which has displays of exquisite gold jewellery from the second century AD, and – startlingly – the mummified remains of an 8-year-old girl, along with a coin collection. The **ground floor** is devoted to statuary of the early empire, including a gallery with an unparalleled selection of unidentified busts found all over Rome – amazing pieces of portraiture, and as vivid a representation of patrician Roman life as you'll find. There are also identifiable faces from the so-called imperial family – a bronze of Germanicus, a marvellous small bust of Caligula, several representations of Livia, Antonia and Drusus and a hooded statue of Augustus. On the far side of the **courtyard** is Greek sculpture, including bronzes of a Hellenistic prince holding a spear and a wounded pugilist at rest.

The gallery on the **first floor** has groupings of later imperial dynasties in roughly chronological order, starting with the Flavian emperors and ending with the Severans, with the fierce-looking Caracalla looking across past his father Septimius Severus to his brother Geta, whom he later murdered.

The **second floor** takes in some of the finest Roman frescoes and mosaics ever found. There is a stunning set of frescoes from the Casa di Livia (see p.71), depicting an orchard dense with fruit and flowers and patrolled by partridges and doves; wall paintings rescued from what was perhaps the riverside villa of Julia and Agrippa; and mosaics showing naturalistic scenes – sea creatures, people boating – as well as four finely crafted chariot drivers and their horses.

SAN LORENZO FUORI LE MURA

Piazzale del Verano 3. Daily 7.30am–12.30pm & 4–8pm (winter 3.30–7pm). MAP PP.94–95, POCKET MAP K4

The student neighbourhood of San Lorenzo, behind Termini, is home to **San Lorenzo fuori le Mura**, one of the seven great pilgrimage churches of Rome, and a typical Roman basilica, fronted by a columned portico and with a lovely twelfth-century cloister to its side. The original church was built by Constantine over the site of St Lawrence's martyrdom – the saint was reputedly burned to death on a gridiron, halfway through his ordeal apparently uttering the immortal words, "Turn me, I am done on this side." Because of its proximity to Rome's rail yards, the church was bombed heavily during World War II, but it has been rebuilt with sensitivity, and remains much as it was originally. Inside there are features from all periods, including a Cosmati mosaic floor and thirteenth-century pulpits. The mosaic on the inside of the triumphal arch is a sixth-century depiction of the founder offering his church to Christ. The catacombs below (rarely open) are where St Lawrence was apparently buried – a dank path leads to the pillars of Constantine's original structure. There's also a Romanesque cloister with a well-tended garden.

PIGNETO

Tram #5 or bus #105 from Termini.

Once a gritty inner-city district, **Pigneto** has been gentrified in recent years and is now firmly on the radar of Rome's cool set. The area has transformed itself into one of the city's best areas for a night out, with a selection of laidback bars and intimate restaurants, particularly around Via del Pigneto, which is home to a lively morning **market** from Monday to Saturday.

Pigneto is a twenty-minute taxi ride from Termini, or a short hop on the tram or bus, but well worth the trek.

SAN LORENZO FUORI LE MURA

Shops

BLUE GOOSE

Via del Boschetto 4. Daily 11am–8pm; closed Sun in winter. MAP PP.94–95, POCKET MAP G5

This tiny store is crammed full of rails of vintage designer clothing, all in good condition and at reasonable (if not rock-bottom) prices. There's a good selection of bags and jewellery too.

BOSCHETTO TRE

Via del Boschetto 3. Daily 10.30am–8pm. MAP PP.94–95, POCKET MAP G5

Cool little homeware store, with lots of northern European design-led knick-knacks that make great presents. You can pick up anything from a novelty lemon squeezer to a pop art-influenced watch, at affordable prices.

FELTRINELLI INTERNATIONAL

Via Emanuele Orlando 84. Daily 9am–8pm. MAP PP.94–95, POCKET MAP G4

This international branch of the nationwide chain has an excellent stock of books in English, as well as in French, German, Spanish and Portuguese.

LOL

Via Urbana 89a. Daily 10am–1.30pm & 2–8pm. MAP PP.94–95, POCKET MAP G5

Ultra-stylish Monti boutique stocking niche womenswear brands such as Forte Forte and Soho de Luxe, with an emphasis on beautiful, unusual pieces in precious fabrics, from €100 and up.

PIFEBO

Via dei Serpenti 135. Mon–Sat 11am–8pm, Sun noon–8pm. MAP PP.94–95, POCKET MAP G5

Two floors of vintage clothes and accessories for men and

BOSCHETTO TRE

women, with a great selection of sunglasses and bags too. Pifebo Chilo Shop, a few doors down at no. 141, sells clothes by the kilo at rock-bottom prices.

SUPER

Via Leonina 42. Daily 10.30am–8pm. MAP PP.94–95, POCKET MAP G5

Monti's original concept store is still going strong. Though space is tight, they manage to pack in a well-curated selection of cool womenswear, menswear and quirky homeware, with niche brands you won't find anywhere else.

TRIMANI

Via Goito 20 www.trimani.com. Mon–Sat 9am–8.30pm. MAP PP.94–95, POCKET MAP H3

One of the city's best wine shops, *Trimani* has been in business since 1876 and is still run by the same family. It's close to Termini if you want to stock up before heading off to the airport; otherwise, they can ship anywhere. There's also a wine bar around the corner serving decent food (see p.105).

Cafés and snacks

DAGNINO

Galleria Esedra, Via E. Orlando 75. Daily 7am–11pm. MAP PP.94–95, POCKET MAP G4

Good for a coffee, snack or light lunch, this long-established Sicilian bakery – ricotta-stuffed *cannoli* are a speciality – is a peaceful retreat in the Termini area, with tables outside in a small shopping arcade.

LA BOTTEGA DEL CAFFÈ

Piazza Madonna dei Monti 5. Daily 8am–2am. MAP PP.94–95, POCKET MAP G5

Right in the heart of Monti, this is a good place for breakfast, a lunchtime snack or an early-evening drink, with tables outside on a picturesque square.

PALAZZO DEL FREDDO DI GIOVANNI FASSI

Via Principe Eugenio 65. Mon–Thurs noon–midnight, Fri & Sat noon–12.30am, Sun 10am–midnight; winter closes 10pm Mon–Thurs & Sun. MAP PP.94–95, POCKET MAP J6

A wonderful, airy 1920s ice cream parlour. Brilliant fruit ice creams and great *frullati*, too.

PANELLA

Via Merulana 54. Mon–Sat 8am–midnight, Sun 8.30am–4pm. MAP PP.94–95, POCKET MAP H5

This Sicilian bakery serves superior pastries and excellent coffee, and is great for breakfast, a light lunch at its shady outdoor tables or an *aperitivo* at the bar.

Restaurants

ALLE CARRETTE

Via Madonna dei Monti 95 ⓣ 06 679 2770. Daily noon–3pm & 7.30–11.30pm; in winter open dinner daily, lunch Fri–Sun. MAP PP.94–95, POCKET MAP G5

Inexpensive large pizzeria just up Via Cavour that normally has long queues for the exceptional pizza and phenomenal desserts they serve here.

NECCI DAL 1924

DOOZO

Via Palermo 51/53 ⓣ 06 481 5655, ⓦ doozo.it. Tues–Sat 12.30–3pm & 7.30–11pm, Sun 7.30–10.30pm. MAP PP.94–95, POCKET MAP G4

Arguably the best Japanese restaurant in Monti. Part restaurant and tearoom, part art gallery and bookshop, *Doozo* serves affordable lunch menus (around €15); dinner is pricier (€60 for the multi-course *kaiseki* feast). Outdoor seating is in a leafy courtyard with an ancient wall.

L'ASINO D'ORO

Via del Boschetto 73 ⓣ 06 4891 3832. Tues–Sat 12.30–2.30pm & 7.30–11pm. MAP PP.94–95, POCKET MAP G5

The Rome location of legendary chef Lucio Sforza, who blends traditional Roman ingredients in both complex and simple combinations that you won't find anywhere else in the city. Great value at lunch (€16 for three courses). Credit cards not accepted at lunch.

LA CARBONARA

Via Panisperna 213 ⓣ 06 482 5176. Mon–Sat 12.30–2.30pm & 7–11pm. MAP PP.94–95, POCKET MAP G5

Legions of satisfied diners have scribbled their signature on the walls of this Monti favourite. Locals flock here for old-school *osteria* classics at rock-bottom prices (spaghetti alla carbonara €7), and it's packed most nights; book ahead.

MONTI DOC

Via G. Lanza 93 ☎ 06 4893 0427. Tues–Sun 11.30am–3pm & 6pm–1am. MAP PP.94–95, POCKET MAP H5

Comfortable Santa Maria Maggiore-neighbourhood wine bar, with a comprehensive wine list and nice food: cold cuts and cheese, soups and a few pastas and *secondi*. There's a good *aperitivo* buffet too (6–8pm).

NECCI DAL 1924

Via Fanfulla da Lodi 68 ☎ 06 9760 1552. Daily 8am–1.30am. Bus #105 or tram #5 or #14 from Termini. MAP PP.94–95, POCKET MAP K6

Pasolini shot some of his films in Pigneto, and this bar-restaurant was apparently one of his favourite haunts. Now a trendy, buzzing spot throughout the day, it has a lovely shady garden where you can have a drink, snack or a full meal, with its creative dishes chalked afresh on the blackboard each day.

PIGNETO QUARANTUNO

Via del Pigneto 41–43 ☎ 06 7039 9483. Tues–Fri 7pm–midnight, Sat & Sun noon–4pm & 7pm–midnight. Bus #105 or tram #5 or #14 from Termini. MAP PP.94–95, POCKET MAP K6

In the heart of the action, on Via del Pigneto's pedestrianized strip, this excellent-value trattoria has a short but ever-changing menu, though their fantastic carbonara (€8) is always on the menu.

POMMIDORO

Piazza dei Sanniti 46 ☎ 06 445 2692. Mon–Sat 12.30–3pm & 7–11pm. MAP PP.94–95, POCKET MAP K4

This family-run Roman trattoria has a breezy open veranda in summer and a fireplace in winter, and a great menu: try the tasty *pappardelle* with a wild boar sauce, and *abbacchio allo scottadito*, perfectly grilled lamb.

PRIMO AL PIGNETO

Via del Pigneto 46 ☎ 06 701 3827. Tues–Sat 7pm–midnight, Sun 1–3.30pm & 7pm–midnight. Bus #105 or tram #5 or #14 from Termini. MAP PP.94–95, POCKET MAP K6

The top Pigneto restaurant, distinguished by its clean, contemporary interior and short menu of unfussy, seasonal dishes made using the freshest of ingredients – the *mezze maniche* pasta with *amatriciana* sauce is a favourite. Primi €11–14, secondi €18–20. It's a good idea to book.

TRAM TRAM

Via dei Reti 44 ☎ 06 490 416. Tues–Sun 12.30–3.30pm & 7.30–11.30pm. MAP PP.94–95, POCKET MAP K5

Despite the grungy location, this trendy San Lorenzo restaurant is a cosy spot, and serves good pasta dishes, seafood and unusual salads. Reserve ahead. There's a bar if you want to carry on drinking after dinner.

TRAM TRAM

TRATTORIA MONTI

Via di San Vito 13a ⓣ 06 446 6573. Tues–Sat 1–2.45pm & 8– 10.45pm, Sun 1–2.45pm. MAP PP.94–95, POCKET MAP H5

A small, homely family-run restaurant specializing in the cuisine of the Marche region, meaning hearty food from a short menu. It's pricey (at least €45/person) but popular – book at least two days in advance.

VALENTINO

Via del Boschetto 37 ⓣ 06 488 0643. Mon–Sat 1–3pm & 7.45–11.15pm. MAP PP.94–95, POCKET MAP G5

With only a faded Peroni sign above the door, this trattoria on an atmospheric street is easy to miss. Inside, it's buzzing, with waiters zipping between the closely packed tables. You'll find grilled meat options, and a *scamorza* (grilled cheese) menu.

Bars

AI TRE SCALINI

Via Panisperna 251 ⓣ 06 4890 7495. Daily 12.30pm– 1am. MAP PP.94–95, POCKET MAP G5

Easy-to-miss, cosy Monti bar, with a great wine list but beer too, and decent food – cheese and salami plates, porchetta, salads and a few hot dishes.

AL VINO AL VINO

Via dei Serpenti 19. Mon–Fri 10.30am–2.30pm & 6pm–12.30am, Sat 10.30am–1.30pm & 6pm–1.30am, Sun 11.30am–1pm & 6pm–12.30am. MAP PP.94–95, POCKET MAP G5

Seriously good wine bar with a choice of over 500 labels, many by the glass. Snacks are generally Sicilian specialities.

BLACK MARKET

Via Panisperna 101 ⓣ 339 822 7541. Daily 5.30pm–2am. MAP PP.94–95, POCKET MAP G5

This bar/art gallery/tearoom filled with mismatched vintage furniture is very Monti. Drop by for the *aperitivo* buffet (6.30–9pm; €10 including a drink), or for cocktails later on, when the warren of rooms is lit by flickering candlelight. Live music Fri & Sat nights.

WINE LIST AT CAVOUR 313

CAVOUR 313

Via Cavour 313. Mon–Thurs 12.30–2.45pm & 6–11.30pm, Fri & Sat 12.30–2.45pm & 6pm–midnight, Sun 12.30–2.45pm & 7–11pm. MAP PP.94–95, POCKET MAP G5

A lovely old wine bar that makes a handy retreat after seeing the ancient sites. The interior is cosy and wood-panelled, and delicious (though not cheap) snacks are served – cheese platters, salads and the like.

FINNEGAN

Via Leonina 66 ⓣ 06 474 7026. Mon–Thurs 1pm–12.30am, Fri 1pm–1am, Sat noon–1am, Sun noon–12.30am. MAP PP.94–95, POCKET MAP G5

Decent Irish pub with live football on TV, pool and a friendly expat crowd. There's seating outside, too, on this bustling Monti street.

IL TIASO

Via Ascoli Piceno 20 ⓣ 333 284 5283. Daily 6pm–2am. Bus #105 or tram #5 or #14 from Termini. MAP PP.94–95, POCKET MAP K6

This relaxed wine bar with free wi-fi has book-lined shelves and a large selection of wines to try by the glass, accompanied by cheese and salami platters, as well as some more substantial meals. There are often live acoustic sets, too.

LA BARRIQUE

Via del Boschetto 41b ⓣ 06 4782 5953. Mon–Sat 1–3.30pm & 7pm–midnight. MAP PP.94–95, POCKET MAP G5

This labyrinthine wine bar is a great spot for an *aperitivo*. French and Italian wines are the main attraction – champagne is a speciality – and there are platters of meats and cheeses, as well as full meals.

TRIMANI

Via Cernaia 37b. Mon–Sat 11.30am–3pm & 5.30pm–midnight. MAP PP.94–95, POCKET MAP H3

Classy wine bar that's good for a lunchtime tipple. You'll spend around €20 to sample a range of cheeses and cured pork, or soup and salad, with a glass of wine.

Clubs and venues

LE MURA

Via di Porta Labicana 24 ⓣ 06 6401 1757, ⓦ lemuramusicbar.com. Tues–Sat

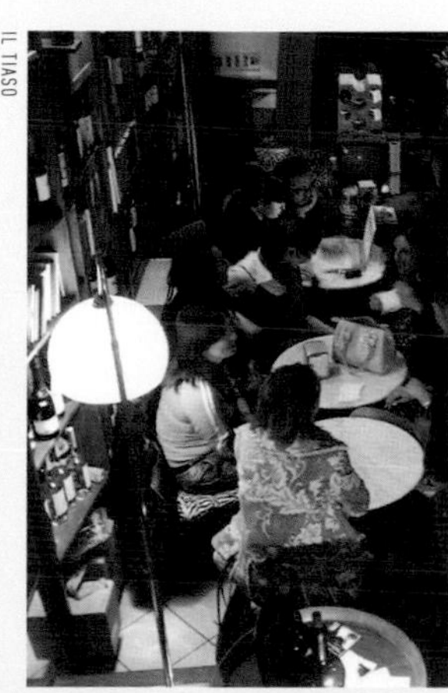

IL TIASO

6.30pm–2am, Sun 5.30pm–1am. MAP PP.94–95, POCKET MAP K5

This little San Lorenzo live music bar has quality live acts every night except Monday, plus craft cocktails and a friendly, laidback atmosphere.

MONK

Via Giuseppe Mirri 35 ⓣ 06 6485 0987, ⓦ monkroma.club. Bus #409 from Tiburtina (Metro B). MAP PP.94–95, POCKET MAP K4

One of the city's hottest summer hangouts, thanks to a great live music programme, plus dj sets, food stalls, stripy deckchairs and ping-pong tables in a multipurpose open space.

TEATRO DELL'OPERA DI ROMA

Piazza Beniamino Gigli 1 ⓣ 06 4816 0255, ⓦ operaroma.it. Box office Mon–Sat 10am–6pm, Sun 9am–1.30pm. MAP PP.94–95, POCKET MAP H4

Nobody compares it to La Scala, but cheap tickets are a lot easier to come by at Rome's opera and ballet venue – they start at around €20 for opera, less for ballet. If you buy the very cheapest tickets, bring some high-powered binoculars: you'll need them in order to see anything at all.

VICIOUS CLUB

Via Achille Grandi 7/a ⓣ 06 7061 4349, ⓦ viciousclub.com. Tues–Sat 10pm–4am. MAP PP.94–95, POCKET MAP K6

Its interior lined with mirrors and black walls, *Vicious Club*'s underground feel marks it out from many Roman clubs. It's a cocktail bar on Tuesday and Wednesday, and the rest of the week it hosts djs. Friday's Rock'n Yolk night (indie, nu-wave, electronica, rap) is popular, and there's a monthly gay night.

The Celian Hill and San Giovanni

Just behind the Colosseum, the Celian Hill is the most southerly of Rome's seven hills, and one of its most peaceful, home to a handful of churches and a quiet park. Just to the south and east are some of Rome's most interesting churches: triple-layered San Clemente and nearby Quattro Coronati, and the complex of San Giovanni in Laterano – which gives its name to the surrounding San Giovanni district – all well worth the walk from the Colosseum. Nearby also is the wartime headquarters of the Nazi SS, now the home of an affecting commemorative museum.

VILLA CELIMONTANA

Via della Navicella 12. MAP PP.108–109, POCKET MAP G7

Much of the Celian Hill is taken up by the park of **Villa Celimontana**, whose gardens make a nice spot for a picnic, with lots of leafy walkways and grassy slopes. There are pony rides and a playground, and outdoor jazz concerts are performed on summer evenings.

SANTO STEFANO ROTONDO

SANTA MARIA IN DOMINICA

Via della Navicella 10. Daily 9am–noon & 3.30–6pm. MAP PP.108–109, POCKET MAP H7

Also known as Santa Maria in Navicella after the ancient Roman stone boat that sits outside, this sixth-century church is just outside the entrance to the Villa Celimontana, and is worth visiting for the ninth-century mosaic above the apse, which shows Pope Paschal I, who restored the church, kneeling at the feet of the Virgin.

SANTO STEFANO ROTONDO

Via di Santo Stefano Rotondo 7. Tues–Sat 9.30am–12.30pm & 3–6pm (2–5pm in winter), Sun 9.30am–12.30pm. MAP PP.108–109, POCKET MAP H7

This church is an ancient structure, illuminated by 22 windows – a magnificent and wonderfully moody circular space, though the feature that really sticks in the mind is the series of stomach-churning frescoes that grace the walls, showing various saints being martyred in different ways, all in graphic and vividly restored detail.

SANTI GIOVANNI E PAOLO

SANTI GIOVANNI E PAOLO

Piazza dei Santi Giovanni e Paolo 13. Daily 8.30am–noon & 3.30–6pm. MAP PP.108–109, POCKET MAP G7

Recognized by its colourful campanile, this church is dedicated to two dignitaries in the court of Constantine who were beheaded here in 361 AD after refusing military service. A railed-off tablet in mid-nave marks the shrine where the saints were martyred and buried. The church is best known today as a wedding venue.

CASE ROMANE

Clivo di Scauro ☎ 06 7045 4544. Daily except Tues & Wed 10am–1pm & 3–6pm. €8. MAP PP.108–109, POCKET MAP G7

The relics of what is believed to be the residence of the martyrs Giovanni and Paolo (see above) – ten rooms, patchily frescoed with pagan and Christian subjects. Standouts include the **Casa dei Genii,** frescoed with winged youths and cupids, and the courtyard or nymphaeum, which has a marvellous fresco of a goddess preparing for her marriage to Pluto, sandwiched between cupids in boats, fishing and loading supplies. There's also an interesting antiquarium, with a good haul of finds from the site.

SAN GREGORIO MAGNO

Piazza di San Gregorio 1. Daily 9am–1pm & 3.30–7.30pm; ring the bell marked "portinare" to gain admission. MAP PP.108–109, POCKET MAP G7

St Gregory the Great founded a monastery that still exists, and was a monk here before becoming pope in 590 AD. The church's interior is fairly ordinary, but the lovely Cosmati floor remains intact, and the saint's chapel at the end of the south aisle has a beautiful altar showing scenes from St Gregory's life, along with his marble throne, which actually pre-dates the saint by 500 years.

SANTI QUATTRO CORONATI

Via dei Querceti. Daily 9.30am–noon & 4.30–6pm. Cloister and chapel at San Silvestro €1. MAP PP.108–109, POCKET MAP H6–H7

Originally built in 1110, the interior feels a world away from the crowds around the nearby Colosseum – an atmosphere that is intensified by the pretty cloister (ring the bell for access), where the community of nuns sings beautifully at Mass. But its real treasure is the chapel of San Silvestro, whose frescoes, painted in 1248, relate the story of how the fourth-century pope cured the emperor Constantine of leprosy and then went on to baptize him.

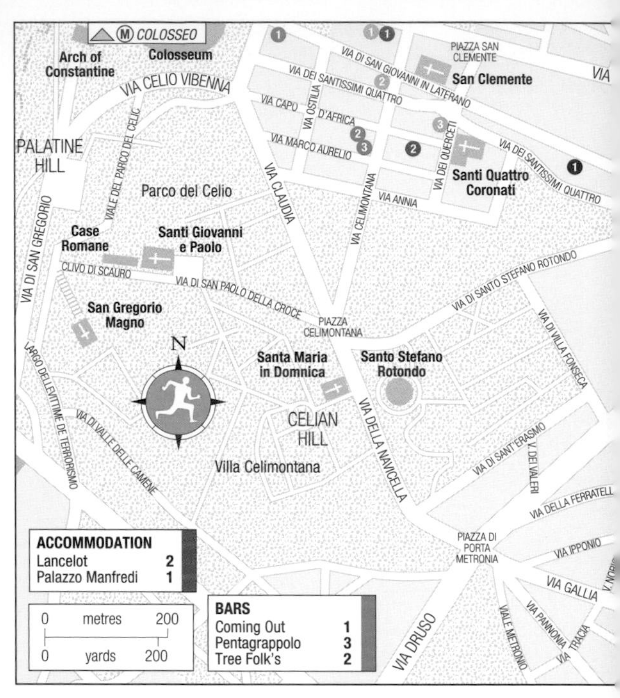

SAN CLEMENTE

Via Labicana 95. Mon–Sat 9am–12.30pm & 3–6pm, Sun noon–6pm. Church free, excavations €10. MAP PP.108–109, POCKET MAP H6

This church perhaps encapsulates better than any other the continuity of history in Rome – a conglomeration of three places of worship from three very different eras. The ground-floor church is a superb example of a medieval basilica, with some fine mosaics in the apse and some beautiful and vivid fifteenth-century frescoes. Downstairs there's the nave of an earlier church, dating back to 392 AD, and the **tomb of Pope Clement I**, the saint to whom the church is dedicated. Steps lead down to the labyrinthine third level, which contains a dank temple of the late second century, alongside several rooms of a Roman house. The temple, used by members of the all-male cult of Mithras, holds a statue of the god slaying a bull, as well as the seats upon which the worshippers sat during their ceremonies.

SAN GIOVANNI IN LATERANO

Piazza di San Giovanni in Laterano. Daily 7am–6.30pm. Cloisters daily 9am–6pm. MAP PP.108–109, POCKET MAP J7

The area immediately south and east of the Esquiline Hill is known as **San Giovanni**, after the great basilica that lies at its heart – the city's cathedral, and the headquarters of the Catholic Church before the creation of the Vatican state. There has been a church on this site since the fourth century, and the present building evokes Rome's staggering wealth of

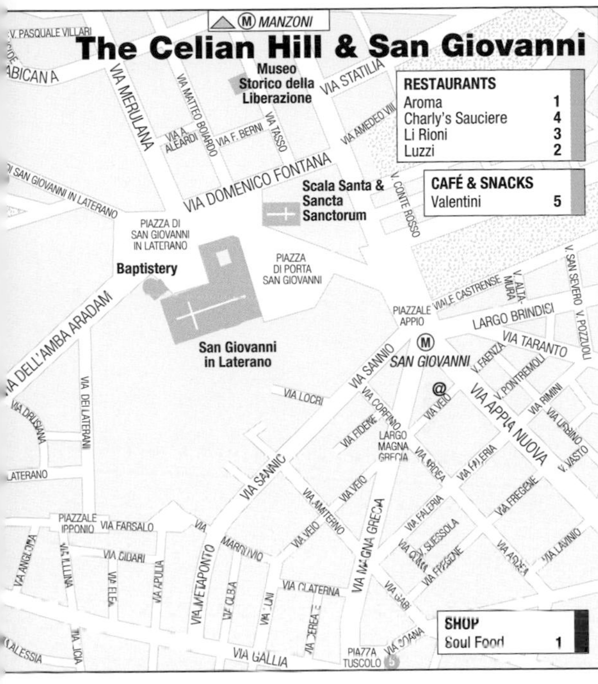

history, with features from different periods. The doors to the church were taken from the Roman Curia or Senate House, while the obelisk outside dates from the fifteenth century BC. Inside, the first pillar on the left of the right-hand aisle shows a fragment of Giotto's fresco of Boniface VIII proclaiming the first Holy Year in 1300. On the next pillar, a more recent monument commemorates Sylvester I, and incorporates part of his original tomb, said to sweat and rattle its bones when a pope is about to die. The nave itself is lined with eighteenth-century statues of the apostles: St Matthew, the tax collector, is shown with coins falling out of a sack; St Bartholomew holds a knife and his own skin (he was flayed alive); St Thomas holds a set square (he's the patron saint of architects) and St Simon a saw (he was, apparently, sawn to death). The heads of St Peter and St Paul are kept secure behind the altar, while the baldacchino just in front is a splash of Gothic grandeur made by the Tuscan sculptor Giovanni di Stefano in the fourteenth century: it shelters the glassed-over bronze tomb of Martin V, the Colonna pope who was responsible for returning the papacy to Rome from Avignon in 1419. Outside the church, the cloisters are decorated with early thirteenth-century Cosmati work, while next door the Lateran Palace (no public access) was home of the popes in the Middle Ages, and is still formally part of Vatican territory.

SAN GIOVANNI IN LATERANO

THE BAPTISTERY

San Giovanni in Laterano. Daily 9am–12.30pm & 4–6.30pm. Free. MAP PP.108–109, POCKET MAP J7

San Giovanni's **baptistery** is the oldest surviving in the Christian world – the octagonal structure was built during the fifth century and has been the model for many such buildings since. Even though it doesn't feel this old, the mosaics in the side chapels and the bronze doors to the chapel on the right, brought here from the Baths of Caracalla, quickly remind you that you're in an ancient church.

THE SCALA SANTA AND SANCTA SANCTORUM

Piazza di San Giovanni in Laterano 14. ☎ 329 75 11 111, Ⓦ scala-santa.it. Scala Santa: April–Sept Mon–Sat 6.30am–7pm, Sun 7am–7pm; Oct–March Mon–Sat 6.30am–6.30pm, Sun 7am–6.30pm; Sancta Sanctorum: Mon–Sat 9.30am–12.40pm & 3–5.10pm. Scala Santa free; Sancta Sanctorum €3.50. MAP PP.108–109, POCKET MAP J7

The **Scala Santa** is claimed to be the staircase from Pontius Pilate's house down which Christ walked after his trial. The 28 steps are protected by boards, and the only way you're allowed to climb them is on your knees, which pilgrims do regularly – although there are other staircases either side for the less penitent. At the top, the **Sancta Sanctorum** holds an ancient (sixth- or seventh-century) painting of Christ said to be the work of an angel, hence its name – *acheiropoeton*, Greek for "not done by human hands".

MUSEO STORICO DELLA LIBERAZIONE

Via Tasso 145. Tues–Sun 9.30am–12.30pm, Tues, Thurs, Fri also 3.30–7.30pm. Free. MAP PP.108–109, POCKET MAP J6

Occupying two floors of the building the Nazis used as a prison during World War II, this museum incorporates the prison cells, left deliberately untouched. It's extremely well done, and perhaps the most seriously affecting free attraction in town.

Shop

SOUL FOOD

Via San Giovanni in Laterano 192. Tues–Sat 10.30am–1.30pm & 3.30–8pm. MAP PP.108–109, POCKET MAP H7

Great music store, mainly vinyl, with lots of rare as well as mainstream rock and punk.

Café

VALENTINI

Piazza Tuscolo 2. Mon–Sat 6am–11pm, Sun 7am–11pm. MAP PP.108–109, POCKET MAP J8

Café, pastry shop and *tavola calda*, just five minutes' from San Giovanni and a great spot for lunch, with outside seating too.

Restaurants

AROMA

Palazzo Manfredi, Via Labicana 125 ⓣ 06 7759 1380, ⓦ aromarestaurant.it. MAP PP.108–109, POCKET MAP H6

A meal at Michelin-starred *Aroma* is worth the splurge for the unsurpassed views of the Colosseum alone, but the food – Italian with a twist – is superb. As you'd expect, it's not cheap (primi around €35, secondi €50, seven-course tasting menu €140).

CHARLY'S SAUCIERE

Via San Giovanni in Laterano 270 ⓣ 06 7049 5666. Mon–Sat noon–2pm & 8–11pm. MAP PP.108–109, POCKET MAP H7

Lots of French classics – including fondues (the owner is Swiss), onion soup and excellent steaks, not to mention a good selection of real French cheeses. Moderate to high prices, but food, service and overall atmosphere are worth every penny. Best to book.

LI RIONI

Via SS. Quattro 24 ⓣ 06 7045 0605. Mon & Wed–Sun 7pm–midnight. MAP PP.108–109, POCKET MAP H6

With its street lamps and tiled roofs, *Li Rioni*'s interior resembles an Italian piazza, especially after trying the robust house wine. At dinner it's packed with locals enjoying crispy Roman-style pizza; a meal with wine costs less than €20.

LUZZI

Via San Giovanni in Laterano 88 ⓣ 06 709 6332. Mon, Tues & Thurs–Sun noon–midnight. MAP PP.108–109, POCKET MAP H6

Between San Giovanni in Laterano and the Colosseum, *Luzzi* sits amid the tourist joints of the neighbourhood. There's hearty food and outside seating. It's very cheap – *secondi* are €8–10 and they do pizzas too.

Bars

COMING OUT

Via San Giovanni in Laterano 8 ⓣ 06 700 9871 ⓦ www.comingout.it. Daily 7am–2am MAP PP.108–109, POCKET MAP G6

Laid-back gay bar that serves food and hosts karaoke and live music nights.

PENTAGRAPPOLO

Via Celimontana 21b ⓣ 06 709 6301. Mon noon–3pm, Tues–Fri noon–3pm & 6pm–1am, Sat & Sun 6pm–1am. MAP PP.108–109, POCKET MAP H6

Celian Hill wine bar with good wines by the glass, cheese plates and cold meats. Live music plus a lively *aperitivo* with tapas Thursday to Sunday.

TREE FOLK'S

Via Capo d'Africa 31. Daily 6pm–2am. MAP PP.108–109, POCKET MAP H6

Lots of Belgian and German brews, plus cider and surely the city's best selection of single malt whisky. Food served, too.

The Aventine Hill and south

The leafy Aventine Hill – once the heart of plebeian Rome – is now an upscale residential area and one of the city's most pleasant corners. South and west from the hill are two distinct neighbourhoods: Testaccio, a working-class enclave that's become increasingly hip and gentrified (and home to much of the city's nightlife), and the more up-and-coming Ostiense, beyond the ancient city wall, worth a visit for the Centrale Montemartini branch of the Capitoline Museums. Between these districts is Rome's Protestant Cemetery, where the poets Keats and Shelley are buried. Further south lie the magnificent basilica of San Paolo fuori le Mura and the Via Appia Antica with its atmospheric catacombs, and beyond, EUR: Rome's futuristic 1930s experiment in town planning.

THE BATHS OF CARACALLA

Viale Terme di Caracalla 52 ⓣ 06 3996 7700. Daily from 9am until 1hr before sunset. €6 joint ticket includes Tomb of Cecilia Metella & Villa dei Quintili (valid for 7 days); free first Sun of the month. Tours (Sun 3pm; Italian only) free. MAP PP.114–115, POCKET MAP H8

The remains of this ancient Roman leisure centre give a far better sense of the monumental scale of Roman architecture than most of the extant ruins in the city – so much so that Shelley was moved to write *Prometheus Unbound* here in 1819. The walls still rise to very nearly their original height and there are many fragments of mosaics – none spectacular, but quite a few bright and well preserved. The complex included gymnasiums, gardens and an open-air swimming pool as well as the hot, tepid and cold series of baths. As for Caracalla, he was one of Rome's worst and shortest-lived rulers, so it's no wonder there's nothing else in the city built by him. The baths make an atmospheric setting for opera and ballet performances during the summer (one of Mussolini's better ideas); for tickets and programme information, see ⓦ operaroma.it.

SANTA SABINA

Piazza Pietro d'Illiria. Daily 8.15am–12.30pm & 3.30–6pm. MAP PP.114–115, POCKET MAP E7

Crowning the Aventine Hill, **Santa Sabina** is a strong contender for Rome's most beautiful basilica. Look

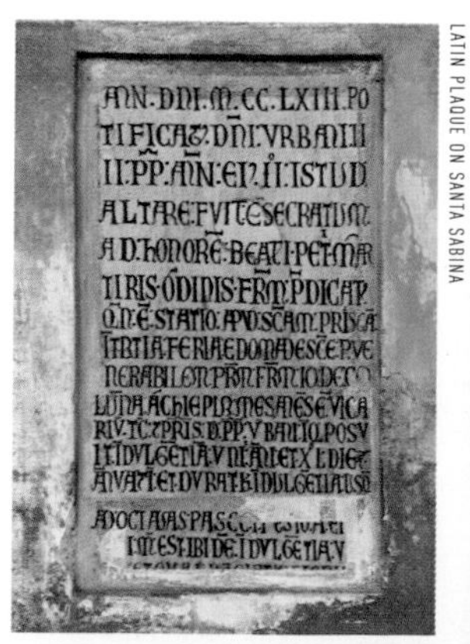
LATIN PLAQUE ON SANTA SABINA

VIEW THROUGH THE KEYHOLE AT THE PRIORY OF THE KNIGHTS OF MALTA

at the main doors, which are contemporary with the church and boast eighteen panels carved with Christian scenes (including one of the oldest representations of the Crucifixion). Santa Sabina is also the principal church of the Dominicans, and inside, just near the doors, a smooth piece of black marble, pitted with holes, was apparently thrown by the devil at St Dominic himself while at prayer, shattering the marble pavement but miraculously not harming the saint. It's also claimed that the orange trees behind, which you can glimpse on your way to a room once occupied by St Dominic himself, are descendants of those planted by the saint. Wherever the truth lies, the views from the park are splendid – across the Tiber to the centre of Rome and St Peter's.

PIAZZA DEI CAVALIERI DI MALTA

MAP PP.114–115, POCKET MAP E7

As if to reward those who venture this far up the Aventine Hill, the minuscule **Piazza dei Cavalieri di Malta** holds an intriguing attraction: the imposing doorway to the **Priory of the Knights of Malta** is kept firmly closed to the public, but you can peek through the keyhole for a perfectly framed, dead-ahead view of St Peter's: the work of Giovanni Battista Piranesi.

TESTACCIO

MAP PP.114–115, POCKET MAP E9

The working-class neighbourhood of **Testaccio** was for many years synonymous with its slaughterhouse, or *mattatoio*. In recent years the area has become gentrified, and is best known for its clubs. For a taste of old Testaccio, head for one of the district's many **restaurants**; this is the best place in town to sample traditional *cucina povera* – offal-heavy "poor cuisine", best sampled at *Checchino dal 1887* (see p.122). Testaccio's historic **market** (Mon–Sat 6am–3pm) is now in bright new premises between Via Galvani and Via Alessandro Volta, and is a great place to pick up a picnic lunch. Near the old slaughterhouse at Piazza Giustiniani 4 is a branch of the **Museum of Contemporary Art of Rome** (MACRO Testaccio; Tues–Sun 2–8pm; €8.50; ⓦ museomacro.org), home to innovative temporary exhibitions.

MONTE TESTACCIO

MAP PP.114–115, POCKET MAP E9

Monte Testaccio, which gives the area its name, is a 35m-high mound created out of the shards of Roman amphorae that were dumped here over several centuries. It's an odd sight, the ceramic curls clearly visible through the tufts of grass that crown its higher reaches, the bottom layers hollowed out by the workshops of car and bike mechanics – and, now, clubs and bars.

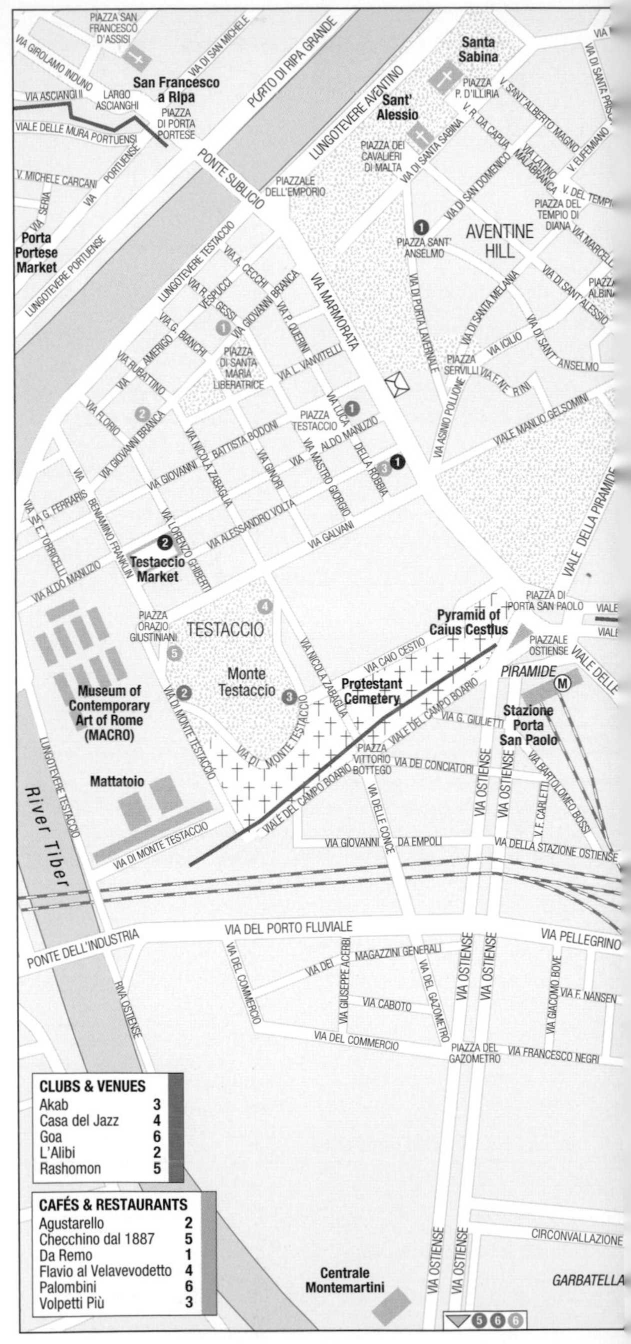
San Francesco a Ripa
Santa Sabina
Sant' Alessio
Porta Portese Market
AVENTINE HILL
Testaccio Market
TESTACCIO
Monte Testaccio
Pyramid of Caius Cestius
Protestant Cemetery
Museum of Contemporary Art of Rome (MACRO)
Mattatoio
Stazione Porta San Paolo
PIRAMIDE
River Tiber
Centrale Montemartini
GARBATELLA
PONTE SUBLICIO
PORTO DI RIPA GRANDE
LUNGOTEVERE AVENTINO
LUNGOTEVERE TESTACCIO
LUNGOTEVERE PORTUENSE
VIA MARMORATA
VIALE MANLIO GELSOMINI
VIALE DELLA PIRAMIDE
VIA OSTIENSE
VIA DEL PORTO FLUVIALE
PONTE DELL'INDUSTRIA
VIA PELLEGRINO
CIRCONVALLAZIONE
CLUBS & VENUES
Akab 3
Casa del Jazz 4
Goa 6
L'Alibi 2
Rashomon 5
CAFÉS & RESTAURANTS
Agustarello 2
Checchino dal 1887 5
Da Remo 1
Flavio al Velavevodetto 4
Palombini 6
Volpetti Più 3

CENTRALE MONTEMARTINI

Via Ostiense 106 ⓣ 06 0608, ⓦ centralemontemartini.org. Tues–Sun 9am–7pm. €7.50, or €12.50 for joint ticket with Capitoline Museums, valid 7 days; free first Sun of the month. Metro B Garbatella. MAP PP.114–115, POCKET MAP E11

This former power station is a permanent outpost of the **Capitoline Museums**, attracting visitors to formerly industrial Ostiense. The huge rooms are suited to showcasing ancient sculpture, although the massive turbines and furnaces have a fascination of their own. Among many compelling objects are the head, feet and an arm from a colossal statue, once 8m high, found in Largo Torre Argentina, a large Roman copy of Athena, a fragmented mosaic of hunting scenes, and a lovely naturalistic statue of a girl seated on a stool with her legs crossed, from the third century BC. There's also a figure of Hercules and next to it a soft Muse Polymnia, the former braced for activity, the latter leaning on a rock and staring into the distance.

SAN PAOLO FUORI LE MURA

Via Ostiense 190. Basilica daily 7am–6.30pm, cloister daily 8am–6.15pm. Cloisters and excavations €4. Metro B San Paolo. MAP PP.114–115, POCKET MAP E12

The basilica of **San Paolo fuori le Mura** (St Paul's Outside the Walls) is one of Rome's five patriarchal basilicas, occupying the site of St Paul's tomb. Victim of a devastating fire in 1823, today it is largely a nineteenth-century reconstruction. The huge structure has a powerful and authentic sense of occasion, evidenced by the medallions of the popes fringing the nave and transepts above, starting with St Peter to the right of the apse and ending with Benedict XVI at the top of the south aisle. The cloister holds probably Rome's finest piece of Cosmati work, its spiralling, mosaic-encrusted columns enclosing a peaceful rose garden. Beyond is the **pinacoteca**, a gallery of ecclesiastical art, vestments and the like, while off the cloister an **exhibition gallery** holds fragments of statuary recently unearthed in the early medieval monastic complex south of the basilica. The **excavations** themselves are a work in progress, but you can explore the site on raised walkways.

CENTRALE MONTEMARTINI

THE AURELIAN WALL

MAP PP.114–115, POCKET MAP E10–H9

Built by the Emperor Aurelian in 275 AD to enclose Rome's hills and protect the city from invasion, the Aurelian Wall still surrounds much of the city, but its best-preserved stretch runs 2km between Porta San Paolo and Porta San Sebastiano (which lies a few hundred metres east of Largo Terme di Caracalla). Here, the **Museo delle Mura** at Via di Porta San Sebastiano 18 (T 06 0608, W museodellemuraroma .it; Tues–Sun 9am–2pm; €5) occupies two floors of the city gate and has displays showing Aurelian's original plans and lots of photos of the walls past and present. You can climb up to the top of the gate for great views over the Roman countryside beyond, and walk a few hundred metres along the wall itself. From here it's only a short walk up Via di Porta San Sebastiano to the Baths of Caracalla.

VIA APPIA ANTICA

POCKET MAP H10–K12

The **Via Appia Antica**, which starts at the Porta San Sebastiano, is the most famous of the consular roads that used to strike out in each direction from ancient Rome. It was built by one Appio Claudio in 312 BC, and is the only Roman landmark mentioned in the Bible. During classical times the "Appian Way" was the most important of all the Roman trade routes, carrying supplies right down through Campania to the port of Brindisi. It's no longer the main route south out of the city – that's Via Appia Nuova from nearby Porta San Giovanni – but it remains an important part of early Christian Rome, its verges lined with numerous pagan and Christian sites, including, most famously, the underground burial cemeteries, or catacombs, of the first Christians.

THE AURELIAN WALL

Visiting Via Appia Antica and the catacombs

Buses run south along **Via Appia Antica** and conveniently stop at, or near to, most of the main attractions, starting with Porta San Sebastiano. You can walk it, but bear in mind that much of the Via Appia Antica isn't particularly picturesque, at least until you get down to the **Catacombs of San Sebastiano**, and the best thing to do is take a bus to San Sebastiano and double back or walk on further for the attractions you want to see. Bus #118 stops at Via del Teatro di Marcello (to the right of the staircase up to the Campidoglio), the Colosseum, the Circus Maximus and Terme di Caracalla, and makes several stops on Via Appia Antica, including Domine Quo Vadis, San Sebastiano and San Callisto; you can also take bus #218 from Piazza San Giovanni, which goes down Via Ardeatina, or bus #660 from Colli Albani metro station (line A), which goes beyond the Tomb of Cecilia Metella. Or you could walk from Porta San Sebastiano and take everything in on foot, which allows you to stop off at the Parco Regionale dell'Appia Antica **information office** for the area – it's actually classified as a national park – at Via Appia Antica 58, on the right just before you get to Domine Quo Vadis (Mon–Sat 9.30am–1.30pm & 2–5/5.30pm, Sun 9.30am–5/6.30pm; 06 513 5316, www.parcoappiaantica.it). You can pick up a good **map** and other information on the various Appia Antica sights here, as well as hire bikes (€3/hour or €15/day). You can **take a tour** of the catacombs and nearby sights with Enjoy Rome (see p.185; Mon, Thurs & Sat at 10am; 3hr; €55). Finally, there are a couple of decent restaurants down by San Sebastiano: *L'Archeologia* (06 788 0494; closed Tues), just past the church, and the *Cecilia Metella* (06 512 6769; closed Mon) right opposite.

DOMINE QUO VADIS

Via Appia Antica 51. Daily 8am–7pm, 6pm in winter. POCKET MAP J11

About 500m from Porta San Sebastiano, where the road forks, the church of Domine Quo Vadis is the first sight on Via Appia. Legend has this as the place where St Peter saw Christ while fleeing from certain death in Rome and asked "Where goest thou, Lord?", to which Christ replied that he was going to be crucified once more, leading Peter to turn around and accept his fate. The small church is ordinary enough inside, except for its replica of a piece of marble that's said to be marked with the footprints of Christ – the original is in the church of San Sebastiano (see p.120).

VIA APPIA ANTICA

CATACOMBS OF SAN CALLISTO

Via Appia Antica 110/126 T 06 513 0151, W catacombe.roma.it. Thurs–Tues 9am–noon & 2–5pm; closed end Jan to end Feb. €8. POCKET MAP J12

The largest of Rome's catacombs, the Catacombs of San Callisto were founded in the second century AD and many of the early popes are buried here. There are regular free tours (40min) in English, and the site also features some seventh- and eighth-century frescoes, and the crypt of Santa Cecilia. She was buried here after her martyrdom, before being moved to the church dedicated to her in Trastevere – a copy of Carlo Maderno's famous statue marks the spot.

MAUSOLEO DELLE FOSSE ARDEATINE

Via Ardeatina 174 T 06 513 6742. Mon–Fri 8.15am–3.15pm, Sat & Sun 8.15am–4.45pm. Free. POCKET MAP K12

A ten-minute walk from San Callisto, close by the #218 bus stop, is a site that remembers the **massacre** of over 300 civilians during the Nazi occupation of Rome, after the Resistance had ambushed and killed 32 soldiers in the centre of the city. The Nazis exacted a harsh vengeance, killing ten civilians for every dead German, burying the bodies here and then exploding mines to cover up their crime. The bodies were dug up after the war and reinterred in the mausoleum here. A small museum tells the story of the event.

CATACOMBS OF SAN SEBASTIANO

Via Appia Antica 136 T 06 785 0350, W catacombe.org. Mon–Sat 10am–4.30pm; closed Dec. €8. POCKET MAP K12

These **catacombs** sit under a much-renovated basilica that was originally built by Constantine on the spot where the bodies of the apostles Peter and Paul are said to have lain for a time. Half-hour tours take in paintings of doves and fish, a contemporary carved oil lamp and inscriptions dating the tombs themselves. The most striking features are three pagan tombs (one painted, two stuccoed) discovered when archeologists were investigating the floor of the basilica upstairs. Just above here, Constantine reputedly raised his chapel, and although St Peter was later removed to the Vatican and St Paul to San Paolo fuori le Mura, the graffiti records the fact that this was indeed where the two apostles' remains rested.

TOMB OF CECILIA METELLA

VILLA AND CIRCUS OF MAXENTIUS

Via Appia Antica 153 ⓣ06 0608, ⓦwww.villadimassenzio.it. Tues–Sun 10am–4pm. Free. POCKET MAP K12

A few hundred metres on from the San Sebastiano catacombs, the group of brick ruins trailing off into the fields to the left are the remains of the **Villa and Circus of Maxentius**, a complex built by the emperor in the early fourth century AD before his defeat by Constantine. It's a clear, long oval of grass, similar to the Circus Maximus (see p.72), but slightly better preserved.

TOMB OF CECILIA METELLA

Via Appia Antica 161 ⓣ06 3996 7700. Tues–Sun 9am–1hr before sunset. €6 joint ticket including Baths of Caracalla and Villa dei Quintili; free first Sun of the month. POCKET MAP K12

Further along the Via Appia, this circular tomb dates from the Augustan period, and was converted into a castle in the fourteenth century. Known as "Capo di Bove" for the bulls on the frieze around it, the tomb itself, a huge brick-built drum, is little more than a large pigeon coop these days; various fragments and finds are littered around the adjacent, later courtyards, and down below you can see what's left of an ancient lava flow from thousands of years earlier. The medieval building next door houses sculpture fragments from Roman tombs along the Via Appia Antica.

EUR

Main piazzas at south end of Via Cristoforo Colombo. Bus #714 from Termini to Via Cristoforo Colombo or metro line B to EUR Fermi. POCKET MAP E12

The **EUR** district was planned by Mussolini for the 1942 Esposizione Universale Roma, but not finished until after the war. Its monumental Fascist architecture and grand processional boulevards recall Imperial Rome (especially the Palazzo della Civilità or "Square Colosseum"). Overall it's a pretty strange and soulless place, something of a white elephant despite the busy offices. Apart from the **shops** – the city's biggest mall, Euroma2, is on Via Cristoforo Colombo (Metro EUR Fermi, then bus 70, 700 or 709) – EUR's main attraction is its museums. The **Museo della Civilità Romana**, Piazza Agnelli 10 (closed for renovation at the time of writing; ⓦmuseociviltaromana.it) has a large model of the fourth-century city and also incorporates the Planetario e Museo Astronomico.

Shops

LO SPACCIO DI TESTACCIO

Stall no. 39, Testaccio market, between Via Galvani and Via Alessandro Volta. Mon–Sat 8.30am–2pm. MAP PP.114–115, POCKET MAP E9

Amid the hustle and bustle of Testaccio market is this little kitchenware stall with a vintage feel, selling enamel saucepans, glassware and all manner of wooden utensils that you soon won't be able to do without.

VOLPETTI

VOLPETTI

Via Marmorata 47. Mon–Wed 8.30am–2pm & 4.30–8.15pm, Thurs–Sat 8.30am–8.15pm. MAP PP.114–115, POCKET MAP E8

It's worth seeking out this Testaccio deli, truly one of Rome's very best, with a fantastic selection of cold meats and cheeses.

Cafés and restaurants

AGUSTARELLO

Via Giovanni Branca 98–100 ☎06 574 6585. Mon–Sat 12.30–3pm & 7.30pm–midnight. MAP PP.114–115, POCKET MAP E8

Just off busy Piazza di Santa Maria Liberatrice, this small and simple trattoria is strong on the *quinto quarto* (offal) dishes that Testaccio is known for, and also serves all the classics of Roman cuisine (roast lamb with potatoes €18).

CHECCHINO DAL 1887

Via di Monte Testaccio 30 ☎06 574 6318. Tues–Sat 12.30–3pm & 8pm–midnight, Sun 12.30–3pm. MAP PP.114–115, POCKET MAP E9

A historic symbol of Testaccio cookery, with an excellent wine cellar, too. Expensive, but worth it for its rustic atmosphere and excellent menu of authentic Roman meat and offal dishes.

DA REMO

Piazza Santa Maria Liberatrice 44 ☎06 574 6270. Mon–Sat 7pm–1am; closed three weeks in Aug. MAP PP.114–115, POCKET MAP E8

Remo is the best kind of pizzeria: usually crowded with locals, very basic and serving the thinnest, crispiest Roman pizza you'll find. It's also worth trying the heavenly *bruschette* and other snacks like *supplì* and *fiori di zucca*. Perfect pre-clubbing food – and very cheap (pizzas from €6).

FLAVIO AL VELAVEVODETTO

Via di Monte Testaccio 97 ☎06 574 4194, ⓦristorantevelavevodetto.it. Daily 12.30–3pm & 7.45–11pm. MAP PP.114–115, POCKET MAP E9

Top-notch ingredients (meat from the restaurant's own herds and own-grown veg) go into Roman classics such as *coratella con carciofi* (lamb's offal with artichokes; €12) and meatball stew (€14) at this perennially popular Testaccio trattoria.

PALOMBINI

Piazzale Adenauer 12. Mon–Thurs 7am–10pm, Fri & Sat 7am–1am, Sun 8am–10pm. MAP PP.114–115, POCKET MAP H12

Great EUR café whose outside terrace and large interior are

a haven amidst EUR's brutal boulevards. Appropriately housed on the ground floor of EUR's official "restaurant building", it's a café, *tabacchi* and wine shop all rolled into one, and serves excellent cakes and sandwiches.

VOLPETTI PIÙ

Via Alessandro Volta 8. Mon–Thurs 10.30am–3.30pm & 5.30–10pm, Fri & Sat 10.30am–3.30pm & 5.30–11pm; closed afternoons in Aug. MAP PP.114–115, POCKET MAP E8

Tavola calda that's attached to the famous deli a few doors down. Great pizza, *supplì*, chicken, deep-fried veg and much more.

Bar

OASI DELLA BIRRA

Piazza Testaccio 41. Mon–Sat 4.30pm–midnight, Sun 7pm–midnight. MAP PP.114–115, POCKET MAP E8

Unassumingly situated under a Piazza Testaccio wine bar, the cosy basement rooms here house an international selection of beers that arguably rivals anywhere in the world – 500 in all, and with plenty of wines to choose from as well. You can eat generously assembled plates of cheese and salami, as well as a great selection of *bruschette* and polenta dishes.

Clubs & venues

AKAB

Via di Monte Testaccio 69 ⓣ06 5725 0585, ⓦakabclub.com. Metro B Piramide or bus #23. Wed–Sat 10pm–4am. €10–20, including 1 drink. MAP PP.114–115, POCKET MAP E9

This club is built into an old carpenter's shop on two floors, one on ground level, the other a cave-like room below. Head down for Thursday's popular "Milkshake" (r'n'b, hip-hop) night.

CASA DEL JAZZ

Viale di Porta Ardeatina 55 ⓣ06 0608, ⓦcasajazz.it. Metro #B to Piramide or bus #714. Admission €8–20. MAP PP.114–115, POCKET MAP G9

Sponsored by the city, this converted villa in leafy surroundings is the ultimate jazz-lovers' complex, with a restaurant, recording studios and a 150-seat auditorium that hosts gigs on most nights.

GOA

Via Libetta 13 ⓣ06 574 8277 ⓦgoaclub.com. Metro B Garbatella or bus #29, 769, 770. Thurs–Sat 11.30pm–5am. Admission around €15. MAP PP.114–115, POCKET MAP E11

Long-running Ostiense club near the Basilica San Paolo, playing techno, house and drum'n'bass, with a top-of-the-range sound system and a loungey bar area.

L'ALIBI

Via di Monte Testaccio 44 ⓣ06 574 3448, ⓦlalibi.it. Metro B Piramide or bus #23. Fri–Sun 11.30pm–4am. Admission €10–€15, including 1 drink. MAP PP.114–115, POCKET MAP E9

Predominantly – but by no means exclusively – male venue that's one of Rome's oldest and best gay clubs. Downstairs there's a multi-room cellar disco and upstairs an open-air bar. The big terrace is perfect during the warm months, with dancing under the stars.

RASHOMON

Via degli Argonauti 16 ⓦrashomonclub.com. Metro B Garbatella. Fri & Sat 11pm–4am. Admission around €10. MAP PP.114–115, POCKET MAP F11

A two-room live music space with good music and dj sets at weekends. There's also a late-night cocktail bar, open from Tuesday to Saturday.

Trastevere and the Janiculum Hill

Across the river from the centre of town, Trastevere (the name means literally "across the Tiber") was the artisan area of the city in classical times, neatly placed for the trade that came upriver from Ostia. Nowadays the area is a long way from its working-class roots, and its many bars and restaurants can be thronged with tourists. But its narrow streets and closeted squares are charming, peaceful in the morning, lively come the evening, with dozens of trattorias setting tables out along the cobbled streets – and still buzzing late at night, when its lively bars take over.

SAN FRANCESCO A RIPA

Piazza San Francesco d'Assisi 88. Daily 7am–1pm & 2–7.30pm. MAP PP.126–127, POCKET MAP D7–E7

The church of **San Francesco a Ripa** is best known for two things: the fact that St Francis himself once stayed here – you can see the actual room he stayed in if you're lucky enough to find it open – and the writhing, orgasmic statue of a minor saint, the Blessed Ludovica Albertoni, sculpted by Bernini towards the end of his career. As a work of Baroque emotiveness, it's perhaps even more frank in its depiction of an earthily realized divine ecstasy than his more famous *Ecstasy of St Theresa* in the church of Santa Maria della Vittoria (see p.86).

SANTA CECILIA IN TRASTEVERE

Piazza Santa Cecilia 22. Basilica and excavations daily 10am–1pm & 4–7pm; singing gallery Mon–Sat 10am–12.30pm. Basilica free, singing gallery €2.50, excavations €2.50. MAP PP.126–127, POCKET MAP E18

In its own quiet piazza off Via Anicia, the basilica of **Santa Cecilia in Trastevere** was

BLESSED LUDOVICA ALBERTONI, SAN FRANCESCO A RIPA

MOSAICS IN SANTA MARIA IN TRASTEVERE

originally built over the site of the second-century home of St Cecilia, who was – along with her husband – persecuted for her Christian beliefs. The story has it that Cecilia was locked in the caldarium of her own baths for several days but refused to die, singing her way through the ordeal (Cecilia is patron saint of music). Her head was finally half hacked off with an axe, though it took several blows before she died. Below the high altar, under a Gothic baldacchino, Stefano Maderno's statue of the limp saint shows her incorruptible body as it was found when exhumed in 1599, with three deep cuts in her neck. Downstairs, **excavations** of the baths and the rest of the Roman house are on view in the crypt. But more alluring by far is the **singing gallery** above the nave of the church (ring the bell to the left of the church door), where **Pietro Cavallini**'s late thirteenth-century fresco of the *Last Judgement* – all that remains of the decoration that once covered the entire church – is a powerful, amazingly naturalistic piece of work for its time, centring on Christ in quiet majesty, flanked by angels.

SANTA MARIA IN TRASTEVERE

Piazza Santa Maria in Trastevere. Daily 7.30am–9pm; Aug 8am–noon & 4–9pm. MAP PP.126–127, POCKET MAP C18

In the heart of old Trastevere, Piazza **Santa Maria in Trastevere** is named after the church in its northwest corner. Held to be the first Christian place of worship in Rome, it was built on a site where a fountain of oil is said to have sprung on the day of Christ's birth. The church's mosaics are among the city's most impressive: mostly Byzantine-inspired works depicting a solemn yet sensitive parade of saints thronged around Christ and Mary – the *Coronation of the Virgin* – beneath which are scenes from her life by the Santa Cecilia artist, Pietro Cavallini. Under the high altar on the right, an inscription – "FONS OLEI" – marks the spot where the oil is supposed to have sprung up.

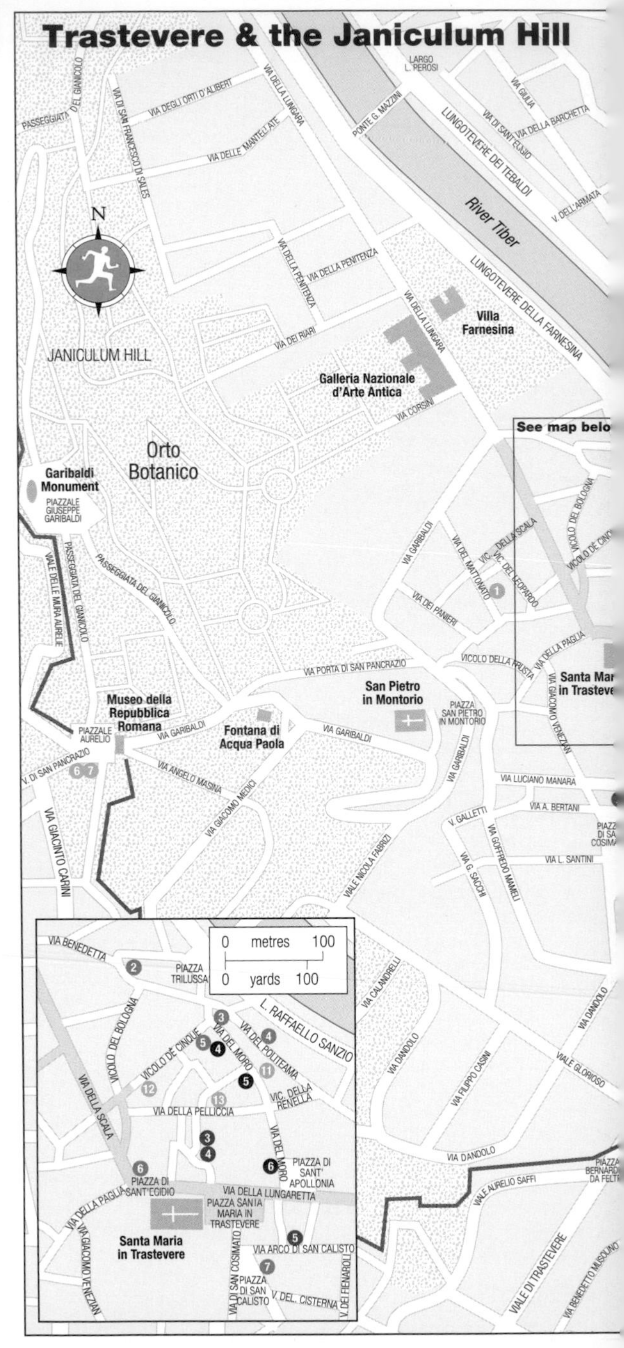
Trastevere & the Janiculum Hill
N
JANICULUM HILL
Orto Botanico
Garibaldi Monument
PIAZZALE GIUSEPPE GARIBALDI
Villa Farnesina
Galleria Nazionale d'Arte Antica
River Tiber
See map below
San Pietro in Montorio
PIAZZA SAN PIETRO IN MONTORIO
Museo della Repubblica Romana
PIAZZALE AURELIO
Fontana di Acqua Paola
Santa Maria in Trastevere
PIAZZA TRILUSSA
L. RAFFAELLO SANZIO
PIAZZA DI SANT'EGIDIO
PIAZZA DI SANT' APOLLONIA
PIAZZA SANTA MARIA IN TRASTEVERE
PIAZZA DI SAN CALISTO
0 metres 100
0 yards 100
LARGO L. PEROSI
LUNGOTEVERE DEI TEBALDI
LUNGOTEVERE DELLA FARNESINA
VIA DELLA LUNGARA
VIA GARIBALDI
VIA DELLA SCALA
VIA DELLA LUNGARETTA
VIA DELLA PAGLIA
VIA GIACOMO VENEZIAN
VIA DANDOLO
VIALE DI TRASTEVERE

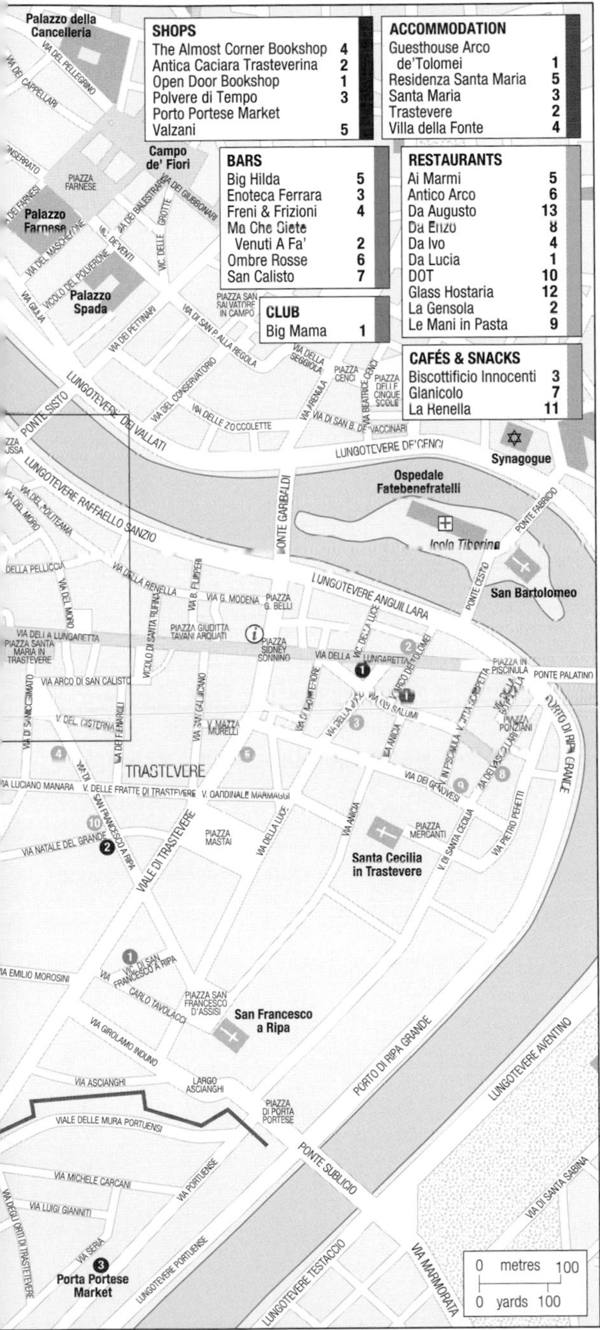
SHOPS
The Almost Corner Bookshop 4
Antica Caciara Trasteverina 2
Open Door Bookshop 1
Polvere di Tempo 3
Porto Portese Market
Valzani 5
ACCOMMODATION
Guesthouse Arco de'Tolomei 1
Residenza Santa Maria 5
Santa Maria 3
Trastevere 2
Villa della Fonte 4
BARS
Big Hilda 5
Enoteca Ferrara 3
Freni & Frizioni 4
Ma Che Siete Venuti A Fa' 2
Ombre Rosse 6
San Calisto 7
CLUB
Big Mama 1
RESTAURANTS
Ai Marmi 5
Antico Arco 6
Da Augusto 13
Da Enzo 8
Da Ivo 4
Da Lucia 1
DOT 10
Glass Hostaria 12
La Gensola 2
Le Mani in Pasta 9
CAFÉS & SNACKS
Biscottificio Innocenti 3
Glanicolo 7
La Renella 11
Palazzo della Cancelleria
Campo de' Fiori
Palazzo Farnese
Palazzo Spada
Synagogue
Ospedale Fatebenefratelli
Isola Tiberina
San Bartolomeo
TRASTEVERE
Santa Cecilia in Trastevere
San Francesco a Ripa
Porta Portese Market
LUNGOTEVERE DEI VALLATI
LUNGOTEVERE DE' CENCI
LUNGOTEVERE RAFFAELLO SANZIO
LUNGOTEVERE ANGUILLARA
PONTE SISTO
PONTE GARIBALDI
PONTE PALATINO
PONTE SUBLICIO
PORTO DI RIPA GRANDE
LUNGOTEVERE AVENTINO
LUNGOTEVERE TESTACCIO
VIA MARMORATA
VIALE DI TRASTEVERE
0 metres 100
0 yards 100

VILLA FARNESINA

Via della Lungara 230 06 6802 7268, villafarnesina.it. Mon–Sat 9am–2pm, second Sun of the month 9am–5pm; guided tours in English on Sat at 10am. €6. MAP PP.126–127, POCKET MAP C16

The early sixteenth-century **Villa Farnesina** was built by Baldassare Peruzzi for the Sienese banker Agostino Chigi. Its opulent rooms are decorated with marvellous frescoes and most people come to view the Raphael-designed painting of *Cupid and Psyche* in the now glassed-in loggia, completed in 1517 by the artist's assistants. The painter and art historian Vasari claims Raphael didn't complete the work because his infatuation with his mistress – "La Fornarina", whose father's bakery was situated nearby – was making it difficult to concentrate. Nonetheless it's very impressive: a flowing, animated work bursting with muscular men and bare-bosomed women, although the only part Raphael is said to have actually completed is the female figure with her back turned on the lunette (to the right of the door leading out to the east). He did, however, apparently manage to finish the *Galatea* in the room next door. The ceiling illustrates Chigi's horoscope constellations, frescoed by the architect of the building, Peruzzi, who also decorated the upstairs Salone delle Prospettive, where trompe l'oeil balconies give views onto contemporary Rome.

PALAZZO CORSINI

Via della Lungara 10 06 6880 2323, galleriacorsini.beniculturali.it. Mon & Wed–Sun 8.30am–7.30pm. €5, or €9 including Palazzo Barberini; valid 3 days; free first Sun of the month. MAP PP.126–127, POCKET MAP C16–17

Housed in the **Palazzo Corsini**, the **Galleria Nazionale d'Arte Antica** is a relatively small collection that takes up a few rooms of the giant palace. There's a grouping of Flemish paintings, including works by Rubens and Van Dyck, and a room full of landscapes, including lush scenes by Dughet. Look out for the famous portrayal of *Salome with the Head of St John the Baptist* by Guido Reni. You can also visit the bedchamber of Queen Christina, who renounced Protestantism and, with it, the Swedish throne in 1655, and brought her library and fortune to Rome – she died, here in the palace, in 1689, and is one of only three women to be buried in St Peter's. Also worth a look are the curious Corsini Throne, thought to be a Roman

PALAZZO CORSINI

VIEW FROM THE JANICULUM HILL

copy of an Etruscan throne of the second or first century, and, further on, Caravaggio's youthful, highly stylized *St John the Baptist*.

THE ORTO BOTANICO

Largo Cristina di Svezia 24 ☎06 4991 7107. Mon–Sat: April–Oct 9am–6.30pm; Nov–March 9am–5.30pm. €8. MAP PP.126–127, POCKET MAP B17

The **Orto Botanico** occupies the eastern side of the Janiculum Hill. It's a pleasantly neglected expanse these days where you can clamber up to high stands of bamboo and ferns cut by rivulets of water, stroll through a wood of century-old oaks, cedars and conifers, and relax in a grove of acclimatized palm trees. There's also a herbal garden with medicinal plants, a collection of orchids that bloom in springtime and early summer, and a garden of aromatic herbs put together for the blind. The garden also has the distinction of being home to one of the oldest plane trees in Rome, between 350 and 400 years old.

THE JANICULUM HILL

MAP PP.126–127, POCKET MAP A17–B17

It's about a fifteen-minute walk up Via Garibaldi from lively Piazza di Sant'Egidio to the summit of the **Janiculum Hill** – not one of the original seven hills of Rome, but the one with the best and most accessible views of the centre. Follow Vicolo del Cedro from Via della Scala and take the steps up from the end, cross the main road, and continue on the steps that lead up to **San Pietro in Montorio**, best known – and worth stopping off for – the Renaissance architect Bramante's little **Tempietto** in its courtyard (Tues–Fri 9.30am–12.30pm & 2–4.30pm, Sat 9am–3pm). Head up from here past the gigantic **Fontana di Acqua Paola** – which starred in the opening scene of Paolo Sorrentino's 2013 film *The Great Beauty* – up to the Porta San Pancrazio, home to the new **Museo della Repubblica Romana e della Memoria Garibaldina** (Tues–Fri 10am–2pm, Sat & Sun 10am–6pm; free). Dedicated to Garibaldi's unsuccessful defence of the Roman republic of 1849, it holds multimedia displays, photographs and artefacts. From here, it's a short stroll uphill to the statues of the 1849 martyrs – as well as spectacular views across the city. Below the equestrian **monument to Garibaldi**, a **cannon** fires a single shot at exactly noon each day that can be heard as far away as the Colosseum.

Shops

THE ALMOST CORNER BOOKSHOP

Via del Moro 45. Mon–Sat 10am–8pm, Sun 11am–8pm. MAP PP.126–127, POCKET MAP D17

Of all Rome's English bookshops, this is the best bet for finding the very latest titles, and staff are helpful too.

ANTICA CACIARA TRASTEVERINA

Via San Francesco a Ripa 140a/b. Mon–Sat 7am–8pm. MAP PP.126–127, POCKET MAP D18

This wonderful cheese shop is piled high with ricotta, *pecorino romano* and creamy *burrata* from Puglia, as well as cold meats, porcini mushrooms and juicy Sicilian olives.

OPEN DOOR BOOKSHOP

Via della Lungaretta 23. Mon–Sat 10am–8pm, Aug closed Sat pm. MAP PP.126–127, POCKET MAP E18

Although they do have some new titles, especially on Rome and Roman history, used books in English dominate the shelves at this friendly bookshop, where you never know what treasures you might happen upon. They also have a selection of books in Italian, German, French and Spanish.

PORTA PORTESE MARKET

POLVERE DI TEMPO

Via del Moro 59. Mon–Fri 10.30am–8pm, Sat 11am–8pm, Sun noon–8pm. MAP PP.126–127, POCKET MAP D17

This treasure trove of a shop selling antique lamps, hourglasses and globes is a great place to pick up unusual gifts.

PORTA PORTESE MARKET

Via Portuense. Sun 7am–2pm. MAP PP.126–127,POCKET MAP D8.

On a Sunday it's worth approaching Trastevere from the south, walking over the Ponte Sublicio to Porta Portese; from here the Porta Portese flea market stretches down Via Portuense to Trastevere train station in a congested medley of antiques, old motor spares, cheap and trendy clothing items, and assorted junk. Haggling is the rule here, and remember to keep a good hold of your wallet or purse. Plan to come early if you want to buy – most of the bargains have gone by 10am, by which time the crush of people can be rather intense.

VALZANI

Via del Moro 37a/b. Tues–Sun 10am–8.30pm. MAP PP.126–127, POCKET MAP D18

Specializing in the art of confectionary since 1925, this small shop is stuffed full of calorific treats. *Valzani* is most famous for its sublime chocolate, but traditional treats such as *mostaccioli* and *pangiallo* are just as hard to resist.

Cafés and snacks

BISCOTTIFICIO INNOCENTI

Via della Luce 21. Mon–Sat 8am–8pm, Sun 9.30am–2pm. MAP PP.126–127, POCKET MAP E18

Tucked away on a Trastevere backstreet is this wonderfully old-fashioned bakery, run by three generations of the same family. Pride of place is given to the enormous 1950s-vintage oven, which wafts out the delicious aroma of freshly baked biscuits.

GIANICOLO

Piazzale Aurelia 5. Tues–Sat 6am–midnight, Sun 6am–10.30pm. MAP PP.126–127, POCKET MAP B13

Quite an ordinary bar, but in a picturesque location and a bit of a hangout for Italian media stars, writers and academics from the nearby Spanish and American academies. Tasty sandwiches, too, and a couple of tables inside as well as out.

LA RENELLA

Via del Moro 15. Summer Mon–Thurs & Sun 7am–midnight, Fri & Sat 7am–3am; winter daily 7am–10pm. MAP PP.126–127, POCKET MAP D17

Arguably the best bakery in Rome, with great foccaccia and superb *pizza al taglio*. Take a number and be prepared to wait at busy times. You can take away or eat on the premises at the long counter.

Restaurants

AI MARMI

Viale di Trastevere 53 ⓣ06 580 0919. Thurs–Tues 7pm–2am. MAP PP.126–127, POCKET MAP D18

Very reasonably priced place, nicknamed "the mortuary" because of its stark interior and marble tables, and serving superior *supplì al telefono* (so named because of the string of mozzarella it forms when you take a bite), fresh *baccalà* and some of Rome's best pizza.

ANTICO ARCO

Piazzale Aurelio 7 ⓣ06 581 5274, ⓦanticoarco.it. Daily noon–midnight. MAP PP.126–127, POCKET MAP A18

Next to the Janiculum Hill, this is one of Rome's best restaurants, serving creative, beautifully presented dishes. The seven-course tasting menu (€78) is good value for cooking of this calibre.

DA AUGUSTO

Piazza de Renzi 15 ⓣ06 580 3798. Daily 12.30–3pm & 8–11pm. MAP PP.126–127, POCKET MAP D17

A Trastevere old-timer serving Roman basics outside on the cobbles in the summer months. You can get a good meal for about €14 here, including a glass of robust house wine. Expect offerings such as pasta and soup starters, and daily meat and fish specials – not haute cuisine, but decent, hearty Roman cooking. No bookings taken, and no credit cards.

ANTICO ARCO

DA ENZO

Via dei Vascellari 29 ⓣ06 581 2260. Mon–Sat 12.30–3pm & 7.30–11pm. MAP PP.126–127, POCKET MAP E18

This simple backstreet trattoria, with just a handful of tables and the kitchen in view, has been run by the same family for over thirty years. Great for Roman favourites such as pasta with oxtail sauce (€11).

DA IVO

Via di San Francesco a Ripa 158 ⓣ06 581 7082. Wed–Mon 7.30pm–1am. MAP PP.126–127, POCKET MAP D18

The Trastevere pizzeria, almost in danger of becoming a caricature, but still good and very reasonable. A nice assortment of desserts, too – try the *monte bianco* for the ultimate chestnut cream and meringue confection. Arrive early to avoid a chaotic queue.

DA LUCIA

Vicolo del Mattonato 2 ⓣ06 580 3601. Tues–Sun 12.30–3pm & 7.30–11pm. MAP PP.126–127, POCKET MAP C17

Reliable, moderately priced old Roman trattoria that is the best place for summer outdoor dining in Trastevere. *Spaghetti cacio e pepe* is the speciality here – arrive early for one of the in-demand tables on the attractive alleyway outside.

GLASS HOSTARIA

DOT

Via Natale del Grande 52 ⓣ06 581 7281. Mon–Sat 6pm–2am. MAP PP.126–127, POCKET MAP D18

This classy, low-lit restaurant has a Sicilian-inspired menu, ranging from street-food offerings such as *panelle* (chickpea fritters) to pasta with sea urchins (mains from €15). Fish is especially good here, though non-fish-eaters are also catered for.

GLASS HOSTARIA

Vicolo dè Cinque 58 ⓣ06 5833 5903. Tues–Sun 7.30– 11.30pm. MAP PP.126–127, POCKET MAP C17

Trastevere's smartest dining option is this Michelin-starred restaurant, with brick walls, glass floor and polished service. On the menu you might find tagliatelle with wild asparagus, black garlic and lemon, or crab with truffle sauce. The ten-course tasting menu is €110.

LA GENSOLA

Piazza della Gensola 15 ⓣ06 5833 2758. Daily 1–3pm & 7.45–11.30pm; closed Sun in Aug. MAP PP.126–127, POCKET MAP E18

This place, with charming and simple decor, is a lovely place for a special meal: the Sicilian cuisine is faultless and the atmosphere warm and convivial. The predominantly fishy specialities include tagliolini with tuna and asparagus, and the desserts are excellent too: you can't go wrong with the crumbly apple pie served with deliciously creamy cinnamon ice cream.

LE MANI IN PASTA

Via dei Genovesi 37 ⓣ06 581 6017. Tues–Sun 12.30–3pm & 7.30–11.30pm. MAP PP.126–127, POCKET MAP E18

Tucked down an alley, this small and unassuming place has a tiny kitchen in view and specializes in pasta and fish.

A full – and excellent – meal with wine will set you back around €40–50 per person. It's deservedly busy, so be sure to book.

Bars

BIG HILDA

Vicolo dè Cinque 33. Mon–Fri 9am–2am, Sat & Sun 10am–2am. MAP PP.126–127, POCKET MAP D17

This cosy, English-style pub is always buzzing with an Italian and international crowd. There are plenty of tables, inside and out, so you can settle in and enjoy the ultra-long happy hour (11am until around 10pm).

ENOTECA FERRARA

Piazza Trilussa 41 ⓣ06 5833 5903. Daily 6pm–2am. MAP PP.126–127, POCKET MAP D17

This cavernous place incorporates a pricey restaurant, a cheaper *osteria* and, best of the lot, a cosy wine-bar, *La Mescita*. Drop by in the evening for a superior *aperitivo*: there's a huge selection of wines by the glass, accompanied by free nibbles.

FRENI & FRIZIONI

Via del Politeama 4/6. Daily 6.30pm–2am. MAP PP.126–127, POCKET MAP D17

Just off Piazza Trilussa, this former mechanic's workshop (the name means "Brakes and Clutches") is now home to one of the city's best bars. The *aperitivo* buffet (7–10pm) is worth dropping by for, too.

MA CHE SIETE VENUTI A FA'

Via Benedetta 25. Daily 11am–2am. MAP PP.126–127, POCKET MAP C17

There's an amazing choice of artisanal beers from all over the world in this tiny bar. Some of them can't be found anywhere else in the city, or even Italy,

FRENI & FRIZIONI

and this is a cosy place to work your way through them.

OMBRE ROSSE

Piazza di Sant'Egidio 12 ⓣ06 588 4155. Daily 10am–2am. MAP PP.126–127, POCKET MAP C18

A great place for a morning cappuccino, with seating on one of Trastevere's most charming piazzas. Snacky meals are served, and there's live jazz, blues and rock 'n' roll every night except Saturday.

SAN CALISTO

Piazza San Calisto 4. Mon–Sat 6am–2am. MAP PP.126–127, POCKET MAP D18

This old guard Trastevere bar attracts a huge, mixed crowd on late summer nights; the booze is cheap, and you can sit at outside tables for no extra cost. Things are slightly less *demimonde*-ish during the day, when it's simply a great spot to sip a cappuccino, read and enjoy the sun.

Club

BIG MAMA

Vicolo San Francesco a Ripa 18 ⓣ06 581 2551, ⓦbigmama.it. Tues–Sat (and occasionally on Mon) 9pm–1.30am; concerts start at 10.30pm. MAP PP.126–127, POCKET MAP D7

Trastevere-based jazz/blues club of long standing, hosting nightly acts. Book ahead for star attractions. Food is served too.

Villa Borghese and north

During the Renaissance, the market gardens and olive groves north of the city walls were appropriated as summer estates by Rome's wealthy elite, particularly those affiliated to the papal court. One of the most notable of these, Villa Borghese, was the summer playground of the Borghese family and is now a public park and home to two of Rome's best museums: the unmissable art collection of the Galleria Borghese, and the Villa Giulia, built by Pope Julius II and now the National Etruscan Museum. North of Villa Borghese stretch Rome's nineteenth- and early twentieth-century residential districts – not of much interest in themselves except perhaps for the Mussolini-era Foro Italico and the Auditorium music complex.

VILLA BORGHESE

Metro line A to Barberini or Flaminio or bus #53 from Piazza Barberini or #910 from Termini. MAP PP.136–137, POCKET MAP G2

The vast green expanse of **Villa Borghese** – accessible by way of the Pincio Gardens, or from entrances at the top of Via Veneto or Via Porta Pinciana – is about as near as you can get to peace in the city centre. The beautiful landscaped grounds and palace were designed for Cardinal Scipione Borghese in 1605 and bought by the city at the turn of the nineteenth century; they now form the city's most central park. There are plenty of attractions for those who want to do more than just stroll or sunbathe, not least a zoo and some of the city's finest museums (see below), but it's full of pockets of interest if you just want to wander. You can rent bikes outside the Galleria Nazionale d'Arte Moderna and other places in the Pincio Gardens (from €4/hr, €10/4hr), or take a two- or four-person chariot known as a *risciò*, operated by a mixture of pedal and electrical power, which make for a very relaxed way to see the park (€12–25/hr).

LAKE IN THE GROUNDS OF VILLA BORGHESE

GALLERIA BORGHESE

GALLERIA BORGHESE

Piazzale Scipione Borghese ⓣ 06 32 810, ⓦ galleriaborghese.it. Tues–Sun 9am–7pm; admission on timed tickets every 2hr (last entry 5pm); pick up tickets 30min before entry. €11 (including booking fee); free first Sun of the month. Pre-book at least a day in advance (at least two weeks is best in summer); pre-booked visits are obligatory. MAP PP.136–137, POCKET MAP G2

The collection of Cardinal Scipione Borghese in the **Galleria Borghese** is one of the city's most compelling. The first room has as its centrepiece Canova's infamous statue of the half-naked Pauline Borghese posed as Venus, but otherwise the focus is on **Bernini**. The face of his marvellous statue of David is a self-portrait, said to have been carved with the help of a mirror held by Scipione Borghese himself. Other highlights include his dramatic, poised *Apollo and Daphne*; *The Rape of Proserpine* from 1622; and a larger-than-life statue of Aeneas, carrying his father, Anchises, out of the burning city of Troy, sculpted by both Bernini and his then 15-year-old son in 1613. There are paintings, too, including notable works such as Caravaggio's *David Holding the Head of Goliath*, and a self portrait as *Bacchus*, among others, and the upstairs **Pinacoteca** comprises one of the richest collections of paintings in the world, with canvases by Raphael, his teacher Perugino and other masters of the Umbrian school from the late fifteenth and sixteenth centuries. Look for the *Deposition*, *Lady with a Unicorn* and *Portrait of a Man* by Raphael, and a copy of the artist's portrait of a tired-out Julius II, painted in 1513. There's also *Venus and Cupid with a Honeycomb* by Cranach, Lorenzo Lotto's touching *Portrait of a Man* and works by the Venetians of the early 1500s, including Titian's *Sacred and Profane Love*, painted in 1514. The large **Gallery of Lanfranco** at the back of the building holds a series of self-portraits done by Bernini at various stages of his life and a bust of Cardinal Scipione executed in 1632, portraying him as the worldly connoisseur of fine art and living that he was.

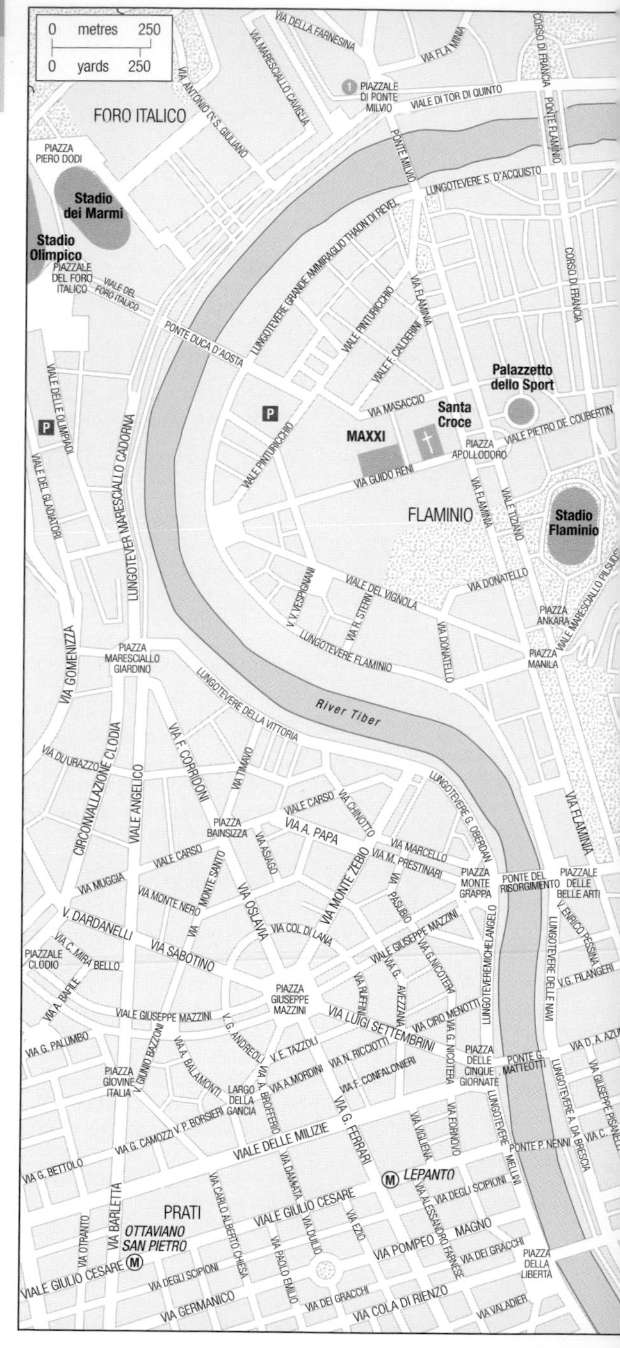
0 metres 250
0 yards 250
VIA DELLA FARNESINA
VIA MARESCIALLO CAVIGLIA
VIA FLAMINIA
CORSO DI FRANCIA
1
PIAZZALE DI PONTE MILVIO
VIALE DI TOR DI QUINTO
PONTE FLAMINIO
FORO ITALICO
VIA ANTONIO DI S. GIULIANO
PIAZZA PIERO DODI
PONTE MILVIO
LUNGOTEVERE S. D'ACQUISTO
Stadio dei Marmi
Stadio Olimpico
PIAZZALE DEL FORO ITALICO
VIALE DEL FORO ITALICO
LUNGOTEVERE GRANDE AMMIRAGLIO THAON DI REVEL
VIALE PINTURICCHIO
VIA FLAMINIA
CORSO DI FRANCIA
PONTE DUCA D'AOSTA
VIALE F. CALDERINI
Palazzetto dello Sport
VIALE DELLE OLIMPIADI
P
P
VIA MASACCIO
Santa Croce
MAXXI
VIALE PIETRO DE COUBERTIN
PIAZZA APOLLODORO
VIALE PINTURICCHIO
VIA GUIDO RENI
VIALE DEL GLADIATORI
LUNGOTEVER MARESCIALLO CADORNA
FLAMINIO
VIA FLAMINIA
VIALE TIZIANO
Stadio Flaminio
VIA DONATELLO
VIALE DEL VIGNOLA
V. V. VESPIGNANI
VIA R. STERN
VIA DONATELLO
PIAZZA ANKARA
VIALE MARESCIALLO PILSUDSKI
LUNGOTEVERE FLAMINIO
PIAZZA MANILA
VIA GOMENIZZA
PIAZZA MARESCIALLO GIARDINO
LUNGOTEVERE DELLA VITTORIA
River Tiber
VIA F. CORRIDONI
CIRCONVALLAZIONE CLODIA
VIA DURAZZO
VIALE ANGELICO
VIA TIMAVO
LUNGOTEVERE G. OBERDAN
VIALE CARSO
VIA CHINOTTO
VIA FLAMINIA
PIAZZA BAINSIZZA
VIA A. PAPA
VIA ASIAGO
VIA MARCELLO
VIA M. PRESTINARI
VIALE CARSO
VIA MONTE SANTO
VIA MONTE ZEBIO
VIA MUGGIA
VIA OSLAVIA
VIA PASUBIO
PIAZZA MONTE GRAPPA
PONTE DEL RISORGIMENTO
PIAZZALE DELLE BELLE ARTI
VIA MONTE NERO
V. DARDANELLI
VIA
VIA COL DI LANA
VIALE GIUSEPPE MAZZINI
V. ENRICO PESSINA
LUNGOTEVERE MICHELANGELO
LUNGOTEVERE DELLE NAVI
VIA C. MIRABELLO
PIAZZALE CLODIO
VIA SABOTINO
VIA G. NICOTERA
VIA G. AVEZZANA
VIA RUFFINI
V.G. FILANGERI
VIA A. BAFILE
PIAZZA GIUSEPPE MAZZINI
VIA LUIGI SETTEMBRINI
VIA CIRO MENOTTI
VIALE GIUSEPPE MAZZINI
V. G. ANDREOLI
V. E. TAZZOLI
VIA N. RICCIOTTI
VIA G. NICOTERA
PIAZZA DELLE CINQUE GIORNATE
PONTE G. MATTEOTTI
VIA D. A. AZUNI
VIA G. PALUMBO
VIA GIUNIO BAZZONI
VIA A. BALAMONTI
VIA A. MORDINI
VIA F. CONFALONIERI
VIA GIUSEPPE PISANELLI
PIAZZA GIOVINE ITALIA
LARGO DELLA GANCIA
VIA A. BROFFERIO
LUNGOTEVERE A. DA BRESCIA
VIA G. CAMOZZI
V. P. BORSIERI
VIA G. FERRARI
VIA VIGLIENA
VIA FORNOVO
LUNGOTEVERE MELLINI
PONTE P. NENNI
VIA C.
VIALE DELLE MILIZIE
VIA G. BETTOLO
VIA DAMIATA
LEPANTO
VIA DEGLI SCIPIONI
VIA CARLO ALBERTO CHIESA
VIALE GIULIO CESARE
VIA ALESSANDRO FARNESE
PRATI
VIA BARLETTA
VIA OTRANTO
OTTAVIANO SAN PIETRO
VIA DUILIO
VIA EZIO
VIA POMPEO MAGNO
VIA DEI GRACCHI
PIAZZA DELLA LIBERTÀ
VIA PAOLO EMILIO
VIALE GIULIO CESARE
VIA DEGLI SCIPIONI
VIA GERMANICO
VIA DEI GRACCHI
VIA COLA DI RIENZO
VIA VALADIER

Villa Borghese & north

ACCOMMODATION	
Next Door	1

CLUB	
Art Café	2

VENUE	
Auditorium	1

RESTAURANTS	
Casina Valadier	5
Metamorfosi	3
ReD	2

CAFÉ & SNACKS	
Caffè delle Arti	4
Gianfornaio	1

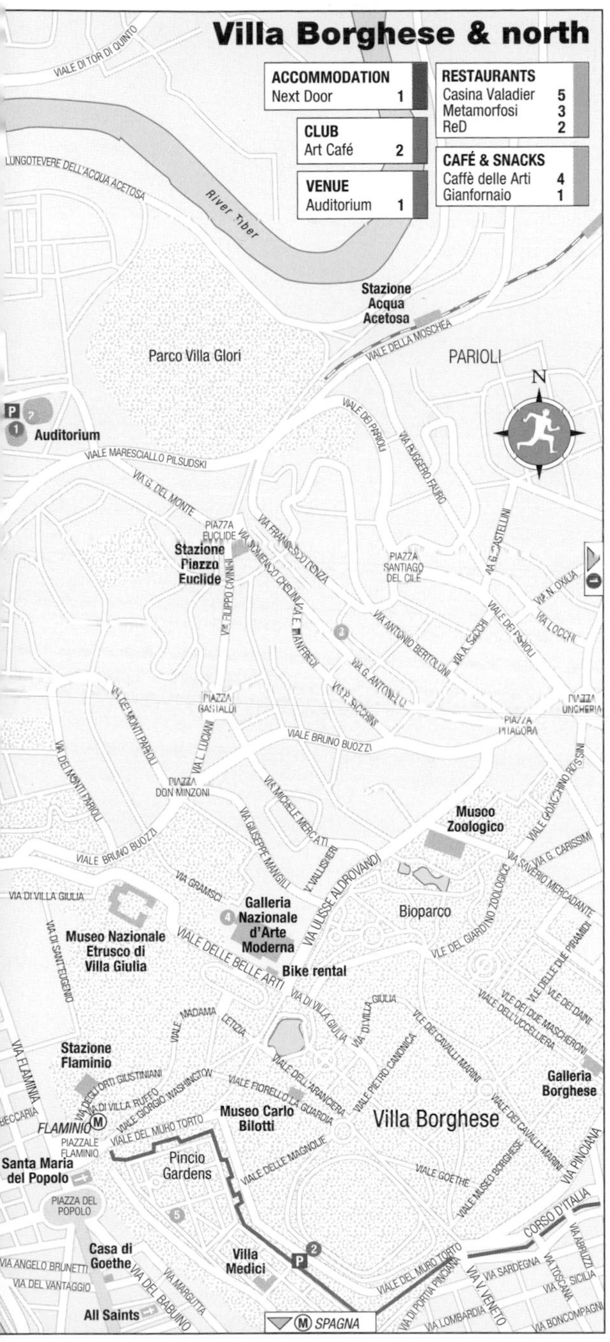

BEARS IN THE BIOPARCO

MUSEO CARLO BILOTTI

Viale Fiorello La Guardia ☎ 06 0608, ⓦ museocarlobilotti.it. June–Sept Tues–Fri 1–7pm, Sat & Sun 10am–7pm; Oct–May Tues–Fri 10am–4pm, Sat & Sun 10am–7pm. Free. MAP PP.136–137, POCKET MAP F2

Housed in the orangery of the Villa Borghese, this museum is, like the Galleria Borghese, made up of a family bequest, this time of **Carlo Bilotti** – a perfume and cosmetics baron who, until his death in 2006, collected art and hobnobbed with the brightest and best in the international art world. Good portraits of him by Larry Rivers, and of his wife and daughter by Andy Warhol, add to the slightly self-congratulatory air of the place, but the real reason for coming is to enjoy the small collection of high-quality works by the great modern Greek-Italian painter, Giorgio De Chirico, who lived in Rome for many years (see p.78).

BIOPARCO

Via del Giardino Zoologico, Villa Borghese ☎ 06 360 8211, ⓦ bioparco.it. Daily: Jan–March & Nov–Dec 9.30am–5pm; April–Oct 9.30am–6pm, open till 7pm Sat & Sun April–Sept. €16 adults, €13 children over 1m tall. MAP PP.136–137, POCKET MAP F1

Large, typical city-centre zoo, much improved and reinvented as the **"Bioparco"**, focusing on conservation and education yet still providing the usual animals kids are after – tigers, apes, giraffes, elephants, hippos and much more. The **zoological museum** next door – accessible from the main road (left out of the zoo and then left again) is less engaging and rather dated but worth a visit, with displays on different animal habitats as well as lots of more traditional stuffed mammals and birds.

GALLERIA NAZIONALE D'ARTE MODERNA

Via delle Belle Arti 131 ☎ 06 322 981, ⓦ www.gnam.beniculturali.it. Tues–Sun 8.30am–7.30pm. €8. MAP PP.136–137, POCKET MAP F1

Rome's **museum of modern art** is a lumbering, Neoclassical building housing a collection of nineteenth- and twentieth-century Italian (and a few foreign) names. It can make a refreshing change after several days of having the senses bombarded with Etruscan, Roman and Renaissance art. The nineteenth-century collection contains a splendid range of paintings by the Tuscan Impressionists (the Macchiaioli school), as well as works by Monet, Van Gogh and Cézanne, not to mention a giant statue of Hercules by the nineteenth-century Italian sculptor Canova and some mighty battle scenes celebrating Italian Unification. The twentieth-century collection features work by Giacomo Balla (a view of the Villa Borghese divided into 15 panels), his student Boccione and other Futurists, along with work by Modigliani and De Chirico. There are also some postwar canvases by the likes of Rothko, Pollock and Cy Twombly, Rome's own American artist, who lived in the city for most of his life.

The sun-trap terrace of the museum's smart **café** is a good spot for a coffee (see p.141).

MUSEO NAZIONALE ETRUSCO DI VILLA GIULIA

Piazzale Villa Giulia 9 Ⓦ villagiulia.beniculturali.it. Tues–Sun 8.30am–7.30pm. €8. MAP PP.136–137, POCKET MAP E1

The Villa Giulia is a lovely collection of courtyards, loggias, gardens and temples put together in a playful Mannerist style for Pope Julius III in the mid-sixteenth century. It now houses the **Museo Nazionale Etrusco di Villa Giulia**, the world's primary collection of Etruscan treasures, along with the Etruscan collection in the Vatican (see p.147). Part of the collection is housed in nearby **Villa Poniatowski**, but you have to prebook to visit these rooms. Not much is known about the Etruscans, but the Roman's predecessors were a creative and civilized people, evidenced here by a wealth of sensual sculpture, jewellery and art. They were also deeply religious and much of the collection focuses on preparing for the afterlife. The most famous exhibit is the remarkable *Sarcophagus of the Married Couple* (in the octagonal room in the east wing) – a touchingly lifelike portrayal of a husband and wife lying on a couch. It dates from the sixth century BC and was discovered in the tombs at Cerveteri. Look also at the delicate and beautiful cistae – drum-like objects, engraved and adorned with figures, that were supposed to hold all the things needed for the care of the body after death. Further on are marvellously intricate pieces of gold jewellery, delicately worked into tiny horses, birds, camels and other animals, as well as mirrors, candelabras and religious statues – votive offerings designed to appease the gods. On the upper floor of the west wing, you'll find a drinking horn in the shape of a dog's head that is so lifelike you almost expect it to bark; a *holmos*, or small table, to which the maker attached 24 little pendants around the edge; and a bronze disc breastplate from the seventh century BC decorated with a weird, almost modern abstract pattern of galloping creatures.

EXHIBIT IN THE MUSEO NAZIONALE ETRUSCO

FORO ITALICO

Metro Ottaviano then bus #32 to Piazza Lauro de Bosis. MAP PP.136–137, POCKET MAP B1

The **Foro Italico** sports complex is one of the few parts of Rome to survive intact pretty much the way Mussolini planned it. The centrepiece is the Ponte Duca d'Aosta, which connects Foro Italico to the town side of the river, and is headed by a white marble obelisk capped with a gold pyramid, engraved MUSSOLINI DUX in beautiful 1930s calligraphy. Beyond the bridge, an avenue patched with mosaics revering the Duce leads up to a fountain surrounded by more mosaics of muscle-bound figures revelling in healthful sporting activities. Either side of the fountain are the two main stadiums: the larger of the two, the Stadio Olimpico on the left, was used for the Olympic Games in 1960 and is still the venue for Rome's two soccer teams, though AS Roma are set to move elsewhere in 2017; the smaller, the **Stadio dei Marmi** ("stadium of marbles"), is ringed by sixty great male statues, groins modestly hidden by fig leaves, in a variety of elegantly macho poses.

MAXXI

Via Guido Reni 4a ⓦfondazionemaxxi.it. Tues–Fri & Sun 11am–7pm, Sat 11am–10pm; €10. Tram #2 from Piazzale Fiaminio (Metro A). MAP PP.136–137, POCKET MAP D1

This museum of twenty-first-century art and architecture is housed in a landmark building by the Anglo-Iraqi architect Zaha Hadid. It mostly hosts temporary exhibitions, but there are small permanent collections too, and the building itself – a jagged, concrete spaceship that looks like it's just landed in this otherwise rather ordinary part of the city – is worth a visit.

PONTE MILVIO

Metro Flaminio then tram #2. MAP PP.136–137, POCKET MAP D1

In 312 AD, Constantine defeated Maxentius at this footbridge across the Tiber, a victory that brought about the end of Roman paganism. More recently, it has been home to numerous padlocks, placed here by lovers who then threw the keys into the river. Once the bridge's lampposts started to collapse beneath the weight, the council removed the padlocks, though the bridge remains a romantic meeting point for local teens.

FORO ITALICO

Café and snacks

CAFFÈ DELLE ARTI

Via Antonio Gramsci 73. Mon 8am–5pm, Tues–Sun 8am–midnight. MAP PP.136–137, POCKET MAP F1

Attached to the modern art gallery (see p.138), this elegant café/restaurant serves up sandwiches and light lunches in the smart dining room or under shady umbrellas on the terrace.

GIANFORNAIO

Largo Maresciallo Piaz 16. Mon–Sat 7.30am–9pm, Sun 9am–3pm. MAP PP.136–137, POCKET MAP D1

Great bakery selling tasty pizza and other goodies.

Restaurants

CASINA VALADIER

Piazza Bucarest ☎06 6992 2090, Ⓦcasinavaladier.com. Tues–Sun 12.30–3pm & 7.30–11pm. MAP PP.136–137, POCKET MAP E2

With views across the city from the Pincio, this restaurant's main draw is its position, but the food isn't bad either (mains around €35), and the Valadier-designed building is a beauty. Also has a café selling lighter lunch dishes.

METAMORFOSI

Via Giovanni Antonelli 30 ☎06 807 6839, Ⓦmetamorfosiroma.it. Mon–Fri 12.30–2.30pm & 8–10.30pm, Sat 8–10.30pm. MAP PP.136–137, POCKET MAP F1

Roy Caceres' Michelin-starred restaurant is a delight, with creative Mediterranean cuisine served in elegant surroundings. The tasting menus are good value for such quality (€100 for six dishes, €130 for ten).

RED

Via Pietro de Coubertin 30 ☎06 8069 1630. Daily 8.30am–1am. MAP PP.136–137, POCKET MAP D1

Part of the Auditorium complex, this sleek designer bar-restaurant is good for a drink or a meal before or after a performance.

Club

ART CAFÉ

Via del Galoppatoio 33 ☎06 322 0994, Ⓦartcafe.it. Fri & Sat 11pm–5am. Admission €15, with a drink. MAP PP.136–137, POCKET MAP F2

In the underground car park in Villa Borghese, this is one of Rome's glitziest clubs. Dress up, and expect to queue.

Venue

AUDITORIUM

Via Pietro de Coubertin 15. Bus #53, 280, 910 or Tram #2, 19. Box office daily 11am–8pm. Concert tickets from around €15. Buy tickets online, or in Italy on ☎892902 or from abroad on ☎06 4411 7799. Tours Sat & Sun every hour 11.30am–4.30pm; book in advance on ☎06 8024 1281, Ⓦauditorium.com; €9. MAP PP.136–137, POCKET MAP D1

Designed by Renzo Piano, this is home to Rome's premier orchestra, the Accademia Nazionale di Santa Cecilia. Two smaller venues host chamber, choral, recital and experimental works, and the complex also sees shows by major rock and jazz names. There's a great book and CD shop on site, plus a decent café and regular tours.

AUDITORIUM

The Vatican

Situated on the west bank of the Tiber, just across from the city centre, the Vatican City has been a sovereign state since 1929, and its 1000 inhabitants have their own radio station, daily newspaper, and postal and security services, the last being the colourfully dressed Swiss Guards. It's believed that St Peter was buried in a pagan cemetery on the Vatican hill; hence the building of a basilica to venerate his name and the siting of the headquarters of the Catholic Church here. Stretching north from St Peter's, the Renaissance papal palaces are now home to the Vatican Museums – quite simply, the largest, richest, most compelling and perhaps most exhausting museum complex in the world. The other main Vatican sight worth visiting is the Castel Sant'Angelo on the riverside, a huge fortress which once harboured the popes in times of danger. Apart from visiting the main attractions, you wouldn't know at any point that you had left Rome and entered the Vatican; indeed the area around it, known as the Borgo, is one of the city's most cosmopolitan districts – full of mid-range hotels, restaurants and scurrying tourists and pilgrims, while the district just beyond, Prati, is a comfortable middle-class neighbourhood that's home to some of Rome's best and often least touristy restaurants.

CASTEL SANT'ANGELO

CASTEL SANT'ANGELO

Lungotevere Castello 50 ⓦ castelsantangelo.com. Daily 9am–7.30pm €10. MAP PP.144–145, POCKET MAP C13

The great circular hulk of the **Castel Sant'Angelo** marks the edge of the Vatican. It was designed and built by Hadrian as his own mausoleum and renamed in the sixth century, when Pope Gregory the Great witnessed a vision of St Michael here that ended a terrible plague. The papal authorities converted the building for use as a fortress and built a passageway to link it with the Vatican as a refuge in times of siege or invasion. Inside, a spiral ramp leads up into the centre of the mausoleum, over a drawbridge, to the main level at the top, where a small palace was built to house the papal residents in appropriate splendour. Pope Paul III had some especially fine renovations made, including the beautiful Paolina rooms, where the gilded ceilings display the Farnese family arms, and you'll also notice the pope's personal motto, *Festina Lente* ("Make haste slowly"), scattered throughout the ceilings and in various corners of all his rooms. Elsewhere, rooms hold swords, armour, guns and the like, while below are dungeons and storerooms which can be glimpsed from the spiralling ramp, testament to the castle's grisly past as the city's most notorious Renaissance prison. Off the Paolina rooms, a terrace runs around the whole building and holds a shady bar for pick-me-up drinks and sandwiches – and some great views of Rome, best from the terrace on the top of the whole structure – from which Tosca famously flung herself in Puccini's eponymous opera.

ST. PETER'S SQUARE

ST PETER'S SQUARE

MAP PP.144–145, POCKET MAP A14

Perhaps the most famous of Rome's many piazzas, Bernini's **St Peter's Square** doesn't disappoint, although its size isn't really apparent until you're right on top of it, its colonnade arms symbolically welcoming the world into the lap of the Catholic Church. The obelisk in the centre was brought to Rome by Caligula in 36 AD, and was moved here in 1586, when Sixtus V ordered that it be erected in front of the basilica, a task that took four months and was apparently done in silence, on pain of death. The matching fountains on either side are the work of Carlo Maderno (on the right) and Bernini (on the left). In between the obelisk and each fountain, a circular stone set into the pavement marks the focal points of an ellipse, from which the four rows of columns on the perimeter of the piazza line up perfectly, making the colonnade appear to be supported by a single line of columns.

The Vatican

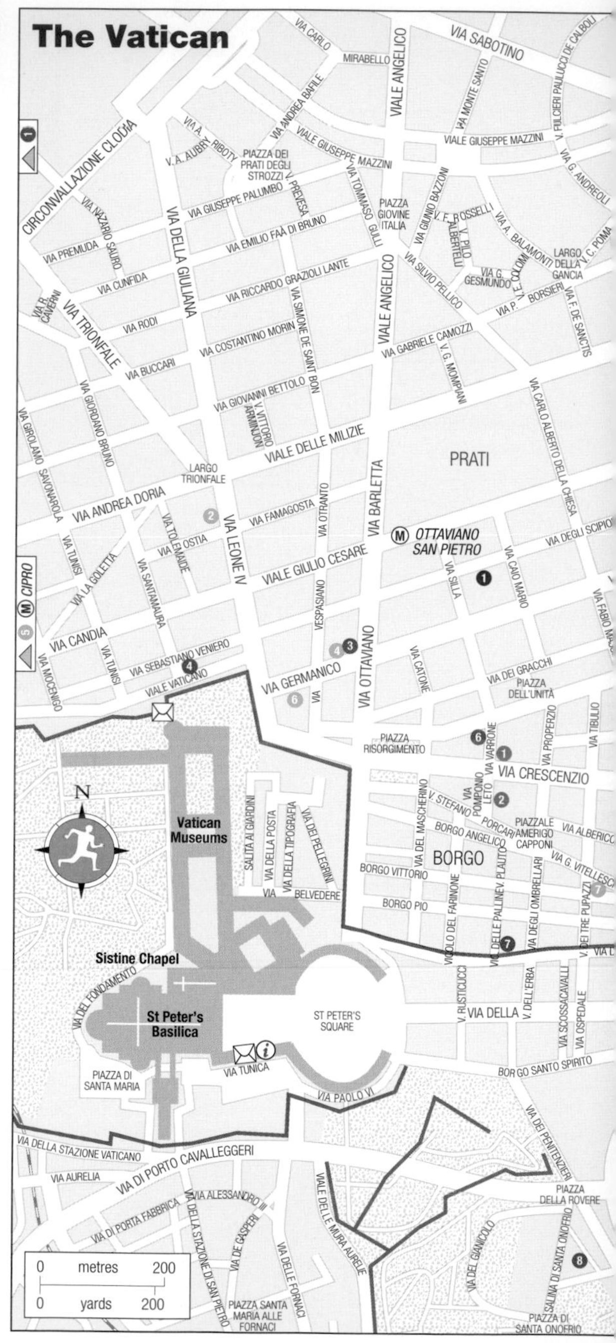

PRATI
BORGO
OTTAVIANO SAN PIETRO
CIPRO
Vatican Museums
Sistine Chapel
St Peter's Basilica
ST PETER'S SQUARE
VIA CRESCENZIO
VIALE GIULIO CESARE
VIALE DELLE MILIZIE
VIA ANDREA DORIA
VIALE ANGELICO
VIA OTTAVIANO
VIA LEONE IV
VIA GERMANICO
VIA DI PORTO CAVALLEGGERI
BORGO SANTO SPIRITO
PIAZZA RISORGIMENTO
LARGO TRIONFALE
VIA TRIONFALE
CIRCONVALLAZIONE CLODIA
VIA DELLA GIULIANA
VIA SABOTINO
VIALE GIUSEPPE MAZZINI
VIA PAOLO VI
VIA AURELIA
VIA DELLA STAZIONE VATICANO
VIALE VATICANO
0 metres 200
0 yards 200

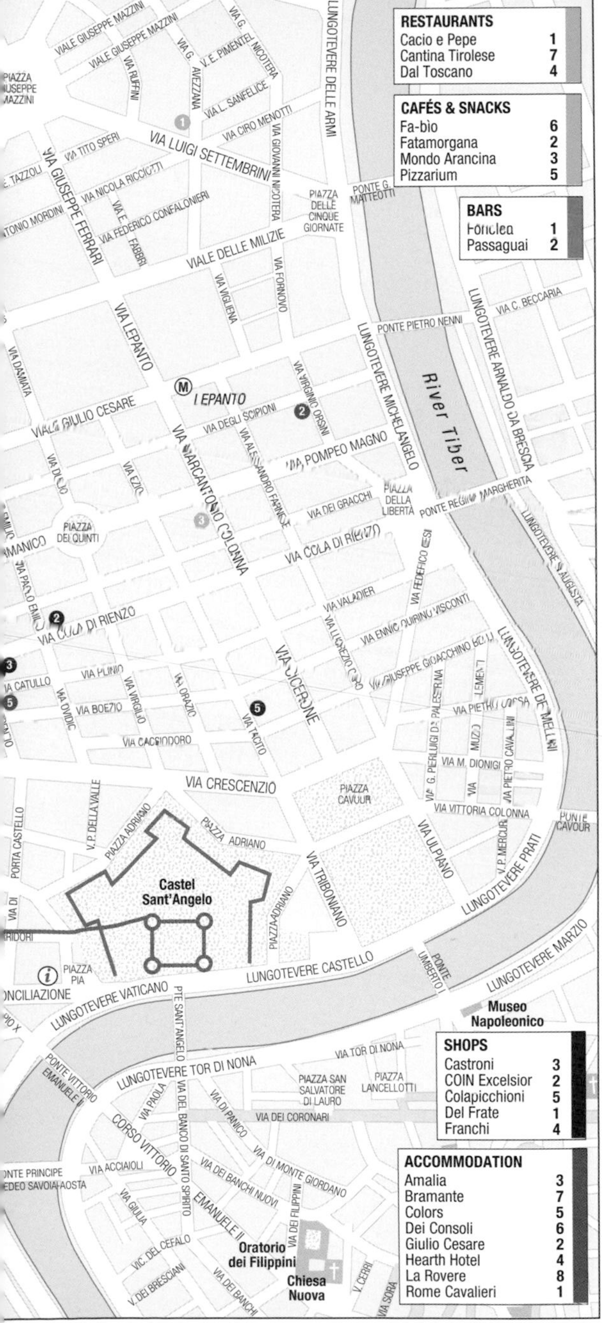
RESTAURANTS
Cacio e Pepe 1
Cantina Tirolese 7
Dal Toscano 4
CAFÉS & SNACKS
Fa-bìo 6
Fatamorgana 2
Mondo Arancina 3
Pizzarium 5
BARS
Fonclea 1
Passaguai 2
SHOPS
Castroni 3
COIN Excelsior 2
Colapicchioni 5
Del Frate 1
Franchi 4
ACCOMMODATION
Amalia 3
Bramante 7
Colors 5
Dei Consoli 6
Giulio Cesare 2
Hearth Hotel 4
La Rovere 8
Rome Cavalieri 1
River Tiber
Castel Sant'Angelo
Museo Napoleonico
Oratorio dei Filippini
Chiesa Nuova
LEPANTO
VIA LUIGI SETTEMBRINI
VIALE DELLE MILIZIE
VIA LEPANTO
VIALE GIULIO CESARE
VIA POMPEO MAGNO
VIA COLA DI RIENZO
VIA CICERONE
VIA CRESCENZIO
PIAZZA CAVOUR
PIAZZA ADRIANO
LUNGOTEVERE CASTELLO
LUNGOTEVERE VATICANO
LUNGOTEVERE TOR DI NONA
LUNGOTEVERE MICHELANGELO
LUNGOTEVERE DELLE ARMI
LUNGOTEVERE ARNALDO DA BRESCIA
LUNGOTEVERE PRATI
LUNGOTEVERE MARZIO
PONTE PIETRO NENNI
PONTE REGINA MARGHERITA
PONTE CAVOUR
PONTE UMBERTO I
PONTE VITTORIO EMANUELE II
CORSO VITTORIO EMANUELE II
VIA DEI CORONARI
VIA GIUSEPPE FERRARI
VIA MARCANTONIO COLONNA
PIAZZA DEI QUINTI
PIAZZA DELLA LIBERTÀ
PIAZZA DELLE CINQUE GIORNATE
PIAZZA PIA
VIA DI MONTE GIORDANO

ST PETER'S

Daily: April–Sept 7am–7pm; Oct–March 7am–6.30pm. Strict dress code – knees and shoulders must be covered. MAP PP.144–145, POCKET MAP B4

The Basilica di San Pietro, better known to many as **St Peter's**, is the principal shrine of the Catholic Church, built on the site of St Peter's tomb, and worked on by the greatest Italian architects of the sixteenth and seventeenth centuries. Not so long ago you could freely stroll around the piazza and wander into the basilica when you felt like it. Now much of the square is fenced off, and you can only enter St Peter's from the right-hand side (exiting to the left); you also have to go through security first, and the queues can be horrendous unless you get here before 9am.

Inside the **basilica**, on the right, is Michelangelo's graceful *Pietà*, completed when he was just 24. Following an attack by a vandal in 1972, it sits behind glass, strangely remote from the rest of the building. Further into the church, the dome is breathtakingly imposing, rising high above the supposed site of St Peter's tomb. With a diameter of 41.5m it is Rome's largest dome, supported by four enormous piers, decorated with reliefs depicting the basilica's so-called "major relics": St Veronica's handkerchief, which was used to wipe the face of Christ; the lance of St Longinus, which pierced Christ's side; and a piece of the True Cross. On the right side of the nave is the bronze statue of St Peter, its right foot polished smooth by the attentions of pilgrims. Bronze was also the material used in Bernini's 26m-high baldacchino, cast out of 927 tonnes of metal removed from the Pantheon roof in 1633. To modern eyes, it's an almost grotesque piece of work, its wild spiralling columns copied from those in the Constantine basilica. Bernini's feverish sculpting decorates the apse too, his bronze *Cattedra* enclosing the supposed chair of St Peter, though his monument to Alexander VII in the south transept is more interesting, its winged skeleton struggling underneath the heavy marble drapes, upon which the Chigi pope is kneeling in prayer.

An entrance off the aisle leads to the steeply priced **Treasury** (daily: April–Sept 8am–7pm; Oct–March 8am–6.15pm; €6), while steps by Bernini's statue of Longinus lead down

MICHELANGELO'S PIETÀ

to the **Grottoes** (daily: April–Sept 8am–6pm; Oct–March 8am–5.30pm), where the majority of the popes are buried. Directly beneath St Peter's baldacchino, the **necropolis** contains a row of Roman tombs with inscriptions confirming that the Vatican Hill was a burial ground in classical times.

Whether the tomb claimed as that of St Peter really is the saint's resting place is unclear, although it does tally with some historical descriptions. To be sure of getting a place on the English-language **tour**, book two or three months in advance via the Scavi office, through the arch to the left of St Peter's (Mon–Sat 9am–3.30pm; €13; no under-15s; ⓣ 06 6988 5318, ⓔ scavi@fsp.va).

The worthwhile ascent to the **roof and dome** (daily: April–Sept 8am–6pm; Oct–March 8am–5pm; €8 via lift, €6 climbing the 551 stairs) is outside by the entrance to the church. The views from the gallery around the interior of the dome give you a sense of the vastness of the church, and the roof grants views all around before the (challenging) climb to the lantern at the top of the dome – the views are as glorious as you'd expect – pretty much the best in the city.

THE VATICAN MUSEUMS

Viale Vaticano 13 ⓦ mv.vatican.va. Mon–Sat 9am–6pm, last entrance at 4pm, last Sun of each month 9am–2pm, last entrance at 12.30pm; Fridays May–July, Sept & Oct open 7–11pm, online booking obligatory; closed public and religious holidays. €16, under-18s and under-26s with student ID €8; €4 extra for online booking; last Sun of the month free. MAP PP.144–145, POCKET MAP B3

If you have found any of Rome's other museums disappointing, the Vatican is probably the reason why: so much booty from the city's history has

THE INTERIOR OF ST PETER'S BASILICA

ended up here, and so many of the Renaissance's finest artists were in the employ of the pope, that the result is a set of museums which put most other European collections to shame. As its name suggests, the complex actually holds a number of museums on very diverse subjects – displays of classical statuary, Renaissance painting, Etruscan relics and Egyptian artefacts, not to mention the furnishings and decoration of the building itself. There's no point in trying to see everything, at least not on one visit, and the only features you really shouldn't miss are the Raphael Rooms and the Sistine Chapel, and perhaps the Museo Pio-Clementino and Pinacoteca. Above all, decide how long you want to spend here, and what you want to see, before you start; it's easy to collapse from museum fatigue before you've even got to your main target of interest. In high season there may be a queue to get in, but getting to the museums late morning or after lunch can mean a shorter wait. Try to avoid Mondays, Saturdays and the days before and after Catholic holidays.Or buy your ticket in advance online and go to the front of the queue.

THE VATICAN MUSEUMS

THE PINACOTECA

Vatican Museums. MAP PP.144–145, POCKET MAP B4

If the **Pinacoteca** is on your list, it's best to visit it first – turn right at the top of the stairs. Housed in a separate building, it ranks among the best of Rome's picture galleries, with works from the early to high Renaissance and right up to the nineteenth century. Among early works, there is an amazing *Last Judgement* by Nicolò and Giovanni from the twelfth century, the stunning *Simoneschi* triptych by Giotto, painted in the early 1300s for the old St Peter's, and fragments of Melozzo de Forlì's *Musical Angels*, painted for the church of Santi Apostoli. Further on are the rich backdrops and elegantly clad figures of the Umbrian School painters, Perugino and Pinturicchio. Raphael has a room to himself, where you'll find his *Transfiguration*, which he had nearly completed when he died in 1520, *The Coronation of the Virgin*, painted when he was only 19 years old, and, on the left, the *Madonna of Foligno*, showing Sts John the Baptist, Francis of Assisi and Jerome. Leonardo's *St Jerome*, in the next room, is a remarkable piece of work with Jerome a rake-like ascetic torn between suffering and a good meal, while Caravaggio's *Descent from the Cross*, two rooms on, is a warts-and-all canvas that unusually shows the Virgin Mary as a middle-aged mother grieving over her dead son. Take a look too at the most gruesome painting in the collection, Poussin's *Martyrdom of St Erasmus*, which shows the saint stretched out on a table with his hands bound above his head in the process of having his small intestine wound onto a drum – basically being "drawn" prior to "quartering".

MUSEO PIO-CLEMENTINO

Vatican Museums. MAP PP.144–145, POCKET MAP B3

To the left of the entrance, the **Museo Pio-Clementino** is home to some of the Vatican's best classical statuary, including two pieces that influenced Renaissance artists more than any others – the serene *Apollo Belvedere*, a Roman copy of a fourth-century BC original, and the first-century BC *Laocoön*. The former is generally thought to be a near-perfect example of male anatomy and was studied by Michelangelo; the latter depicts the prophetic Trojan priest being crushed by a serpent as he warned of the danger of the Trojan horse, and is perhaps the most famous classical statue of all time. Beyond here there are busts of Roman emperors, the statue of *Venus of Cnidos*, the first known representation of the goddess, the so-called *Belvedere Torso*, found in the Campo de' Fiori during the reign of Julius II, and much, much more sublime classical statuary.

MUSEO GREGORIANO EGIZIO

Vatican Museums. MAP PP.144–145, POCKET MAP B3

It may not be one of the Vatican's highlights, but the **Museo Gregoriano Egizio** holds a distinguished collection of ancient Egyptian artefacts, including some vividly painted mummy cases (and two mummies), along with canopic jars, the alabaster vessels into which the entrails of the deceased were placed.

MUSEO GREGORIANO ETRUSCO

Vatican Museums. MAP PP.144–145, POCKET MAP B3

The **Museo Gregoriano Etrusco** holds Etruscan sculpture, funerary art and applied art. Especially worth seeing are the finds from the Regolini-Galassi tomb, from the seventh century BC, discovered near Cerveteri, which contained the remains of three Etruscan nobles. There's gold armour, a bronze bedstead, a funeral chariot and a wagon, as well as a great number of enormous storage jars, in which food, oil and wine were contained for use in the afterlife.

GALLERIA DEI CANDELABRI, DEGLI ARAZZI, AND DELLE CARTE GEOGRAFICHE

Vatican Museums. MAP PP.144–145, POCKET MAP B3

Outside the Etruscan Museum, a large monumental staircase leads back down to the **Galleria dei Candelabri**, the niches of which are adorned with huge candelabras taken from imperial Roman villas. This gallery is also stuffed with ancient sculpture, its most memorable piece being a copy of the famous statue of *Diana of Ephesus*, whose multiple breasts are, according to the Vatican official line, in fact bees' eggs. Beyond here, the **Galleria degli Arazzi** has Belgian tapestries to designs by the school of Raphael and tapestries made in Rome during the 1600s. The **Galleria delle Carte Geografiche** was decorated in the late sixteenth century with maps of all Italy, the major islands in the Mediterranean, the papal possessions in France, as well as large-scale maps of the maritime republics of Venice and Genoa.

GALLERIA DELLE CARTE GEOGRAFICHE

RAPHAEL ROOMS

Vatican Museums. MAP PP.144–145, POCKET MAP B3

At the end of the various galleries, the **Raphael Rooms** formed the private apartments of Pope Julius II, and when he moved in here he commissioned Raphael to redecorate them in a style more in tune with the times. Raphael died in 1520 before the scheme was complete, but the two rooms that were painted by him, as well as others completed by pupils, stand as one of the highlights of the Renaissance. The **Stanza di Eliodoro**, the first room you come to, was painted by three of Raphael's students five years after his death, and is best known for its painting of the *Mass of Bolsena* which relates a miracle that occurred in the town in northern Lazio in the 1260s, and, on the window wall opposite, the *Deliverance of St Peter*. The other main room, the **Stanza della Segnatura**, or pope's study, was painted between 1508 and 1511, when Raphael first came to Rome, and comes close to the peak of the painter's art. *The School of Athens*, on the near wall as you come in, steals the show, a representation of the triumph of scientific truth in which all the great minds from antiquity are represented. It pairs with the *Disputation of the Sacrament* opposite, which is a reassertion of religious dogma – an allegorical mass of popes, cardinals, bishops, doctors and even the poet Dante.

THE TRANSFIGURATION

APPARTAMENTO BORGIA

Vatican Museums. MAP PP.144–145, POCKET MAP B3

Outside the Raphael Rooms, the **Appartamento Borgia** was inhabited by Julius II's hated predecessor, Alexander VI, and is host to a large collection of modern religious art, although its ceiling frescoes, the work of Pinturicchio between 1492 and 1495, are really the main reason to visit, especially those of the Sala dei Santi, where the figure of St Catherine is said to be a portrait of Lucrezia Borgia.

SISTINE CHAPEL

Vatican Museums. MAP PP.144–145, POCKET MAP B4

Steps lead from the Raphael Rooms to the **Sistine Chapel**, a huge barn-like structure that is the pope's official private chapel and the scene of the conclaves of cardinals for the election of each new pontiff. The walls of the chapel were decorated by several prominent painters of the Renaissance – Pinturicchio, Perugino, Botticelli and Ghirlandaio. However they are entirely overshadowed by Michelangelo's more famous **ceiling frescoes**, commissioned by Pope Julius II in 1508, and

perhaps the most viewed set of paintings in the world. The frescoes were done by **Michelangelo** single-handed over a four-year period and depict scenes from the Old Testament, from the *Creation of Light* at the altar end to *The Drunkenness of Noah* over the door. Look also at the pagan sibyls and biblical prophets which Michelangelo incorporated in his scheme – some of the most dramatic figures in the entire work, and all clearly labelled by the painter, from the sensitive figure of the Delphic Sybil to the hag-like Cumaean Sybil and the prophet Jeremiah – a brooding self-portrait of an exhausted-looking Michelangelo. Julius II lived only a few months after the Sistine Chapel ceiling was finished, but the fame of the work he had commissioned spread. It's staggeringly impressive, all the more so for its restoration, which lifted centuries of accumulated soot and candle grime off the paintings to reveal a much brighter painting. Michaelangelo's other great work here, *The Last Judgement*, is on the altar wall of the chapel, and was painted by the artist more than twenty years later. Michelangelo wasn't especially keen to work on this, but Pope Paul III, an old acquaintance of the artist, was keen to complete the decoration of the chapel. The painting took five years, again single-handed, and is probably the most inspired and most homogeneous large-scale painting you're ever likely to see. The centre is occupied by Christ, turning angrily as he gestures the condemned to the underworld. St Peter, carrying his keys, looks on in astonishment, while Mary averts her eyes from the scene. Below Christ a group of angels blast their trumpets to summon the dead from their sleep. On the left, the dead awaken from their graves, tombs and sarcophagi, and are levitating into the heavens or being pulled by ropes and the napes of their necks by angels who take them before Christ. At the bottom right, Charon, keeper of the underworld, swings his oar at the damned souls as they fall off the boat into the waiting gates of hell.

THE SISTINE CHAPEL

MUSEUM OF CHRISTIAN ART AND THE VATICAN LIBRARY

Vatican Museums. MAP PP.144–145, POCKET MAP B4
After the Sistine Chapel, you're channelled to the exit by way of the **Museum of Christian Art**, which is not of great interest in itself, but does give access to a small room off to the left that contains a number of ancient Roman frescoes and mosaics, among them the *Aldobrandini Wedding*, a first-century BC Roman fresco that shows the preparations for a wedding in touching detail. Back down the main corridor, the **Vatican Library** is decorated with scenes of Rome and the Vatican, and beyond, the corridor opens out into the dramatic **Library of Sixtus V**, a vast hall built across the courtyard in the late sixteenth century to glorify literature – and of course Sixtus V himself.

BRACCIO NUOVO AND MUSEO CHIARAMONTI

Vatican Museums. MAP PP.144–145, POCKET MAP B4
The **Braccio Nuovo** and **Museo Chiaramonti** both hold classical sculpture, although they are the Vatican at its most overwhelming – close on a thousand statues crammed into two long galleries. The Braccio Nuovo was built in the early 1800s and it contains, among other things, probably the most famous extant image of Augustus, and a bizarre-looking statue depicting the Nile. The 300-metre-long Chiaramonti gallery is lined with the chill marble busts of hundreds of nameless ancient Romans, along with the odd deity. It pays to have a leisurely wander, for there are some real characters here: sour, thin-lipped matrons with their hair tortured into pleats, curls and spirals; kids, caught in a sulk or mid-chortle; and ancient old men, their flesh sagging and wrinkling to reveal the skull beneath.

MUSEI GREGORIANO PROFANO, PIO CRISTIANO AND ETNOLOGICO

Vatican Museums. MAP PP.144–145, POCKET MAP B4
Next door to the Pinacoteca, the **Museo Gregoriano Profano** holds more classical sculpture, mounted on scaffolds for all-round viewing, including mosaics of athletes

from the Baths of Caracalla and Roman funerary work, notably the Haterii tomb friezes, which show backdrops of ancient Rome and realistic portrayals of contemporary life. The adjacent **Museo Pio Cristiano** has intricate early Christian sarcophagi and, most famously, an expressive third-century AD statue of the Good Shepherd. The **Museo Etnologico** displays art and artefacts from all over the world, collected by Catholic missionaries.

VATICAN GARDENS

Daily except Wed & Sun; €32, includes access to the Vatican Museums; visits last about two hours; 40min bus tours also available, €36; tickets must be booked in advance on Ⓣ 06 6988 4676, Ⓦ mv.vatican.va. MAP PP.144–145, POCKET MAP A4

It's possible to visit the lovely **Vatican Gardens** on a guided tour – well worth doing for the great views of St Peter's. But you have to be organized and book in advance. The dress code is as for St Peter's – so no bare knees or shoulders.

THE VATICAN GARDENS

Shops

CASTRONI

Via Cola di Rienzo 196. Mon–Sat 7.30am–8pm, Sun 9.30am–8pm; closed Sun mid-June to mid-Sept. MAP PP.144–145, POCKET MAP C3

Huge, labyrinthine food store with a large selection of Italian treats as well as hard-to-find international favourites – plus a café with coffee, cakes and sandwiches. There's another branch at Via Frattina 79, near the Spanish Steps.

COIN EXCELSIOR

Via Cola di Rienzo 173. Mon–Sat 10am–8pm, Sun 10.30am–8pm. MAP PP.144–145, POCKET MAP C3

This swish new department store at the heart of shop-lined Via Cola di Rienzo has three floors of designer labels, niche perfume brands, jewellery and furnishings, with a smart food hall in the basement.

COLAPICCHIONI

Via Tacito 76/78. Mon–Fri 7.30am–2.30pm & 5–7.30pm, Sat 7am–2.30pm. MAP PP.144–145, POCKET MAP D3

Long-running food store, mainly a bakery, selling the family's excellent *pangiallo* and other foodie goodies.

FRANCHI

DEL FRATE

Via degli Scipioni 118/124 ☎06 323 6437. Tues–Sat 9am–1.30pm & 4–8pm. MAP PP.144–145, POCKET MAP C3

This large wine and spirits shop is located on a quiet street near the Vatican, and has all the Barolos and Chiantis you could want, alongside shelves full of *grappa* in all shapes and sizes. There's a wine bar/restaurant attached, too.

FRANCHI

Via Cola di Rienzo 200. Mon–Sat 9am–8.30pm. MAP PP.144–145, POCKET MAP C3

One of the best delis in Rome – a triumph of cheeses and sausages with an ample choice of cold or hot food to go, including delicious *torta rustica* and roast chicken. They'll make up a customized lunch for you, and they have the wines to go with it.

Cafés and snacks

FA-BÌO

Via Germanico 43. Mon–Fri 10.30am–5.30pm, Sat 10.30am–4pm. MAP PP.144–145, POCKET MAP B3

All-organic, mainly veggie ingredients go into the tasty soups, salads and sandwiches (around €6) at this hole-in-the-wall café near the Vatican Museums. There are bar stools inside, or take away to nearby Piazza Risorgimento.

FATAMORGANA

Via Leone IV 50–52 ☎06 3751 9093. Daily: summer noon–midnight; winter noon–9pm. MAP PP.144–145, POCKET MAP B2

This is undoubtedly one of the top three *gelaterie* in Rome. *Fatamorgana* serves up scoops of creative and seasonal flavours, and is just a short walk from the Vatican Museums.

MONDO ARANCINA

Via Marcantonio Colonna 38 T 06 9761 9213. Daily 10am–midnight. MAP PP.144–145, POCKET MAP D2

Great *pizza al taglio* at this Prati Sicilian takeaway, but the real treats are the *arancini* – any number of varieties, from tomato and mozzarella to Bolognese, and cheap too, at €2.50 each. Just the thing for post-Vatican recovery.

PIZZARIUM

Via della Meloria 43 T 06 3974 5416. Mon–Sat 11am–10pm, Sun noon–4pm & 6–10pm. MAP PP.144–145, POCKET MAP A3

Celebrity *pizzaiolo* Gabriele Bonci lures foodies to this hole-in-the-wall spot near Cipro metro. Join the hordes for top-notch pizza by the slice, made with slow-leavened dough. Little seating, but it's perfect for lunch on the run.

Restaurants

CACIO E PEPE

Via Avezzana 11 T 06 321 7268. Mon–Fri 12.30pm–3pm & 7.30–11.30pm, Sat 12.30pm–3pm. MAP PP.144–145, POCKET MAP D1

Rough-and-ready Prati cheapie with a menu taped to the wall but the food can't be beat. You can't book, and should expect to wait for a table, but it's well worth it: great *cacio e pepe* (naturally), *alla gricia*, *carbonara* and other pasta staples, and good *secondi* too.

CANTINA TIROLESE

Via Vitelleschi 23 T 06 6813 5297. Tues–Fri & Sun noon–3pm & 7pm–midnight, Sat 7pm–midnight. MAP PP.144–145, POCKET MAP B13

The hearty and wholesome Austrian and German fare served at this long-established Prati standby is excellent – and there's lots of it. A nice change from Rome's usual offerings.

DAL TOSCANO

DAL TOSCANO

Via Germanico 58/60 T 06 3972 5717. Tues–Sun 12.30–3pm & 8–11.15pm. MAP PP.144–145, POCKET MAP B3

Tuscan food, and very popular, with great steaks and other meat dishes, perfectly grilled on charcoal, delicious *pici* (thick home-made spaghetti) and *ribollita* (veg & bread soup) – all at moderate prices. A treat, and very handy for the Vatican.

Bars

FONCLEA

Via Crescenzio 82a T 06 689 6302. Daily 7pm–2am; concerts start at 9.30pm. MAP PP.144–145, POCKET MAP C3

This historic basement joint is loaded both with devoted regulars and visitors who have happily discovered that there is life in the Vatican's sometimes somnolent Borgo and Prati area. Free live music every evening, and happy hour 7–8.30pm.

PASSAGUAI

Via Pomponio Leto 1 T 06 8745 1358. Mon–Fri 10am–2am, Sat & Sun 6pm–2am. MAP PP.144–145, POCKET MAP A13

Busy basement wine bar that serves great platters of cheese, meats and salads to go with its excellent wine. Unusually, there's no cover or bread charge.

Day-trips

You may find there's quite enough in Rome to keep you occupied during your stay. But it can be a hot, oppressive city, and its churches, museums and ruins are sometimes wearing – so if you're around long enough it's worth getting out to see something of the countryside or going to the beach. Two of the main attractions close to Rome are among the most compelling attractions in the country, let alone the Rome area: Tivoli, less than an hour by bus northeast of Rome, is a small provincial town famous not only for the travertine quarries nearby, but also for its villas, complete with landscaped gardens and parks; southwest of Rome, Ostia is the city's busiest seaside resort, but more importantly was the site of the port of Rome in classical times, the ruins of which – Ostia Antica – are well preserved and worth seeing.

Tivoli

COTRAL buses leave Rome for Tivoli every 10min from Ponte Mammolo metro station (line B); journey time 45min, or 30–50min by train from Tiburtina station.

Perched high on a hill, with fresh mountain air and a pleasant position on the Aniene River, **Tivoli** has always been a retreat from the city. In classical days it was a retirement town for wealthy Romans; during the Renaissance it again became the playground of the moneyed classes, attracting some of the city's most well-to-do families and their new-built villas. Nowadays the leisured classes have mostly gone, but Tivoli does very nicely on the fruits of its still-thriving travertine business and the relics from its ritzier days. To do justice to the gardens and villas – especially if Villa Adriana is on your list – you'll need the whole day.

VILLA D'ESTE

THE TEMPLE OF VESTA

VILLA D'ESTE

Piazza Trento 5 ⓣ 0774 332 920, ⓦ villadestetivoli.info. Tues–Sun 8.30am–1hr before sunset. €8.

Tivoli's major sight is the **Villa d'Este**, across the main square of Largo Garibaldi. This was the country villa of Cardinal Ippolito d'Este, and has since been restored to its original state. Beautiful Mannerist frescoes in its rooms show scenes from the history of the d'Este family in Tivoli, but it's the gardens that most people come to see, peeling away down the hill in a succession of terraces, their carefully tended lawns, shrubs and hedges interrupted by one fountain after another. Among the highlights, the central, almost Gaudí-like Fontana del Bicchierone, by Bernini, is one of the most elegant; to the right of this is the Fontana dell'Ovato, fringed with statues, underneath which is a rather dank arcade, in which you can walk. On the far side of the garden, the Rometta, or "Little Rome", has reproductions of the city's major buildings and a boat holding an obelisk.

VILLA GREGORIANA

Piazza Tempio di Vesta ⓣ 0774 332 650, ⓦ visitfai.it/parcovillagregoriana. Tues–Sun: April–Oct 10am–6.30pm, March, Nov & Dec 10am–4pm. €6.

Tivoli's other main attraction, the **Villa Gregoriana**, was created in 1831 when Pope Gregory XVI diverted the flow of the river here to ease the periodic flooding of the town. As interesting and beautiful as the d'Este estate, it remains less visited, and has none of the latter's conceits – its vegetation is lush and overgrown, descending into a gorge over 60m deep. There are two main waterfalls – the larger Grande Cascata on the far side, and a smaller one at the neck of the gorge. Cross the bridge and go in the back entrance, from where the path winds down to the bottom of the canyon, passing a ruined Roman villa. Climb up the other side through hollowed-out rock and you can get right up to the roaring falls; beyond, the path leads to the far side to the main entrance and the substantial remains of a **Temple of Vesta**, clinging to the side of the hill. The paths can be steep and slippery, so wear sturdy shoes.

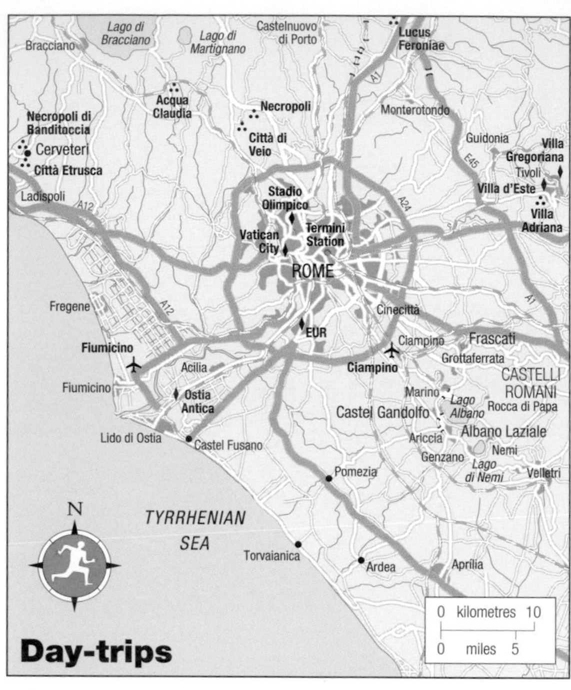

VILLA ADRIANA

Largo Yourcenar ☎ 0774 382 733, 🌐 coopculture.it. Daily 9am–1hr before sunset; €8. Ask the Rome–Tivoli bus to drop you off or take the local CAT #4 or #4X bus from Largo Garibaldi in Tivoli (roughly every 45min).

Probably the largest and most sumptuous villa in the Roman Empire, **Villa Adriana**, just outside Tivoli, was the retirement home of the Emperor Hadrian for a short while between 135 AD and his death three years later. Hadrian was a great traveller and a keen architect, and parts of the enormous site were inspired by buildings he had seen around the world. The massive Pecile, for instance, through which you enter, is a reproduction of a building in Athens; the Canopus, on the opposite side of the site, is a copy of the sanctuary of Serapis near Alexandria, its long, elegant channel of water fringed by sporadic columns and statues leading up to a temple of Serapis at the far end. Near the Canopus, a museum displays the latest finds from the ongoing excavations here, though most of the discoveries have found their way to museums in Rome. Back towards the entrance there are the remains of two bath complexes, a fishpond with a cryptoporticus (underground passageway) underneath, marked with the names of the seventeenth- and eighteenth-century artists who visited here, and finally the Teatro Marittimo, with its island in the middle of a circular pond – the place to which it's believed Hadrian would retire for a siesta.

Hitting the beach

OSTIA

Trains run from Porta San Paolo station, next door to Piramide metro on line #B; get off at Lido Centro or the last stop, Cristoforo Colombo, where the crowds might be thinner. A €1.50 BIT ticket is sufficient.

Lido di Ostia has for years been the number one, or at any rate the closest and most accessible seaside resort for Romans. The beaches are OK, and much cleaner than they used to be, but you have to pay to use them and the town doesn't have a great deal to recommend it apart from its thumping nightlife in summer, and with a little more time you could do better. Ostia is, however, easy to get to, just half an hour by train from Rome.

TORVAIANICA

In summer, buses run from Cristoforo Colombo station in Ostia; take #07.

South of Ostia, towards **Torvaianica**, the water is cleaner and the crowds not so thick, plus there are gay and nudist sections of the beach if these are your fancy, and not a lot of development.

SANTA MARINELLA

Trains are every 30min from Termini, and take about an hour.

Santa Marinella is one of the most popular spots north of the capital. It has a lovely crescent beach, 5min walk from the train station, and although most of it is pay-only the sand is fine and clean and the water shallow – perfect for kids.

SANTA MARINELLA

ANZIO

ANZIO

There are trains every hour from Termini; the journey takes an hour.

About 40km south of the capital, and fairly free of its pull, **Anzio** is worth visiting both for its beaches and its history – much of the town was damaged during a difficult Allied landing here on January 22, 1944, to which two military cemeteries (one British, another, at nearby Nettuno, American), plus a small museum, bear testimony. It was also a favoured spot of the Roman emperor, the ruins of whose villa spread along the cliffs above and even down onto the beach. Anzio has a thriving fishing fleet and there are some great restaurants down on the harbour. From the station, it's just a ten-minute walk down to the main square and harbour, with the beaches stretching out north of the centre.

Castelli Romani

South of Rome, the towns that make up the **Castelli Romani** have historic centres, hearty local cuisine and good white wines, making them popular with weekending Romans, especially in summer.

FRASCATI

COTRAL buses run to Frascati from Rome's Anagnina metro station (line A) every 15–30min (30min). Trains run hourly from Termini (30min).

At just 20km from Rome, **Frascati** is the nearest of the Castelli towns and also the most striking, with an atmospheric old centre and some great places to eat and drink. Its main square, Piazza Marconi, is dominated by the majestic Villa Aldobrandini, designed by Giacomo della Porta at the start of the seventeenth century. The Baroque *palazzo* is off-limits, but you can visit the gardens (Mon–Fri: summer 9am–1pm & 3–6pm; winter 9am–1pm & 3–5pm; free). The pedestrianized old centre revolves around the two squares of Piazza San Pietro and Piazza del Mercato. Frascati is also the most famous of the **Colli Albani wine towns**: ask at the tourist office in Piazza Marconi for details of winery tours, tastings and local *fraschette* – rustic, rough-and-ready bars serving up local wine, often produced in the owner's vineyard.

CASTEL GANDOLFO

There are nine daily buses from Anagnina metro station (line A), taking 35min.

Southeast of Frascati, **Castel Gandolfo** is best known as the pope's summer retreat: between July and September the pope usually gives sporadic midday addresses on Sundays, though it depends on the individual – Pope Francis is an infrequent visitor. Set 400m above Lago Albano, the town is a pleasantly airy place, and enjoys great views over the lake from its terraces. The Barberini Garden attached to the papal palace has recently been opened to the public for the first time (tours on Sat at 10am & 11am; 1hr 30min; €20; book in advance through Ⓦ museivaticani.va). Nearby, the main Piazza della Libertà is a pleasant oblong of cafés and papal souvenir shops, at the end of which is the imposing bulk of the Papal Palace itself. Below the town, there are lots of restaurants along the lakeshore.

ARICCIA

Take a train from Termini to Albano Laziale (hourly; 55min), from where it's a 20min walk to Ariccia.

Poised between two gorges, **Ariccia** enjoys a dramatic location on the ancient Via Appia, with spectacular views on all sides. The main road crosses the town's central piazza, a well-proportioned square designed by Bernini. On one side of the square is the town's main sight: the huge **Palazzo Chigi** built by Bernini for Pope Alexander VII, whose *piano nobile* is home to the Chigi collections of paintings, sculpture and objects of applied art (guided tours only Tues–Fri at 11am, 4pm & 5.30pm, Sat & Sun hourly 10.30am–12.30pm & 4–7pm, opens and closes one hour earlier Oct–March afternoons; €8).

CASTEL GANDOLFO

Ostia Antica

Viale dei Romagnoli 717 06 5635 0215, www.ostiaantica.beniculturali.it. Tues–Sun: end March to Aug 8.30am–7.15pm; Sept 8.30am–7pm; Oct 8.30am–6.30pm; Nov to mid-Feb 8.30am–4.30pm; mid-Feb to mid-March 8.30am–5pm; mid to late March 8.30am–5.30pm. €8; free first Sun of the month. Regular trains from Roma–Porta San Paolo (next door to Piramide metro station, on line B); journey time 30min.

The excavations of the port of Ostia – **Ostia Antica** – are one of the finest ancient Roman sites you'll see anywhere. Until its harbour silted up and the town was abandoned in the fourth century, Ostia was Rome's principal port and a commercial hub. Over the centuries, the Tiber's mud preserved its buildings incredibly well and the place is now an evocative sight: it's easier to visualize a Roman town here than at the Forum – and it compares pretty well with celebrated sights like Pompeii.

From the entrance, the **Decumanus Maximus**, Ostia's main street, leads west, past the **Baths of Neptune** on the right (with its interesting mosaic) to the town's commercial centre, the **Piazzale delle Corporazioni**. On the way, detour down **Via della Fontana**, which gives a good idea of the typical Roman street layout: ground-floor shops; upper-floor apartments. There are more shops on Piazzale delle Corporazioni, which specialized in enterprises from all over the ancient world, each once fronted by a mosaic denoting their trade – grain merchants, ship-fitters, ropemakers and the like. On one side of the square, Ostia's theatre has been much restored and hosts classical drama performances in summer.

Further on, turn right up Via dei Molini, then left, to reach the **House of Diana**, probably the best-preserved private house in Ostia, with a set of rooms around a central courtyard, and Mithraeum at the back (tours can be pre-booked for Sun 10.30am). Cross the road to the **Thermopolium**, an ancient Roman café, complete with seats outside, a high counter, display shelves and wall paintings of parts of the menu. North of the House of Diana, the **museum** holds wall paintings depicting domestic life in Ostia and some fine sarcophagi and statuary from the site, notably *Mithras Slaying the Bull* from one of Ostia's Mithraeums. Left from here, the **Forum** centres on the **Capitolium**, reached by a wide flight of steps, and fringed by the remains of baths and a basilica. Further on, at the Porta Occidentale, or western gate, veer right along Via delle Foce to visit a cluster of three Republican temples. The ruins are a little hard to decipher, but beyond them is the third-century **House of Cupid and Psyche**, whose courtyard holds a copy of the statue of Cupid and Psyche that you can see in the museum. Further along Via delle Foce is the **Baths of the Seven Sages** complex, with a wonderfully intact floor mosaic and atmospheric arcaded passageways that lead to the large **House of the Charioteers**. From the roof you can enjoy great views over the whole site.

Near the entrance, the **Castle of Julius II** was commissioned by the future pope; it's closed for long-term restoration, but it's worth a visit when it reopens for the lovely views from the third-floor walkway.

OSTIA ANTICA

ACCOMMODATION

Hotels and B&Bs

There's no shortage of places to stay in Rome – but accommodation here tends to be pricier than in other European cities. Location is important: many of the cheaper options are clustered around Termini district, which, despite having improved dramatically in recent years, is not the city's most picturesque. Via Veneto is traditionally home to Rome's fanciest five-stars, and is somewhere to consider if you're looking for some old-world luxury, though much trendier these days are the cobbled lanes of the Monti district, a stone's throw from the Colosseum. You'll feel more in the thick of things in the Tridente area near the Spanish Steps or in the Centro Storico and around Campo de' Fiori, from where you can walk just about everywhere. Across the river, Prati is a pleasant, well-heeled neighbourhood handy for the Vatican. Trastevere is close to the main sights and comes into its own after dark.

Accommodation prices

All accommodation prices in this chapter are for the cheapest double room in high season but remember that rates are very much driven by demand – never be afraid to ask for a better rate; they can only say no. Most hotels now offer **discounted online rates** – anything from ten to forty percent off the official price – when you make a non-refundable booking in advance; the prices quoted below are the standard rates, without discounts. Note that rates do not include Rome's **accommodation tax** (€3–7 per person, per night, for up to ten consecutive nights), which will be added to your bill. Children under the age of 10 are exempt, and you pay nothing after ten days. **Breakfast** is included in all but the five-stars, where you can expect to be charged an extra €28–38. Book in advance if you want to snag a bargain, especially when the city is at its busiest (March–July, Sept, Oct and Christmas). There are often deals to be had out of season, particularly in the heat of August.

If you arrive without a reservation, Enjoy Rome is your best bet (see p.185), or try the usual international hotel booking sites such as Ⓦ booking.com or Ⓦ expedia.com. However, you can often get better rates by booking directly with the hotel.

The Centro Storico

ALBERGO DEL SENATO > Piazza della Rotonda 73, Bus #116 ⓣ 06 678 4343, ⓦ albergodelsenato.it. MAP PP.36–37, POCKET MAP E15. A classy choice next door to the Pantheon, with friendly service and knockout views of the city from the roof and the Pantheon from some of the rooms. **€290**

CESÀRI > Via di Pietra 89a, Bus #116 ⓣ 06 674 9701, ⓦ albergocesari.it. MAP PP.36–37, POCKET MAP F14. In a perfect position close to the Pantheon, this has been a hotel since 1787 – as they will be sure to tell you. The comfortable rooms are elegantly and traditionally furnished and you can enjoy the roof terrace at breakfast and for drinks on summer evenings. **€219**

DUE TORRI > Vicolo del Leonetto 23, Bus #116 ⓣ 06 6000 6956, ⓦ hotelduetorriroma.com. MAP PP.36–37, POCKET MAP E14. Cosy hotel with a personal touch tucked away in a warren of streets a couple of minutes from Piazza Navona. Once a residence for cardinals, then a brothel, some rooms are on the small side but have been well renovated, and there's a comfy reception area. Family rooms available too. **€170**

NAVONA > Via dei Sediari 8, Bus #492 ⓣ 06 6821 1392, ⓦ hotelnavona .com. MAP PP.36–37, POCKET MAP E15. Constructed on the site of the ancient Baths of Agrippa, this is a moderately priced hotel located between the Pantheon and Piazza Navona – really you couldn't ask for a better location if you want to be in the centre of Rome. Rooms are decently furnished, with their own bathrooms, and the welcome is warm. They also have a sister hotel, the *Zanardelli* (see p.168). **€189**

PORTOGHESI > Via dei Portoghesi 1, Bus #116 ⓣ 06 686 4231, ⓦ hotelportoghesiroma.it. MAP PP.36–37, POCKET MAP E14. Decent and well-equipped modern rooms 5min from most Centro Storico attractions. Breakfast is served on the roof terrace upstairs. It's worth paying a little extra for one of the roomier junior suites (€230). **€200**

RAPHAËL > Largo Febo 2, Bus #64 ⓣ 06 682 831, ⓦ raphaelhotel.com. MAP PP.36–37, POCKET MAP D14. Set on a quiet, picturesque piazza just off Piazza Navona, the *Raphaël* is a mix of plush traditional style – antiques and rich colours – and sleek contemporary rooms designed by American architect Richard Meier (of Ara Pacis fame). There's also a rooftop terrace – one of Rome's loveliest – where you can try to identify the city's domes over a cocktail. **€480**

RESIDENZA CANALI > Via dei Tre Archi 13, Bus #492 ⓣ 06 6830 9541, ⓦ residenzacanali.com. MAP PP.36–37, POCKET MAP D14. Tucked away on a side street just a 3min walk from Piazza Navona, this family-run hotel is hard to beat for location and service. The bright rooms, with wood-beamed ceilings and modern en-suite bathrooms, are great value too, especially the suites, each with its own terrace. Note that there are several flights of stairs – and no lift. **€195**

Apartments and B&Bs

A few hotels rent out apartments, and a number of agencies specialize in short lets. One of the best options is Rome Apartments (UK ⓣ 0203 608 0580, US ⓣ 202 618 9600, ⓦ romeapartments.com). Cross-Pollinate (ⓦ cross-pollinate.com), run by the owners of *The Beehive* (see p.172), is a good source of budget apartments; ⓦ romeloft.com and ⓦ aplaceinrome.com are also worth a browse. See ⓦ b-b.rm.it for a good range of B&Bs all over the city. Prices start relatively low – around €60 for a double – with the more upscale options going for up to €180.

RESIDENZA ZANARDELLI > Via G. Zanardelli 7, Bus #492 T 06 6821 1392, W residenzazanardelli.com. MAP PP.36–37, POCKET MAP D14. Run by the same family as the *Navona* (see p.167). Located just north of Piazza Navona, the building used to be a papal residence and has many original fixtures and furnishings. The elegant rooms are decently priced, especially considering the location. **€189**

SANTA CHIARA > Via Santa Chiara 21, Bus #116 T 06 687 2979, W albergosantachiara.com. MAP PP.36–37, POCKET MAP E15. The *Santa Chiara's* location is superb: on a quiet piazza right behind the Pantheon. Some rooms overlook the Santa Maria sopra Minerva church. Ask for a renovated room; they are bright, modern and comfortable. **€270**

TEATRO PACE > Via del Teatro Pace 33, Bus #64 T 06 687 9075, W hotelteatropace.com. MAP PP.36–37, POCKET MAP D15. This beautifully restored *palazzo*, a few paces from Piazza Navona, was once home to a prominent Vatican cardinal. Leading off an impressive Baroque spiral staircase (no lift) are four floors of elegant, spacious rooms with original wood beams, floor-sweeping drapes and luxurious bathrooms. **€205**

Campo de' Fiori and the Ghetto

ARGENTINA RESIDENZA > Via di Torre Argentina 47, Bus #64 T 06 6819 3267, W argentinaresidenza.com. MAP PP.52–53, POCKET MAP E16. This former noble carriage house has been converted to a six-room hotel and it's an elegant affair, with antique ceilings combining with well-chosen modern furnishings and amenities. It's in a perfect location, too, close to the major transport hub of Largo Argentina. **€200**

CAMPO DE' FIORI > Via del Biscione 6, Bus #64 T 06 6880 6865, W hotelcampodefiori.com. MAP PP.52–53, POCKET MAP D16. A friendly place in a good location just off Campo de' Fiori with 23 individually designed rooms, each a different colour. The sixth-floor roof terrace has great views and the hotel owns a number of recently restored apartments nearby if you're keen to self-cater (from €260 for two, €364 for four). **€336**

DOM HOTEL > Via Giulia 131, Bus #40 T 06 683 2144, W domhotelroma.com. MAP PP.52–53, POCKET MAP C15.This luxury boutique hotel goes all out for opulence in its rooms and suites, all moody tones, statement lighting and splashy art. There's a gem of a terrace on the top floor with views across the rooftops, while on the ground floor, boudoir-esque restaurant and cocktail bar *The Deer Club* is thronged with hip young things after dark: great if you want to be in the thick of the action, not so much if you just want a quiet beer before bed. **€460**

DOMUS ESTER > Via di San Salvatore in Campo 38, Bus #64 T 06 6813 9414, W new.estercampodefiori.com. MAP PP.52–53, POCKET MAP D16. Tucked away in the heart of the Ghetto, this little hotel is great value for money given its fantastic location, a 5min walk from Campo de' Fiori. The rooms are on the small side but spotless and crisply painted, with wood-beamed ceilings and gleaming bathrooms. Breakfast is delivered to your room in the morning. There are several flights of stairs and no lift. **€149**

FORTYSEVEN > Via Petroselli 47, Bus #170 T 06 678 7816, W fortysevenhotel.com. MAP PP.52–53, POCKET MAP F17. Tasteful, elegant rooms above the ancient cattle market just outside the Ghetto. Within striking distance of the Forum, Trastevere and the Ghetto, it has a rooftop bar and restaurant too. **€315**

HOTEL RESIDENZA IN FARNESE > Via del Mascherone 59, Bus #64 T 06 6821 0980, W residenzafarneseroma.it. MAP PP.52–53, POCKET MAP D16. Situated on a quiet side street right by the Palazzo Farnese, this hotel has tastefully appointed rooms – though some are showing signs of wear and tear – and helpful staff. The location is excellent too – it's great for both the Centro Storico and Trastevere, just across the water by way of the Ponte Sisto footbridge. Do ask, though, to see several rooms – they vary a lot and some can be on the small side. **€199**

INDIGO ROME – ST GEORGE > Via Giulia 62, Bus #40 06 686 611, hotelindigorome.com. MAP PP.52–53, POCKET MAP C15. This five-star has recently been given a top-to-toe revamp, and its plush rooms now sport playful touches such as outsize photos of the Fiat 500 emblazoned across the walls, and bold geometric linens. There's a spa with Turkish bath (free access to guests), plus a smart restaurant, *I Sofà*, and a rooftop bar and restaurant in the summer months. **€438**

TEATRO DI POMPEO > Largo del Pallaro 8, Bus #64 06 687 2812, hotelteatrodipompeo.it. MAP PP.52–53, POCKET MAP D16. Built above the remains of Pompey's ancient Roman theatre, this moderately priced hotel has a great location just off the Campo, and comfortable rooms, with high beamed wooden ceilings, marble-topped furniture and – in some – great views. **€140**

The Tridente, Trevi and Quirinale

BABUINO 181 > Via del Babuino 181 Spagna 06 3229 5295, romeluxurysuites.com. MAP PP.76–77, POCKET MAP E2. *Rome Luxury Suites* operates this and two other locations (Via Margutta 54 and Via Mario de'Fiori 37). Decorated with contemporary Italian flair, the accommodation is stylishly comfortable and includes breakfast and concierge service. **€400**

CASA HOWARD > Via Capo le Case 18; Via Sistina 149 Spagna 06 6992 4555, casahoward.com. MAP PP.76–77, POCKET MAP F4. This small boutique hotel offers a series of themed rooms, varying considerably in price, in two locations: one close to Piazza di Spagna, the other just off Piazza Barberini. Rooms are on the small side, but elegantly and stylishly furnished; service is very personal and welcoming. Breakfast is served to you in your room. **€122**

CASA MONTANI > Piazzale Flaminio 9 Flaminio 06 3260 0421, casamontani.com. MAP PP.76–77, POCKET MAP E2. This self-styled "luxury town house" is a boutique hotel with a personal feel. The rooms – all designed by the owners, a friendly French-Italian couple – are decked out in a chic palette of neutrals, with touches of luxury: designer bathrooms, wide-screen TVs and breakfast served on fine porcelain. The five rooms are rightly popular – book well ahead. **€218**

CONDOTTI > Via Mario de' Fiori 37 Spagna 06 679 4661, hotelcondotti.com. MAP PP.76–77, POCKET MAP E3. This cosy and inviting three-star, with comfortable rooms and cheery, welcoming staff also has a sister hotel nearby, the *Condotti Palace* at Via della Croce 15, whose luxury suites have a refined, elegant feel. **€261**

CROSSING CONDOTTI > Via Mario de' Fiori 28, Spagna 06 6992 0633, crossingcondotti.com. MAP PP.76–77, POCKET MAP E3. This superior boutique hotel combines a cosy, warm feel with five-star service – one of two super-efficient but friendly concierges are on hand all day. The elegant suites and apartments, which marry antiques from the owner's private collection with modern designer furniture, have access to a kitchenette stocked with free snacks and drinks (you help yourself to breakfast), and some rooms come with rudimentary kitchen facilities. All this, plus a great location close to the Spanish Steps. **€345**

DAPHNE TREVI > Via degli Avignonesi 20 Barberini, 06 8916 3892, daphne-rome.com. MAP PP.76–77, POCKET MAP F4. Welcoming place on a quiet street leading from Piazza Barberini to the Trevi fountain, run by an American woman and her Roman husband. Most of the rooms are bright, modern and spacious, and you can choose between shared bathrooms and en-suite. **€175**

DE RUSSIE > Via del Babuino 9 Flaminio 06 328 881, roccofortehotels.com. MAP PP.76–77, POCKET MAP E2. Coolly elegant and gorgeously understated, this hotel's emphasis on comfort and quality, not to mention its stellar location just off Piazza del Popolo, makes it first choice for the hip traveller spending someone else's money – it's popular among visiting movie

Our picks

Budget choice: *Blue Hostel* p.172
Central hotel: *Navona* p.167
Boutique: *Portrait Roma* p.171
Room with a view: *Hassler* p.170
Romance: *Casa Howard* p.169
Luxury: *De Russie* p.169
Local charm: *B&B La Scalinatella* p.172

stars. If you're not staying here, you can still experience the buzz in the courtyard *Stravinskij Bar* (see p.91). **€898**

DEI BORGOGNONI > Via del Bufalo 126, Bus #175 **T 06 6994 1505, W hotelborgognoni.com.** MAP PP.76–77, POCKET MAP G13. Nicely situated four-star that has pleasant, well-renovated rooms. A surprisingly large hotel, considering its location down a side street not far from Piazza di Spagna, and handy for this part of town and for the Centro Storico. **€281**

DEKO ROME > Via Toscana 1, M Barberini **T 06 4202 0032, W dekorome.com.** MAP PP.76–77, POCKET MAP G3. This little hotel, run by the ever-helpful Marco and Serena, gets everything right, from the glass of prosecco on arrival to the complimentary iPad in your room. The rooms are modern and spotless, and it's in a great location too. It's understandably popular, so book ahead. **€230**

HASSLER > Piazza Trinità dei Monti 6 M Spagna **T 06 699 340, W hotelhasslerroma.com.** MAP PP.76–77, POCKET MAP F3. You can't get much closer to the heart of Rome than this – and you certainly can't get a much better view. Situated right at the top of the Spanish Steps, this luxury hotel has elegant rooms and every convenience a guest could possibly require. **€630**

HOTEL ART > Via Margutta 56 M Spagna **T 06 328 711, W hotelartrome.com.** MAP PP.76–77, POCKET MAP E3. Tucked away on Via Margutta, this has an impressive bar and lobby fashioned out of a vaulted chapel. Rooms are excellent, too, with plenty of luxurious touches – Frette linens, Etro toiletries – and breakfast is a feast. **€295**

HOTEL BAROCCO > Via della Purificazione 4, M Barberini **T 06 487 2001, W hotelbarocco.com.** MAP PP.76–77, POCKET MAP F3. Overlooking Bernini's Fontana del Tritone in Piazza Barberini, this smart four-star is within walking distance of all the main sights. Extremely comfortable, if a little old-fashioned, the rooms are all thick carpets, swagged curtains and gilt-framed art. Great breakfasts, too. **€310**

HOTEL D'INGHILTERRA > Via Bocca di Leone 14 M Spagna **T 06 699 811, W niquesatravel.com.** MAP PP.76–77, POCKET MAP F13. This old favourite, formerly the apartments of the princes of Torlonia, combines design touches with old-world elegance. Rooms are furnished with antiques and have Murano glass chandeliers and marble bathrooms. **€478**

HOTEL PANDA > Via della Croce 35, M Spagna **T 06 678 0179, W hotelpanda.it.** MAP PP.76–77, POCKET MAP E3. If you don't mind lugging your cases up two floors (there's no lift), this no-frills little hotel, just steps from Piazza di Spagna, is a bargain. Rooms – both en suite and with shared bathroom – are on the small side but are clean and comfortable. Breakfast is not included but there are plenty of cafés nearby. **€85**

IL PALAZZETTO > Vicolo del Bottino 8 M Spagna **T 06 6993 41000, W ilpalazzettoroma.com.** MAP PP.76–77, POCKET MAP F3. Located at the top of the Spanish Steps, this is an elegant hotel with just four rooms, all differently designed in chic monochrome. It also has a panoramic rooftop bar and guests can use the facilities of the *Hassler* (see p.170). **€360**

JK PLACE ROMA > Via di Monte d'Oro 30, Spagna **06 982 634**, **jkroma.com**. MAP PP.76–77, POCKET MAP E13. This chic bolthole in the centre of Rome oozes sophisticated style, from the tasteful rooms – whose marble-clad bathrooms are bigger than most hotel bedrooms – to the airy lounge, dotted with art and sculpture, and the mirror-lined dining room, which sparkles like a jewellery box. Expensive, but a Roman one-off. **€800**

LOCARNO > Via della Penna 22 Flaminio **06 361 0841**, **hotellocarno.com**. MAP PP.76–77, POCKET MAP E2. Arguably the most characterful and inviting hotel in central Rome, a quirky and engaging place whose courtyard bar draws a crowd every evening. The rooms aren't the most luxurious or facility-laden but they're comfy and individually furnished. Considering the location, it's well priced, and there is a fleet of bikes for guests' use. **€210**

MODIGLIANI > Via della Purifacazione 42 Barberini **06 4281 5226**, **hotelmodigliani.com**. MAP PP.76–77, POCKET MAP F3. A friendly, modern hotel on a quiet street just off Piazza Barberini. Rooms are comfortable, and have a/c. Splash out on a superior room – they have views of St Peter's. There's a small garden courtyard. **€170**

PIAZZA DI SPAGNA > Via Mario de' Fiori 61 Spagna **06 679 3061**, **hotelpiazzadispagnarome .com**. MAP PP.76–77, POCKET MAP F3. This small hotel, just a few minutes' walk from the Spanish Steps, is a good alternative to the opulent palaces that dominate the area. Rooms are comfortable, and all have a/c. Friendly staff too. **€210**

PORTRAIT ROMA > Via Bocca di Leone 23 Spagna **06 6938 0742**, **lungarnocollection.com**. MAP PP.76–77, POCKET MAP F13. This converted town house with fourteen rooms, owned by the Salvatore Ferragamo fashion house, is a bastion of luxury and comfort. Prices are high – but the suites are superbly appointed, and there's a lovely rooftop bar. **€612**

RESIDENZA DI RIPETTA > Via di Ripetta 231, Spagna **06 323 1144**, **residenzadiripetta.com**. MAP PP.76–77, POCKET MAP E3. Set in a seventeenth-century cloister, the *Hotel d'Inghilterra*'s sister hotel has very comfortably furnished rooms; it's worth paying a little extra for the superior and deluxe rooms, which come with hidden kitchenettes and marble bathrooms. The hotel's biggest draw, though, is its large plant-filled terrace – a rarity in the centre of Rome. It also has an intimate restaurant. **€302**

RESIDENZA NAPOLEONE III > Largo Goldoni 56, Spagna **06 6880 8083**, **residenzanapoleone.com**. MAP PP.76–77, POCKET MAP E13. These two suites in the sixteenth-century Palazzo Ruspoli should be top of your list if someone else is footing the bill. The opulent Napoleone Suite is furnished with priceless antiques and huge oil paintings – a level of luxury of which the famous one-time resident obviously approved – while the Roof Garden Suite is wonderfully homely, filled with books and antiques, and with a vast roof terrace overlooking the city's rooftops. **€900**

VILLA SPALLETTI TRIVELLI > Via Piacenza 4, Bus #64 **06 4890 7934**, **villaspalletti.it**. MAP PP.76–77, POCKET MAP G4. In a fantastic location a five-minute walk from Piazza Venezia, this aristocratic villa is one of Rome's most luxurious accommodation options. The twelve rooms are impeccably furnished with antiques, and the common areas – including a lovely garden – exude an aura of exclusivity. **€625**

The Esquiline, Monti and Termini

1880 ATYPICAL ROOMS > Via Nazionale 66, Bus #40 **06 9761 3452**, **atypicalroomsrome.com**. MAP PP.94–95, POCKET MAP G4. There are plenty of hotels lining busy Via Nazionale, but this is a cut above: a reworked *pensione* completely remodelled by a firm of architects, it has five large, high-ceilinged rooms and one suite, with contemporary bare-brick or wallpaper feature walls, and most with the bathroom in view. Soundproofed rooms and memory-foam mattresses make for a comfortable night's sleep. **€210**

ALPI > Via Castelfidardo 84 Ⓜ Termini ⓣ 06 444 1235, ⓦ hotelalpi.com. MAP PP.94–95, POCKET MAP J3. One of the more peaceful hotels close to Termini, with pleasant (if somewhat small) rooms, a terrace and a great buffet breakfast – better than you would normally expect from a hotel in this bracket. **€170**

ARTEMIDE > Via Nazionale 22, Ⓜ Repubblica ⓣ 06 489 911, ⓦ hotelartemide.it. MAP PP.94–95, POCKET MAP G4. If you're after a grand hotel without the five-star price tag, head to the handsome *Artemide*, which combines an imposing, old-world feel with a warm welcome. The comfortable rooms come with a free minibar, and the rooftop bar is a lovely spot on a sunny day. **€499**

ARTORIUS > Via del Boschetto 13, Bus #64 ⓣ 06 482 1196, ⓦ hotelartoriusrome.com. MAP PP.94–95, POCKET MAP G5. On a cobbled Monti street and with just ten rooms, the family-run *Artorius* is an appealing mid-range option. The attractive courtyard makes a pleasant spot for breakfast in fine weather, and for drinks after dark. **€175**

B&B LA SCALINATELLA > Via Urbana 48, Ⓜ Cavour ⓣ 06 488 0547 or 339 5256537, ⓦ lascalinatellaroma.com. MAP PP.94–95, POCKET MAP G5. Set in in a seventeenth-century *palazzo* just a ten-minute walk from the Colosseum, this superb three-room B&B is run by friendly sisters Annamaria and Elisabetta. The rooms are beautifully furnished with whitewashed wood beams, antique furniture and spacious modern bathrooms; book the larger "comfort" room if you can. In the little brick-vaulted breakfast room, tea served in an antique silver teapot and plentiful pastries make a good start to the day. The B&B is on the second floor of the *palazzo*, with no lift. **€120**

THE BEEHIVE > Via Marghera 8 Ⓜ Termini ⓣ 06 4470 4553, ⓦ the-beehive.com. MAP PP.94–95, POCKET MAP J4. This ecological – and economical – hotel run by an American couple is one of Rome's most popular budget options. The doubles – some of which share bathrooms – are basic but stylishly decorated; a few en-suites (€10 extra) are available in a separate part of the building, more spartan dorms go for €35 a head, and you can also stay in a nearby guesthouse with communal kitchen (€80 for a double room). There is also a garden and a restaurant that serves breakfast (extra), as well as vegetarian dinner on some evenings. **€80**

BLUE HOSTEL > Via Carlo Alberto 13, Ⓜ Termini ⓣ 340 925 8503, ⓦ bluehostel.it. MAP PP.94–95, POCKET MAP H5. Elegant, stylish, comfortable and with great attention to detail – not your average "hostel", then, and in fact this is more of a boutique hotel (there are no dorms, only private rooms). The spacious rooms are painted in restful muted tones and have wood-beamed ceilings, parquet floors and arty black-and-white prints on the walls, and the ultra-helpful Ercole and Andrea go out of their way to make sure you have an enjoyable stay. **€160**

DES ARTISTES > Via Villafranca 20 Ⓜ Castro Pretorio ⓣ 06 445 4365, ⓦ hoteldesartistes.com. MAP PP.94–95, POCKET MAP J3. Exceptionally good value, spotlessly clean and with a wide range of rooms, including dorm beds from €22 (book through ⓦ hostelrome.com). Doubles are available with and without en-suite facilities. You can eat breakfast or recover from a long day of sightseeing on the lovely roof terrace. **€139**

DUCA D'ALBA > Via Leonina 14, Bus #84 ⓣ 06 484 471, ⓦ hotelducadalba.com. MAP PP.94–95, POCKET MAP G5. A stylish four-star in the heart of Monti, just steps from the district's best restaurants and nightlife. All of the attractively furnished rooms have en-suite bathrooms and a/c, and some have balconies. Rooms are heavily discounted in low season. **€195**

LEON'S PLACE > Via XX Settembre 90/94 Ⓜ Termini ⓣ 06 890 871, ⓦ leonsplacehotel.it. MAP PP.94–95, POCKET MAP H3. Walking distance from

Termini but near an upscale residential area. The rooms are smallish but sleekly modern, all black and white with splashes of colour and trendy design touches. €257

NERVA > Via Tor de' Conti 3, Bus #40 Ⓣ 06 679 3764, Ⓦ hotelnerva.com. MAP PP.94–95, POCKET MAP F5. This stylish boutique hotel is fashionably dressed in cool monochrome with pops of colour in the cushions and art, while the houndstooth fabric used for the outsize headboards lends a touch of vintage style, and the marble bathrooms add more glamour. Breakfast (an extra €10) is a five-star feast, and the location – right by the Roman Forum – is pretty special too. €279

NICOLAS INN > Via Cavour 295 Ⓜ Cavour Ⓣ 06 9761 8483, Ⓦ nicolasinn.com. MAP PP.94–95, POCKET MAP G5. A brief stroll from the Colosseum, this B&B is run by a friendly American-Italian couple, who are keen to make guests feel at home. The rooms are a good size, spotless and elegant. Breakfast is served in a nearby bar. €180

RESIDENZA CELLINI > Via Modena 5, Ⓜ Repubblica Ⓣ 06 4782 5204, Ⓦ residenzacellini.it. MAP PP.94–95, POCKET MAP G4. The rooms here are large with a slightly old-fashioned feel; it's worth paying the extra for a spacious junior suite (€240), which comes with a hydromassage bath. Staff are extremely friendly. €220

SUITE DREAMS > Via Modena 5 Ⓜ Repubblica Ⓣ 06 4891 3907, Ⓦ suitedreams.it. MAP PP.94–95, POCKET MAP G4. The rooms at this mid-range hotel are simple but stylish, with generous bathrooms, but it's the attention to detail and friendly customer care that really stand out. Services such as free bottled water and a DVD library for guests' use are an unexpected bonus for a place in this price bracket. €164

VILLA DELLE ROSE > Via Vicenza 5 Ⓜ Termini Ⓣ 06 445 1788, Ⓦ villadellerose.it. MAP PP.94–95, POCKET MAP J4. This centuries-old villa sits amid its own tranquil rose gardens, belying the fact that it's only a block from Termini train station. The decor is a little tired, but it has bags of old-world charm, and staff are friendly. Ask for one of the rooms with a terrace. €130

YES HOTEL > Via Magenta 15 Ⓜ Termini Ⓣ 06 4436 3836, Ⓦ yeshotelrome.com. MAP PP.94–95, POCKET MAP H4. The location – just down the road from Termini – ain't brilliant, but *Yes* is a huge step up from the grotty options that litter the area, and you'll pay considerably less here than for a similar room in the centre. Tailored to the needs of Termini's business travellers – rooms are comfortable but bland. €154

The Celian and Aventine Hills

LANCELOT > Via Capo d'Africa 47 Ⓜ Colosseo Ⓣ 06 7045 0615, Ⓦ lancelothotel.com. MAP PP.108–109, POCKET MAP H6. This friendly family-run hotel has rooms with views of the Colosseum, which is just two minutes' away, and staff that are well-informed and helpful. €196

PALAZZO MANFREDI > Via Labicana 125, Ⓜ Colosseo Ⓣ 06 7759 1380, Ⓦ palazzomanfredi.com. MAP PP.108–109, POCKET MAP H6. An oasis of peace and tranquillity in one of Rome's busiest tourist hotspots, this hotel has fourteen sumptuous rooms and suites, all thoughtfully and stylishly furnished, with big beds, beautiful bathrooms, Nespresso machines, iPads and more, plus marvellous views of the neighbouring Colosseum from some rooms. There's a fabulous restaurant, *Aroma*, on site too (see p.111). All in all, a genuinely luxurious boutique hotel experience, and one that's rare in Rome – hence the high prices. €550

SAN ANSELMO > Piazza Sant'Anselmo 2 Ⓜ Piramide Ⓣ 06 570 057, Ⓦ aventinohotels.com. MAP PP.114–115, POCKET MAP E8. One of the most peaceful places you could stay, and arguably in central Rome's most upscale residential neighbourhood, the *San Anselmo* has beautifully furnished rooms (each with a different theme). Breakfast is good, there's a nice lounge and garden, and parking is free. Deals available outside high season. €144

Trastevere

GUESTHOUSE ARCO DE'TOLOMEI > Via Arco de' Tolomei 27, Tram #8 Ⓣ 06 5832 0819, Ⓦ bbarcodeitolomei.com. MAP PP.126–127, POCKET MAP E18. In an attractively crumbling *palazzo* on Trastevere's quieter, eastern side, this old-world B&B is full of antiques passed down from generation to generation of the owners' family, but the atmosphere is anything but stuffy. The generous breakfast is served in the conservatory. Ten percent discount for cash payment. **€210**

RESIDENZA SANTA MARIA > Via dell'Arco di San Calisto 20, Tram #8 Ⓣ 06 5833 5103, Ⓦ residenzasantamaria.com. MAP PP.126–127, POCKET MAP D18. In an eighteenth-century building – which once housed crafts workshops – this intimate hotel has been attractively restored, with features such as brick arches, wood-beamed ceilings and an internal courtyard giving it a welcoming feel. It's especially recommended for families: four of the six rooms are triples or quads. **€202**

SANTA MARIA > Vicolo del Piede 2, Tram #8 Ⓣ 06 589 4626, Ⓦ hotelsantamariatrastevere.it. MAP PP.126–127, POCKET MAP D17. Just off Piazza Santa Maria in the heart of Trastevere, the rooms of this friendly three-star surround a garden filled with lovely orange trees. There's free internet access, and bikes are provided for guests' use. **€270**

TRASTEVERE > Via Luciano Manara 24a/25, Tram #8 Ⓣ 06 581 4713, Ⓦ hoteltrastevere.net. MAP PP.126–127, POCKET MAP C18. A good choice if you want to be in the heart of Trastevere, with nicely decorated – though small – doubles, and apartments to rent for up to five people. Request a room overlooking the little piazza, rather than the interior courtyard. **€115**

VILLA DELLA FONTE > Via della Fonte d'Olio 8, Tram #8 Ⓣ 06 580 3797, Ⓦ villafonte.com. MAP PP.126–127, POCKET MAP D18. This attractive hidden-away place feels almost secret, yet it is just a few steps from Piazza Santa Maria in Trastevere. The rooms are cosy and comfortable and there's a lovely sun-trap terrace. **€134**

Vatican

AMALIA > Via Germanico 66 Ⓜ Ottaviano Ⓣ 06 3972 3356, Ⓦ hotelamalia.com. MAP PP.144–145, POCKET MAP B3. Located not far from the Vatican, this place has bright, nicely renovated double rooms with generous en-suite bathrooms. **€99**

BRAMANTE > Vicolo delle Palline 24, Bus #40 Ⓣ 06 6880 6426, Ⓦ hotelbramante.com. MAP PP.144–145, POCKET MAP A13. This little hotel, located right next to the ancient wall running from the Vatican to Castel Sant'Angelo, has charming rooms with original wood-beamed ceilings and antiques. **€160**

COLORS > Via Boezio 31 Ⓜ Ottaviano, Ⓣ 06 687 4030, Ⓦ colorshotel.com. MAP PP.144–145, POCKET MAP C3. This hostel/hotel in a quiet neighbourhood near the Vatican provides kitchen facilities, a lounge with satellite TV and a small roof terrace. Doubles are available both en suite and with shared facilities, and there are sometimes dorm beds available too. No breakfast. **€89**

DEI CONSOLI > Via Varrone 2d, Ⓜ Ottaviano Ⓣ 06 6889 2972, Ⓦ hoteldeiconsoli.com. MAP PP.144–145, POCKET MAP C3. From the elegantly welcoming entrance to the thoughtfully designed rooms, this is one of the best moderately priced choices in the Vatican area, with a lovely roof terrace and excellent service. **€288**

GIULIO CESARE > Via degli Scipioni 287 Ⓜ Lepanto Ⓣ 06 321 0751, Ⓦ hotelgiuliocesare.com. MAP PP.144–145, POCKET MAP D2. This charming hotel is no longer the home of an Italian countess, but you may feel like royalty once you step into the elegant foyer. Friendly staff lead you down mirror-lined hallways to elegant rooms with lovely marble bathrooms. **€170**

HEARTH HOTEL > Via Santamaura 2, Ⓜ Ottaviano Ⓣ 06 3903 8383, Ⓦ hearthhotel.com. MAP PP.144–145, POCKET MAP B3. About as close as you can get to the Vatican – the entrance to the museums is just across the street – this renovated *palazzo* has large, stylishly furnished rooms. If you're a light sleeper request a room on the quieter side of the building or you might be woken by the early-morning chatter from the museums' inevitable queue. **€144**

LA ROVERE > Vicolo S. Onofrio 4–5, Bus #64 T 06 6880 6739, W hotollarovere.biz MAP PP.144–145, POCKET MAP B15. Just across the bridge from Piazza Navona, this attractive hotel is tucked away from Rome's bustle, and offers a terrace garden and antique-filled setting for its guests to relax in. **€212**

ROME CAVALIERI > Via A Cadlolo 101 T 06 350 91, W romecavalieri.com. MAP PP.144–145, POCKET MAP A1. Arguably Rome's smartest hotel is quite a way out of the city centre, but it is worth staying here once, not only to check out Heinz's Beck's legendary three-Michelin-star rooftop restaurant (although you have to book well in advance for this) but also to enjoy its curious mix of Sixties glamour and old-fashioned style. The rooms are large and comfortable, there are three lovely pools, and service is impeccably gracious and professional. The hotel runs regular free shuttle buses to Piazza Barberini. **€328**

Hostels

For dorm accommodation, see also *Des Artistes* (p.172), *The Beehive* (see p.172) and *Colors* (see p.174).

ALESSANDRO PALACE HOSTEL > Via Vicenza 42, M Termini T 06 446 1958, W hostelsalessandro.com. MAP PP.94–95, POCKET MAP J3. This place has been voted one of the top hostels in Europe, and it sparkles with creative style. Pluses include no lock-out or curfew, a good bar with nightly happy hours, free wi-fi and a roof terrace. Breakfast costs extra. **Dorms €26–35; doubles €110**

GENERATOR ROME > Via Principe Amadeo 257, M Termini T 06 492 330, W generatorhostels.com. MAP PP.94–95, POCKET MAP J5. With 78 comfortable rooms – shared en-suite dorms sleeping up to six, plus private rooms – across seven floors, this is a welcome newcomer to Rome's rather lacklustre hostel scene. It's stylish throughout – as you'd expect from this hostel chain – plus there's a deli-style café that uses ingredients from the market across the street, bar and chill-out lounge on site too. **Breakfast €5. Dorms €27, doubles €130**

LA CONTRORA > Via Umbria 7, M Repubblica T 06 9893 7366, W lacontrora.com. MAP PP.76–77, POCKET MAP G3. In an excellent location near Piazza Barberini, this modern hostel has a relaxed, arty feel, funky decor and friendly staff. The spacious lounge has a big-screen TV, free wi-fi, and there's a large communal kitchen. **Dorms €36–38, en-suite doubles €110**

NEXT DOOR > Via Nomentana 316, Bus #90 T 349 522 7371, W nextdoorguesthouse.com. MAP PP.136–137, POCKET MAP F1. Far from your typical hostel, this quirky guesthouse is more about beautiful design than pizza parties. The eight-bed dorm and private rooms are tastefully decorated in moody greys with bursts of vibrant colour, with cleverly upcycled furniture throughout: wooden chairs hung from the walls make offbeat bedside tables, and the table in the common area is made from pinball machines. Breakfast isn't provided but there's a kitchen and large terrace for guests' use. About 20min by bus from Termini. **Dorms €27, doubles €80**

YELLOW > Via Palestro 44 M Termini T 06 4938 2682, W the-yellow.com. MAP PP.94–95, POCKET MAP J4. Self-conciously cool, *Yellow* encourages a lively scene in the downstairs bar and club (open till 4am), so if you're after somewhere quiet it's probably not for you. **Dorms €33–41, en-suite doubles €93**

ESSENTIALS

Arrival

Arriving in Rome is a painless experience if you're travelling by air, by train or even by bus, although negotiating the city's outskirts by car is something you might want to avoid.

By air

Rome has two airports: Leonardo da Vinci, better known simply as Fiumicino, which handles most scheduled flights, and Ciampino, where you'll arrive if you're travelling on a charter or with one of the low-cost European airlines. Information on both airports is available at ⓣ06 65951, ⓦadr.it.

Fiumicino airport

Fiumicino is connected to the centre of Rome by direct trains, which make the 30min ride to Termini for €14; services run every 15min (first train at 5.57am, last train at 11.27pm). In the other direction, the first train is at 4.52am, last train at 10.35pm. Be aware when leaving Rome, that the Fiumicino platform at Termini station is a good 5min schlep from the main part of the station. Alternatively, there are trains every 10–30min to Ostiense and Tiburtina stations, each on the edge of the city centre; tickets to these stations cost less (€8) and Tiburtina and Ostiense are just a short (€1.50) metro ride from Termini. You can also catch bus #23 from Ostiense, or #492 or #649 from Tiburtina, to the town centre (again €1.50). Taxis for the 30–40min journey to and from the airport cost a fixed-rate €48. Several buses go from the airport to Termini. COTRAL have 8 services a day from 1.15am to 7.05pm to Piazza dei Cinquecento (€5 one-way; ⓦcotralspa.it), while SIT bus services run every half hour from 8.30am to 12.30am to Via Marsala and Via Crescenzio in the Vatican (€6 one-way; ⓦsitbusshuttle.com). Terravision runs to Via Marsala 29, by Termini (5.35am–11pm; every 30min; €4 online, €5 on board; ⓦterravision.eu); and T.A.M buses run to Via Giolitti on the south side on Termini, and to Stazione Ostiense (5.40am–11.30pm; roughly every 30min; €5; ⓦtambus.it). All take 50min–1hr.

Ciampino airport

Several companies, including Terravision (ⓦterravision.eu) and SIT bus (ⓦsitbusshuttle.com) run shuttle services to Termini (roughly every 30min; 45min; €4 one-way). They pull up on Via Marsala, right by the station. If you don't want to get off at Termini, and are staying near a metro stop on the A line (near the Spanish Steps or Via Veneto areas, for example), you could take an ATRAL bus (every 40min; 10min; €1.20 one-way, plus €1.20 per suitcase; ⓦatral-lazio.com) from the airport to Anagnina metro station at the end of metro Line A (every 40min; 15min), and take a metro from there to your destination (€1.50). Taxis to and from the airport cost a fixed-rate €30 and take 30–40min.

By train

Most Italian and international trains arrive at Termini station, centrally placed for all parts of the city and the meeting point of the two main metro lines and many city bus routes. Tiburtina (see below) is a stop for some north–south intercity trains. For general enquiries about schedules and prices, call ⓣ892 021 (24hr), or check ⓦtrenitalia.com.

By bus

Most national and international services stop at Tiburtina, Rome's second railway terminal after Termini, which is connected to the city centre by metro line B or buses #492 or #649. Other bus stations, mainly serving the Lazio region, include Ponte Mammolo (trains from Tivoli and Subiaco),

Cornelia (Cerveteri, Civitavecchia), Saxa Rubra (Bracciano area), Laurentina (Nettuno, Anzio, southern Lazio coast) and Anagnina (Castelli Romani); buses are run by Cotral (www.cotralspa.it); all of these stations are on a metro line (except Saxa Rubra, which is on the local rail line from Flaminio).

By car

Driving into Rome can be quite confusing and is best avoided unless you're used to driving in Italy and know where to park (see p.182). Note that much of the Centro Storico is in the **ZTL** (see p.182). It's usually best to get on the Grande Raccordo Anulare (GRA), which circles Rome and is connected with all of the major arteries into the city centre – the Via Cassia from the north, Via Salaria from the northeast, Via Tiburtina or Via Nomentana from the east, Via Prenestina and Via Casilina or Via Cristoforo Colombo from the southeast, Via Appia Nuova and the Pontina from the south, and Via Aurelia from the northwest. From Ciampino, either follow Via Appia Nuova into the centre or join the GRA at junction 23 and follow signs to the centre. From Fiumicino, follow the A12 motorway into the city centre; it crosses the river just north of EUR, from where it's a short drive north up Via Cristoforo Colombo to the city walls and, beyond, to the Baths of Caracalla. In 2017 the ZTL will extend to the *anello ferroviario* (the railway ring around the capital), meaning that cars entering Rome will have to pay a toll charge.

Getting around

The best way to get around is to walk – you'll see more and will better appreciate the city. However, you may need to take public transport to get around quickly or reach the more outlying attractions, and the network is good – a largely efficient blend of buses, a metro with two lines running to central stations and a few trams. ATAC runs the city's bus, tram and metro service. There's an information office in the centre of Piazza dei Cinquecento outside Termini station, their website, atac.roma.it, has information in English and a route planner.

Buses and trams

Buses are cheap and reliable, with several routes for visitors (see box on p.181). Board through the rear doors and punch your ticket as you enter if it's the first time you're using it. There's also a small network of electric minibuses that negotiate the old centre's narrow backstreets, and a few trams, mainly serving outlying areas. After midnight, night buses (*bus notturni*) serve most parts of the city through to

Tickets and travel cards

Flat-fare **tickets** (BIT) cost €1.50 each and are good for any number of bus and tram rides and one metro ride within 100 minutes of validation. Buy them from tobacconists, newsstands and ticket machines located in all metro stations, and validate them in the yellow machines on buses, trams and at the entrance gates in metro stations. You can also get a **day pass** (valid for 24hr on all city transport) for €7, a 48hr pass (€12.50), a 72hr pass (€18), or a seven-day pass for €24. Alternatively, you can travel on public transport for free with the **Roma Pass** and **Omnia Card** (see p.185). A warning: there are hefty fines (€100–500) for fare-dodging, and pleading a foreigner's ignorance will get you nowhere.

Night buses

#N1 follows metro line A; **#N2** calls at all stops along metro line B; and **#N8** runs from Trastevere to Termini station.

about 5.30am (see box above); some have ticket machines on board but it's best to buy a ticket before boarding.

The metro

Rome's metro runs from 5.30am to 11.30pm (1.30am Sat), and although its two main lines – A (red) and B (blue) – don't cover large parts of the city centre, there are a few useful city-centre stations: Termini is the hub of both lines, and there are stops at the Colosseum, Piazza Barberini, Piazza di Spagna and Ottaviano (for the Vatican). A new line, C, will cross line A at San Giovanni; the first section opened in 2014, extending to Pigneto in 2015. The interchange at San Giovanni is due to open in 2016, though funds are running out; planned stations at Piazza Venezia and the Colosseum may not open for years, if at all.

Taxis

Central taxi stands (*fermata dei taxi*) include Termini, Piazza Venezia, Piazza San Silvestro, Piazza di Spagna, Piazza Navona, Largo Argentina, Piazza San Pietro and Piazza Barberini. Or, call a taxi (ⓣ06 0609), but note you pay for the time it takes to get to you. Only take licensed white cabs with the "Comune di Roma" insignia on the door, and check the meter is on; a card in every official taxi explains the extra charges for luggage, late-night, Sundays and holidays, and airport journeys. Pick ups from Termini incur a supplement of €2. Journeys from Termini to the centre should cost around €10–15 and around €15–20 on Sunday or at night.

Bus tours

There are several hop-on-hop-off buses in Rome, operating on much the same route around the main sights, and on similar double-decker buses with audioguide included in the ticket price. The red City Sightseeing tours are the most popular.

City Sightseeing ⓣ06 6979 7554, ⓦcity-sightseeing.com. Good for a quick glance at the sights, this open-top bus has a guided commentary. It leaves from Via Marsala 7 outside Termini station and stops at all the major sights. The trip takes 1hr 40min, and in summer departures are every 10min from 9am until 7pm daily (including hols & Sun). Tickets cost €25 and allow you to get on wherever you like and hop on and off during a 48-hour period. Tickets can be bought on board and discounted fares are available for Roma Pass holders.

Roma Cristiana ⓦoperaromapellegrinaggi.org. The Vatican's tourist bus service links Rome's major basilicas and other Christian sights, starting in Piazza dei Cinquecento and at St Peter's. Services run daily every 30min between 9am (9.30am at St Peter's) and 6pm, and tickets cost €12 for a round trip, €20 for a day or €23 for 24 hours including public transport; buy on board, at Piazza dei Cinquecento or at PIT information kiosks.

Walking tours

Entrance fees are generally not included in the price of tours, so check costs before booking. **Enjoy Rome** (see p.185) is the best all-round operator, offering three-hour tours to groups (maximum 25 people). Most popular are the tours of the ancient sights and the highlights of the Centro Storico (€35). You may prefer the smaller-scale tours of **Context Rome** (ⓣ06 9672 7371, ⓦcontexttravel.com), who run excellent small-group walking tours (maximum 6 people) of sights

Useful bus and tram routes

#3 Tram Viale delle Belle Arti–San Lorenzo–Piazza di Santa Croce in Gerusalemme–Colosseum–Circus Maximus–Piazzale Ostiense.

#8 Tram Piazza Venezia–Via Arenula–Piazza Sonnino–Viale Trastevere–Stazione Trastevere.

#14 Tram Termini–Piazza Vittorio Emanuele–Porta Maggiore–Via Prenestina (Pigneto).

#23 Piazzale Clodio–Piazza Risorgimento–Ponte Vittorio Emanuele II–Ponte Garibaldi–Via Marmorata–Piazzale Ostiense–Centrale Montemartini–Basilica di San Paolo.

#30 Express (Mon–Sat only) Piazzale Clodio–Piazza Mazzini–Piazza Cavour–Corso Rinascimento–Largo Argentina–Piazza Venezia–Lungotevere Aventino–Via Marmorata–Piramide–Via C.Colombo–EUR.

#40 Express Termini–Via Nazionale–Piazza Venezia–Largo Argentina–Borgo Sant'Angelo (Vatican).

#60 Express Piazza Venezia–Via Nazionale–Porta Pia–Via Nomentana

#62 Stazione Tiburtina–Via Nomentana–Porta Pia–Piazza Barberini–Trevi Fountain–Via del Corso–Piazza Venezia– Corso V. Emanuele II–Largo Argentina–Piazza Pia (Vatican).

#64 Termini–Piazza della Repubblica–Via Nazionale–Piazza Venezia–Largo Argentina–Corso Vittorio Emanuele II–Stazione San Pietro.

#75 Via Poerio (Monteverde)–Porta Portese–Testaccio–Piramide–Circus Maximus–Colosseum–Via Cavour–Termini–Via XX Settembre.

#116 Porta Pinciana (Villa Borghese)–Via Veneto–Via del Tritone–Trevi Fountain Campo de' Fiori–Piazza Farnese–Lungotevere Sangallo–Terminal Gianicolo.

#117 San Giovanni in Laterano–Colosseum–Cavour–Via Nazionale–Via del Corso–Piazza Trinità dei Monti–Piazza del Popolo.

#118 Via Appia Antica–Baths of Caracalla–Colosseum–Circus Maximus–Porta San Sebastiano–Via Appia Antica.

#492 Stazione Tiburtina–Piazzale Verano (San Lorenzo)–Termini–Piazza Barberini–Via del Corso–Largo Argentina–Corso del Rinascimento–Piazza Cavour–Piazza Risorgimento–Cipro (Vatican Museums).

#590 Same route as metro line A but with disabled access; runs every 1hr 30min.

#660 Largo Colli Albani–Arco di Travertino–Via Appia Antica–Tomb of Cecilia Metella.

#714 Termini–Santa Maria Maggiore–Via Merulana–San Giovanni in Laterano–Viale Terme di Caracalla–EUR.

#910 Termini–Piazza della Repubblica–Via Piemonte–Via Pinciana (Villa Borghese)–Piazza Euclide–Palazetto dello Sport–Piazza Mancini (Stadio Olimpico).

and neighbourhoods, led by engaging experts, on subjects ranging from architecture to gastronomic Rome. For private walking tours, try **Agnes Crawford** (T 338 1984 375, W understandingrome.com; from €250 for a 3hr tour), whose engaging tailor-made tours of the city delve into Rome's history. **Eating Italy** organizes food tours of Testaccio and Trastevere (from €84; W eatingitalyfoodtours.com).

Bike tours

The best company for bike tours are **TopBike Rental & Tours** (T 06 488 2893, W topbikerental.com), whose small-group tours take interesting routes through the city, with options including a four-hour jaunt through the centre (€45) and a Panoramic Rome tour that takes in the best of Rome's views (4hr 30min; €49). There's also a more challenging ride to the Via Appia Antica and Castelgandolfo lake (€119; 9hr).

Bike, moped and scooter rental

Renting a bike, moped or scooter can be the most efficient way of nipping around Rome's clogged city centre, and there are plenty of places offering this facility (see box, below). Some hotels – such as the *Locarno* (see p.171) – have bikes for guests' use.

Cycling along Rome's first highway and through the Caffarella Valley on a Sunday is a tranquil way of seeing the area. The Appia Antica Visitor Center (see box below) also has good information in English about suggested routes. Bike tours are also available (see above).

Car rental

Driving in central Rome is something to be avoided at all costs. Much of the Centro Storico is within the **ZTL** (*zona di traffico limitato*), in which traffic is restricted during the day; if you are driving to a hotel in the centre, check if they are in the ZTL and if they can get you permission to enter. See W agenziamobilita.roma.it/en for further information. It's generally safe to park your car in the centre, but you might prefer to pay a bit more to keep your car in one of the city's staffed car parks. You can park on the street for around €1.20/hr (8am–8pm), or there are garages in Villa Borghese (€2.20/hr) and in front of Termini station (€2.20/hr for the first three hours, then €1.70/hr). There are car parks next to the terminal metro stations, from where it's easy to get into the city centre.

Car, scooter and bike rental agencies

Cars Avis (Termini T 06 481 4373, Ciampino T 06 7934 0195, Fiumicino T 06 6501 1531); Europcar (Termini T 06 488 2854, Ciampino T 06 7934 0387, Fiumicino T 06 6576 1211); Hertz (Termini T 06 474 0389, Ciampino T 06 7934 0616, Fiumicino T 06 6501 1553); Maggiore (Termini T 06 488 0049, Ciampino T 06 7934 0368, Fiumicino T 06 6501 0678); Sixt (Termini T 06 4782 6000, Ciampino T 06 7934 0802, Fiumicino T 06 6595 3547).

Scooters Barberini (Via della Purificazione 84 T 06 488 5485, W www.rentscooter.it) for €12/day for bikes, mopeds and scooters from €40/day. Treno e Scooter Rent, near the car park in Termini station (T 06 4890 5823, W www.trenoescooter.com. €28–73/day for mopeds or scooters).

Bicycles Appia Antica Visitor Center (Via Appia Antica 58; T 06 513 5316, W www.parcoappiaantica.it; €3/hr or €15/day for bicycles).

Directory A-Z

Cinema

Not many cinemas in Rome screen films in their original language, but the Nuovo Olimpia at Via in Lucina 16g (T 06 6861 1068), off Via del Corso, and Cinema Fiamma at Via L. Bissolati 43 near Piazza Barberini (T 06 485 526) are exceptions. Tickets cost around €7; W www.romereview.com has programme details.

Crime

To call the police, dial T 113. Both the police (Polizia Statale) and the carabinieri (who wear military-style uniforms) have offices in Termini. Otherwise, the questura (main police office) is at Via San Vitale 15, off Via Nazionale; report any thefts to the police here.

Dress

The rules for visiting churches are much as they are all over Italy: dress modestly, which usually means no shorts, short skirts or bare shoulders.

Electricity

220 volts. Both UK and US adaptors are available to buy in Italy, but the latter can be expensive.

Embassies and consulates

Australia Via Bosio 5 T 06 852 721; **Canada** Via Zara 30 T 06 85444 3937; **Ireland** Villa Spada, Via G. Medici T 06 585 2381; **New Zealand** Via Clitunno 44 T 06 853 7501; **UK** Via XX Settembre 80a T 06 4220 0001; **US** Via Veneto 121 T 06 46 741.

Health

Doctors in Italy, Via Frattina 48 (T 06 679 0695, W doctorsinitaly .com; Mon–Fri 10am–8pm), and Aventino 38, Viale Aventino 38 (T 06 5728 9413, W aventino38.it; Mon–Fri 8.30am–7.30pm), are central medical practices with English-speaking doctors; Absolute Dentistry, Via G. Pisanelli 3, has a 24-hour emergency service (T 06 3600 3837).

The most central hospitals with emergency facilities are: Fatebenefratelli, Isola Tiberina (T 06 68371); Rome American Hospital, Via E. Longoni 69 (T 06 22 551), a private multi-speciality hospital with bilingual staff and a 24hr emergency line; San Giovanni at Via A. Aradam 9 (T 06 77051); Santo Spirito at Lungotevere in Sassia 1, near the Vatican (T 6 68 351).

The following pharmacies are open 24hr, year-round: Internazionale, Piazza Barberini 49 T 06 487 1195, Piram, Via Nazionale 228 T 06 488 0754. The pharmacies in Termini station, including Farmacia Cristo Re on the lower level (T 06 488 0776), are open 7.30am–10pm.

Emergencies

For the fire brigade, police or ambulance, call T 113.

Internet

Many of Rome's cafés and bars, and most of its hotels, offer free wi-fi. If you need an internet café, try AntiCafé at Via Veio 4b, near Piazza di San Giovanni in Laterano (Mon–Fri 9am–10pm, Sat & Sun 10am–10pm), where free internet, food and drink, books and board games are included in the hourly rate (€4 for the first hour); or Yex, Piazza Sant'Andrea della Valle 1 (daily 10am–8pm). There are also many internet cafés around Termini station. By law, internet cafés will ask you to show ID such as a passport before allowing you to access the internet. Free wireless hotspots in the city include the Circus Maximus, Villa Borghese, Piazza Navona, Largo Argentina, Trevi Fountain and the Spanish Steps. See W romawireless .com for other locations.

Left luggage

Termini station (daily 6am–11pm; €6 per piece for 5hr, then €0.90 for the sixth to the twelfth hour, then €0.40/hr; T 06 474 4777).

Lost property

For lost property call T 06 6769 3214 (Mon, Tues, Wed & Fri 8.30am–1pm, Thurs 8.30am–5pm); the office is at Circonvallazione Ostiense 191 (Garbatella Metro).

Money

You'll find ATMs throughout the city. Nearly all hotels accept credit cards, though many restaurants are still cash-only. To exchange money, post offices and banks tend to offer the best rates. Banking hours are normally Monday to Friday from 8.30am until 1.30pm, and then for an hour in the afternoon (usually between 2.30 and 4pm). Post offices will exchange American Express travellers' cheques and cash commission-free. For lost or stolen cards, call: American Express T 800 917 8047; MasterCard T 870 866; Visa T 800 819014.

Opening hours

Most museums and galleries are closed on Mondays. Opening hours for state-run museums are generally from 9am until 7pm, Tuesday to Sunday. Most other museums roughly follow this pattern too, although are likely to close for a couple of hours in the afternoon, and have shorter opening hours in winter. Some museums run late-night openings in summer (till 10pm or later Tues–Sat, or 8pm on Sun).

Opening times of ancient sites are more flexible: most are open daily, including Sunday, from 8.30am until the evening – usually one hour before sunset. In winter, times are drastically cut; 4pm is a common closing time.

Most major churches open early, at around 7am or 8am, and close around noon, opening up again at 4pm and closing at 6pm or 7pm.

Phones

If you have a GSM, dual- or tri-band phone which can be unlocked, consider investing in an Italian SIM card, which can be bought for about €10 from Italian providers TIM, Wind, Tre or Vodafone; ask for a "SIM prepagato". To use public telephones, you can buy telephone cards (*carta telefonica*) from *tabacchi* and newsstands in denominations of €3 and €5. You always need to dial the local code; T 06 is the code for Rome and around. Numbers beginning T 800 are free, T 170 will get you through to an English-speaking operator, T 892 412 to international directory enquiries. Any numbers that start with a 3 are mobile numbers. To make long-distance calls, it's cheaper to buy one of the international calling cards, also available from *tabacchi* for upwards of €5. You can make international reversed-charge or collect calls (*chiamata con addebito destinatario*) by dialling T 170 and following the recorded instructions.

Post offices

The main post office is at Piazza San Silvestro 12 (T 06 6973 7216, Mon–Fri 8.20am–7.05pm, Sat 8.20am–12.35pm).

Smoking

Smoking is banned in all public indoor spaces in Italy, including restaurants, bars and clubs.

Time

Rome is one hour ahead of GMT, six hours ahead of Eastern Standard Time, and nine hours ahead of Pacific Standard Time in North America.

Tourist information and passes

There are tourist information booths in Terminal 2 at Fiumicino (daily 9am–6.30pm; T 06 0608), in

Arrivals Hall at Ciampino airport (daily 9am–5.30pm), in Termini station at Via Giolitti 34 (daily 8am–6.45pm; T 06 0608), at Via di San Basilio 51 (daily 9am–7pm) and on the Via dei Fori Imperiali (daily 9.30am–7pm; T 06 0608) although you can also go to **Enjoy Rome** (Via Marghera 8a; Mon–Fri 9am–5.30pm, Sat 8.30am–2pm; T 06 445 1843, W enjoyrome.com), an unofficial but reliable source of information whose English-speaking staff also run a free accommodation-finding service, organize walking and bus tours and can arrange shuttles to the airports. There are also green **information kiosks** (PIT; generally open 9.30am–7pm) near key locations around the city, such as Via Nazionale (Palazzo delle Esposizioni), Piazza Navona (Piazza delle Cinque Lune), Castel Sant'Angelo (Via della Conciliazione 4) and Trastevere (Piazza Sonnino). Rome's tourist information line T 060608 is open daily 9am–9pm; calls are charged at the local rate. The websites W turismoroma.it and W 060608.it are also useful.

For what's-on information, check out W romeing.it or the expat monthly, *Wanted in Rome* (€1; W wantedinrome.com), which is written entirely in English and is also useful if you're looking for an apartment or work. If you understand a bit of Italian, the daily arts pages of the Rome newspaper, *Il Messaggero*, lists movies, plays and major musical events. Newspaper *La Repubblica* includes the "TrovaRoma" section in its Thursday edition, another handy guide to current offerings.

Rome's main museum and transport pass is the **Roma Pass** (W romapass.it). It covers most places you'll want to visit (the notable exception being the Vatican Museums). Available from all museums in the circuit, from tourist information kiosks and online, it costs €36 (valid for three days), or €28 (valid for two days). It entitles you to free admission to the first two participating museums or archeological sites visited, and discounts on visits elsewhere, plus full access to public transport for three days. It also allows you to skip the queue at sights such as the Colosseum and Forum – a huge bonus. The Vatican's **Omnia Card** (W omniakit.org) gives free, fast-track access to the Vatican Museums, St Peter's and the Mamertine Prison, as well as a free Roma Pass; you also get a free trip on the Roma Cristiana bus tour (see p.180). However, it's expensive (€108; valid 72hr), so you're paying a lot to jump the queues, and for the Vatican you can do this anyway simply by booking online for €20. The **Archeologia Card** (€23; valid seven days) covers the Colosseum, Roman Forum, Palatine Hill, Baths of Caracalla, Villa dei Quintili, Tomb of Cecilia Metella and Museo Nazionale Romano. Much of Rome's ancient sculpture has been gathered into the Museo Nazionale Romano, operating in four main sites: Palazzo Massimo, the Terme di Diocleziano, the Crypta Balbi and Palazzo Altemps. You can buy a ticket (at each branch) that grants entry to all for just €7 (valid 3 days). The Colosseum, Roman Forum and Palatine Hill are visitable on a combined ticket.

Travellers with disabilities

Although changes are in the works, Rome can be quite a challenge for those with disabilities. The city's hills, cobbles and steps can make getting around in a wheelchair a challenge, and little of the public transport network is accessible. See W sagetraveling.com for helpful tips on visiting the city. The state-funded Roma Per Tutti service (W www.romapertutti.it; in Italian only) provides information on accessible sights and transport. See also W accessibleitaly.com for information on accessibility and tours.

Festivals and events

Public holidays are denoted by (PH); many sights and shops, and some bars and restaurants close.

NEW YEAR'S DAY (PH)

Jan 1

EPIPHANY (PH)

Jan 6

La Befana, or Epiphany, marks the end of a Christmas fair that fills Piazza Navona from mid-December.

CARNEVALE

Mid-Feb 10 days

Roman kids dress up and are paraded round the city by their proud parents, and clubs put on themed nights. Look out for the carnival delicacies sold throughout the city: *frappe* (deep-fried pastry strips) and *castagnole* (bite-sized pastries).

ROME MARATHON

Sunday in mid-March to early April www.maratonadiroma.it

Thousands of runners take to the streets for Rome's annual marathon; the course takes in many of the major sights en route.

EASTER

During Holy Week, Catholics from across the world descend on Rome to witness the pope's address. On Good Friday, a solemn procession moves from the Colosseum to the Capitoline Hill, while on Easter Sunday the main event is the pope's blessing in St Peter's Square.

PASQUETTA (PH)

Easter Monday

Many Romans head out of town, traditionally for a picnic in the countryside.

NATALE DI ROMA

April 21

A spectacular fireworks display set off from the Campidoglio marks Rome's birthday.

FESTA DELLA PRIMAVERA

Late April

The Spanish Steps are lined with thousands of beautiful blooms.

LIBERATION DAY (PH)

April 25

LABOUR DAY (PH)

May 1

"Primo Maggio" is celebrated with a free rock concert in Piazza San Giovanni.

ROME LITERATURE FESTIVAL

Late May–June www.festivaldelleletterature.it

Readings by well-known authors in various atmospheric locations, including the Campidoglio.

DAY OF THE REPUBLIC

June 2

The day is marked with a military parade along Via dei Fori Imperiali, and the gardens of the Quirinale palace are open to the public.

ESTATE ROMANA

Early June–late Sept

Rome's summer-long cultural extravaganza includes all sorts of events, from open-air film screenings to concerts in atmospheric surroundings. Many events are free; ask at the tourist office for information.

ISOLA DEL CINEMA

Mid-June to early Sept Ⓦisoladelcinema.com

A summertime film festival screening films nightly in the atmospheric setting of the Isola Tiberina, with lots of food stalls too.

ROMA INCONTRA IL MONDO

Mid-June to mid-Sept Ⓦwww.villaada.org

An eclectic programme of pop, rock and indie concerts takes place in Villa Ada. Tickets €5–15.

TEATRO DELL'OPERA

Late June to mid-Aug Ⓦwww.operaroma.it

Teatro dell'Opera's summer season takes place in the floodlit setting of the Baths of Caracalla.

CONCERTI DEL TEMPIETTO

July–mid-Sept Ⓦwww.tempietto.it

Classical concerts with the dramatic backdrop of the ancient Roman Teatro di Marcello.

FESTA DE' NOANTRI

Mid-July Ⓦwww.festadenoantri.it

Two weeks of street performances and events in Trastevere culminate in a huge fireworks display.

FESTA DELLE CATENE

Aug 1

The chains of St Peter are displayed during a special Mass in the church of San Pietro in Vincoli.

FESTA DELLA MADONNA DELLA NEVE

Aug 5

The miracle of a summer snowfall (see p.93) is remembered in the basilica of Santa Maria Maggiore with a shower of white petals on the congregation.

FERRAGOSTO (PH)

August 15

On the Feast of the Assumption of the Virgin, Rome empties as locals in search of cooling breezes head for the sea and mountains.

ROMAEUROPA FESTIVAL

Late Sept to early Dec Ⓦwww.romaeuropa.net

Rome's performing arts festival showcases international talents in music, theatre and dance, in venues around town.

ROME INTERNATIONAL FILM FESTIVAL

Ten days mid-Oct Ⓦwww.romacinemafest.it

Rome's film festival always draws Hollywood talent. The hub of the festival is Rome's Auditorium, but there are venues across town.

OGNISSANTI (PH)

Nov 1

On All Souls' Day, Romans visit family graves in the Verano cemetery in San Lorenzo.

IMMACOLATA CONCEZIONE (PH)

Dec 8

In honour of the Immaculate Conception of the Blessed Virgin Mary, a religious ceremony takes place in the Piazza di Spagna, often attended by the pope.

NATALE / SANTO STEFANO (PH)

Dec 25/Dec 26

NEW YEAR'S EVE/CAPODANNO

Dec 31

New Year's Eve sees a free concert in the Circus Maximus, including a fireworks display.

Chronology

9th century BC > Iron Age village founded on the Palatine Hill.

753 BC > Romulus kills Remus and becomes the city's first ruler.

616–579 BC > Tarquinius Priscus is Rome's first Etruscan king.

509 BC > Tarquinius Superbus, the last Etruscan king, is deposed and the Roman Republic is established.

264–146 BC > Punic Wars against Carthage.

87 BC > Civil war breaks out between Marius and Sulla.

82 BC > Sulla becomes dictator of Rome.

65–63 BC > Marius' nephew, Julius Caesar, establishes a formidable military reputation.

60 BC > Triumvirate of Julius Caesar, Crassus and Pompey rules Rome.

58–51 BC > Caesar colonizes Gaul.

49–45 BC > Caesar marches on Rome, sparking off a civil war between him and Pompey.

44 BC > Caesar is assassinated in Pompey's Theatre on March 15.

43 BC > Leadership is assumed by a triumvirate of Antony, Octavian and Lepidus.

40 BC > Antony marries Octavian's sister, Octavia.

31 BC > Octavian defeats Antony and Cleopatra at the Battle of Actium.

27 BC > Octavian becomes sole ruler as Augustus.

14 AD > Tiberius, Augustus' stepson, assumes power and marries Augustus' daughter, Julia, who gives birth to Caligula, the next emperor.

41 AD > Caligula is assassinated after four years in power. His uncle, Claudius, proves to be a wiser successor.

54 AD > The reign of Claudius' stepson, Nero, is marred by corruption and excess.

69 AD > Emperor Vespasian restores order to Rome and builds the Colosseum in the grounds of Nero's Domus Aurea.

81 AD > Vespasian's son Titus is succeeded by Domitian, who builds the stadium that forms the foundations of today's Piazza Navona.

98 AD > Emperor Trajan expands the empire and Rome grows to a population of around a million.

117 > Trajan is succeeded by Hadrian, a wise and resourceful emperor, who ruled over the empire's golden age.

138–192 > Marcus Aurelius continues to rule a stable city and a rich empire but the Antonine line fizzles out when his son, Commodus, is strangled.

193 > Septimius Severus becomes the first emperor of the Severan dynasty.

211 > Severus' son, Caracalla, murders his brother and assumes power for himself.

275 > The emperor Aurelian builds a wall around the city to keep it safe from invaders.

284 > Diocletian stabilizes Rome and divides the empire into east and west.

306 > Constantine converts to Christianity and defeats his rival Maxentius to claim the Western Empire.

325 > Constantine shifts the seat of power east to Byzantium, renaming it Constantinople.

410 > Rome is captured by the Visigoths, the first time a foreign invader has held the city for 800 years.

5th century > The city declines to a population of around 30,000.

590 > Gregory I becomes pope, revitalizing the city with new basilicas and converting ancient Roman structures like the Pantheon and the Castel Sant'Angelo.

800 > Charlemagne visits Rome and is crowned ruler of the Holy Roman Empire.

850–1300 > Rome is the focus of struggles between the papacy, Holy Roman emperors and its own aristocracy.

1305 > Clement V transfers the papal court to Avignon, France.

1347 > Cola di Rienzo seizes power and re-establishes Rome's Republic for seven years.

1417 > Martin V consolidates papal power in Rome.

1475 > Pope Sixtus IV commissions the Sistine Chapel.

1503 > Julius II becomes pope and commissions frescoes for the Sistine Chapel from Michelangelo.

1513 > Leo X continues Julius's role as patron of the city's greatest artists and architects.

1527 > Holy Roman Emperor Charles V captures Rome and Clement VII flees to the Castel Sant'Angelo.

1534 > Alessandro Farnese is elected pope as Paul III and Michelangelo completes his Sistine Chapel painting of the *Last Judgement*.

1585 > Sixtus V undertakes widespread construction, creating grand vistas and squares.

1605 > St Peter's is completed under the Borghese pope, Paul V.

1623 > Urban VIII ascends the papal throne and becomes the greatest patron of the Baroque's most dominant figure, Gianlorenzo Bernini.

1700 > The city's population is now 150,000, and Rome becomes an essential stop on any traveller's Grand Tour.

1798 > French forces commanded by Napoleon occupy the city; Pius VI is taken as a prisoner to France.

1815 > Papal rule is restored under Pius VII.

1849 > Giuseppe Mazzini forces Pope Pius IX to leave Rome but the papacy is restored four months later by Napoleon III.

1859–64 > Unification forces gather strength and Florence becomes the capital of the new kingdom of Italy.

1870 > Italian forces take Rome and declare the city the capital of the new state under Vittorio Emanuele II. Pope Pius IX is confined to the Vatican.

1922–42 > Mussolini oversees the construction of numerous public works.

1929 > The Lateran Pact is signed by Italy and the Vatican, recognizing the sovereignty of the Vatican City.

1946 > King Vittorio Emanuele III is forced to abdicate and a republic is declared under Alcide de Gasperi.

1960 > Fellini releases *La Dolce Vita*, a film that would define the Sixties in Rome.

1970s > The *anni piombi*, or "years of lead", when Rome became a focus for terrorism, culminating in the murder of politician Aldo Moro.

1990s > Corruption scandals lead to a series of trials and the reconfiguration of the entire Italian political landscape.

2001 > Walter Veltroni is elected mayor of Rome, and oversees a series of prestigious public works.

2005 > Pope John Paul II is succeeded by Josef Ratzinger as Pope Benedict XVI.

2012 > Ignazio Marino becomes mayor of Rome.

2013 > Following the resignation of Pope Benedict XVI, Pope Francis, the first pope from the Americas, is elected. Also this year, after years of scandal, Prime Minister Silvio Berlusconi resigns.

2014 > Two modern-day popes, John Paul II and John XXIII, are canonized at St Peter's, drawing around a million pilgrims from all over the world.

2014 > A huge corruption scandal, implicating top-level politicians and a mafia-like gang, rocks Rome.

2016 > Pope Francis calls an extraordinary Jubilee year: the Holy Year of Mercy. Also this year, Rome's new mayor, Virginia Raggi of the anti-establishment Five Star Movement, becomes the first woman ever to run the capital.

Italian

Speaking some **Italian**, however tentatively, can mark you out from the hordes of tourists in Rome, and having a little more can open up the city no end. What follows is a brief pronunciation guide, some useful words and phrases, and a food and drink glossary. For more detail, *Italian: The Rough Guide Phrasebook* has a huge and accessible vocabulary, a detailed menu reader and conversational examples to get you through most situations.

Pronunciation

Italian **pronunciation** is very simple – generally words are stressed on the penultimate syllable unless an accent (' or ´) denotes otherwise. The only difficulties you're likely to encounter are the few consonants that are different from English:

c before e or i is pronounced as in **ch**urch, while **ch** before the same vowels is hard, as in **c**at.

The same goes with **g** – soft before e or i, as in **g**eranium; hard before h, as in **g**arlic.

sci or **sce** are pronounced as in **sh**eet and **sh**elter respectively.

gn has the ni sound of o**ni**on.

gl in Italian is softened to a sound similar to lyi, as in sta**lli**on.

h is not aspirated, as in **h**onour.

Words and phrases

BASICS

good morning	buongiorno
good afternoon/ evening	buonasera
good night	buonanotte
hello/goodbye	ciao (informal; to strangers use phrases above)
goodbye	arrivederci
yes	si
no	no
please	per favore
thank you (very much)	grazie (molte/mille grazie)
you're welcome	prego
all right/OK	va bene
how are you? (informal/formal)	come stai/sta?
I'm fine	bene
Do you speak English?	parla inglese?
I don't understand	non ho capito
I don't know	non lo so
excuse me (to get attention)	mi scusi
excuse me (in a crowd)	permesso
I'm sorry	mi dispiace
I'm here on holiday	sono qui in vacanza
I'm English	sono inglese
Scottish	scozzese
Welsh	gallese
Irish	irlandese
American (m/f)	americano/a
Australian (m/f)	australiano/a
a New Zealander	neozelandese
today	oggi
tomorrow	domani
day after tomorrow	dopodomani
yesterday	ieri
now	adesso
later	più tardi
tonight	stasera
morning	mattina
afternoon	pomeriggio
evening	sera
wait!	aspetta!
let's go!	andiamo!
here/there	qui/là
good/bad	buono/cattivo
big/small	grande/piccolo
cheap/expensive	economico/caro
early/late	presto/tardi
hot/cold	caldo/freddo
near/far	vicino/lontano
quickly/slowly	velocemente/ lentamente
with/without	con/senza
more/less	più/meno
enough, no more	basta
Mr/Mrs/Miss	signore/signora/ signorina

QUESTIONS AND DIRECTIONS

where?	dove?
Where is/where are...?	Dov'è/Dove sono ... ?
How do I get to ... ?	Per arrivare a ... ?
turn left/right	giri a sinistra/destra
go straight on	vai sempre diritto
How far is it to ... ?	Quant'è lontano a... ?
What time does it open/close?	A che ora apre/ chiude?
What time is it?	Che ore sono?
when?	quando?
what? (what is it?)	cosa? (cos'è?)
How much/many?	Quanto/Quanti?
why?	perché?
It is/there is (is it/is there ...)?	C'è ... ?
How much does it/ they cost?	Quanto costa/ costano?
How do you say it in Italian?	Come si dice in italiano?

TRANSPORT

bus station	autostazione
train station	stazione ferroviaria
a ticket to ...	un biglietto a ...
one-way/return	solo andata/andata e ritorno
Can you tell me when to get off?	Mi può dire dove scendere?
What time does it leave/arrive?	A che ora parte/ arriva?
Where does it leave from?	Da dove parte?

SIGNS

aperto	open
bagno/gabinetto	WC/bathroom
cassa	cash desk
chiuso	closed
chiuso per ferie	closed for holidays
chiuso per restauro	closed for restoration
entrata	entrance
ingresso libero	free entry
signori/signore	gentlemen/ladies
spingere	push
tirare	pull
uscita	exit
vietato fumare	no smoking

ACCOMMODATION

hotel	albergo
hostel	ostello
I'd like to book a room	Vorrei prenotare una camera
Is there a hotel nearby?	C'è un albergo qui vicino?
I have a booking	Ho una prenotazione
Do you have a room ...	Avete una camera
for one/two night/s	per una/due notte/i
for one/two week/s	per una/due settimana/e
with a double bed	con un letto matrimoniale
with twin beds	con due letti
with a shower/ bath	con doccia/ bagno
with a balcony	con balcone
How much is it?	Quanto costa?
It's expensive	È caro
Is breakfast included?	È compresa la colazione?
Do you have anything cheaper?	Ha qualcosa che costa di meno?
Full/half board	Pensione completa/ mezza pensione
Can I see the room?	Posso vedere la camera?
I'll take it	La prendo

NUMBERS

uno	1
due	2
tre	3
quattro	4
cinque	5
sei	6
sette	7
otto	8
nove	9
dieci	10
undici	11
dodici	12
tredici	13
quattordici	14
quindici	15
sedici	16
diciassette	17

diciotto	18
diciannove	19
venti	20
ventuno	21
ventidue	22
trenta	30
quaranta	40
cinquanta	50
sessanta	60
settanta	70
ottanta	80
novanta	90
cento	100
centuno	101
centodieci	110
duecento	200
cinquecento	500
mille	1000
cinquemila	5000
diecimila	10,000

Food and drink terms

BASICS AND SNACKS

aceto	vinegar
aglio	garlic
biscotti	biscuits
burro	butter
caramelle	sweets
cioccolato	chocolate
formaggio	cheese
frittata	omelette
marmellata	jam
olio	oil
olive	olives
pane	bread
pepe	pepper
riso	rice
sale	salt
uova	eggs
zucchero	sugar
zuppa	soup

STARTERS (ANTIPASTI) AND FRIED SNACKS (FRITTI)

antipasto misto mixed cold meats and cheese (and a selection of other things in this list)

arancini fried rice balls with mozzarella and tomato

caponata mixed aubergine, olives, tomatoes and celery

caprese tomato and mozzarella salad

insalata di mare seafood salad

insalata di riso rice salad

melanzane alla parmigiana layers of aubergine, tomato and parmesan

mortadella salami-type cured meat

pancetta bacon

peperonata grilled green, red or yellow peppers stewed in olive oil

pomodori ripieni stuffed tomatoes

prosciutto ham

salame salami

supplì fried rice balls with mozzarella

SOUP (ZUPPA)

brodo clear broth

minestrina any light soup

minestrone thick vegetable soup

pasta e fagioli pasta soup with beans

pastina in brodo pasta in clear broth

stracciatella broth with egg

PASTA

bucatini thick, hollow spaghetti-type pasta.

cannelloni large, stuffed pasta tubes

farfalle literally "bow"- shaped pasta; the word also means "butterflies"

fettuccine flat ribbon egg pasta

paccheri large tubes of pasta

pasta al forno pasta baked with minced meat, eggs, tomato and cheese

penne tubed pasta

rigatoni Large, curved and ridged tubes of pasta – bigger than penne but smaller than paccheri

spaghettini thin spaghetti

strozzapreti literally "strangled priests" – twisted flat noodles

tagliatelle flat ribbon egg noodles, slightly thinner than fettuccine

vermicelli thin strands of pasta often served in soup – literally "little worms"

PASTA SAUCES

aglio e olio with garlic and oil

amatriciana with tomato and *guanciale* (similar to bacon)

arrabbiata ("angry") spicy tomato sauce, with chillies

alla carbonara with beaten egg, pan-fried *guanciale* or bacon, and pecorino cheese

alla gricia with pecorino and *guanciale*

cacio e pepe with pecorino and ground black pepper

con vongole with clams

panna cream

parmigiano parmesan

pasta alla pajata with calf's intestines – a very Roman dish

peperoncino chilli

pomodoro tomato

puttanesca ("whorish") with tomato, anchovy, olive oil and oregano

ragù (or Bolognese) meat sauce

MEAT (CARNE)

abbacchio milk-fed lamb roasted with rosemary and garlic

agnello lamb

bistecca steak

carpaccio slices of raw beef

cervello brain, usually calves'

cinghiale wild boar

coda alla vaccinara oxtail stewed in a rich sauce of tomato and celery

coniglio rabbit

coratella lamb's heart, liver, lungs and spleen cooked in olive oil with lots of black pepper and onions

costolette cutlet, chop

fegato liver

guanciale unsmoked bacon made from pigs' cheeks

maiale pork

manzo beef

milza spleen – sometimes served as a pâté on toasted bread

ossobuco shin of veal

pajata the intestines of a unweaned calf

pancetta bacon

pollo chicken

polpette meatballs

porchetta pork stuffed with herbs and roasted on a spit

rognoni kidneys

salsiccia sausage

saltimbocca alla romana veal cooked with a slice of prosciutto and sage on top, served plain or with a Marsala sauce

scottadito grilled lamb chops, eaten with the fingers

spezzatino stew

trippa tripe

vitello veal

FISH (PESCE) AND SHELLFISH (CROSTACEI)

acciughe anchovies

anguilla eel

aragosta lobster

baccalà cod, best eaten Jewish-style, deep-fried

calamari squid

cozze mussels

dentice sea bream

gamberetti shrimps

gamberi prawns

granchio crab

merluzzo cod

ostriche oysters

pesce spada swordfish

polpo octopus

rospo monkfish

sampiero John Dory

sarde sardines

sogliola sole

tonno tuna

trota trout

vongole clams

VEGETABLES (CONTORNI) AND SALAD (INSALATA)

carciofi... artichokes

...alla romana stuffed with garlic, mint and parsley and stewed in wine

...alla guidia flattened and deep fried in olive oil

carciofini artichoke hearts

cavolfiore cauliflower

cavolo cabbage

cipolla onion

fagioli beans

fagiolini green beans

fiori di zucca batter-fried courgette (zucchini) blossom stuffed with mozzarella and sometimes a sliver of marinated anchovy

finocchio fennel

funghi mushrooms
insalata verde /mista green/mixed salad
melanzane aubergine (eggplant)
patate potatoes
peperoni peppers
piselli peas
pomodori tomatoes
radicchio red salad leaves
spinaci spinach

COOKING TERMS

ai ferri grilled without oil
al dente firm, not overcooked
al forno baked
al sangue rare
alla brace barbecued
alla griglia grilled
alla milanese fried in egg and breadcrumbs
alla pizzaiola cooked with tomato sauce
allo spiedo on the spit
arrosto roast
ben cotto well done
bollito/lesso boiled
cotto cooked (not raw)
crudo raw
fritto fried
in umido stewed
ripieno stuffed
stracotto braised, stewed

CHEESE (FORMAGGI)

dolcelatte creamy blue cheese
fontina northern Italian cheese
pecorino strong, hard sheep's cheese
provola/provolone smooth, round mild cheese, made from buffalo's or sheep's milk, sometimes smoked

FRUIT (FRUTTA) AND NUTS (NOCI)

ananas pineapple
anguria/cocomero watermelon
arance oranges
banane bananas
ciliegie cherries
fichi figs
fichi d'India prickly pears
fragole strawberries
limone lemon
mandorle almonds
mele apples
melone melon
pere pears
pesche peaches
pinoli pine nuts
uva grapes

DESSERTS (DOLCI)

cassata ice-cream cake with candied fruit
crostata pastry tart with fruit, chocolate or ricotta topping
gelato ice cream
macedonia fruit salad
torta cake, tart
zabaglione dessert made with eggs, sugar and Marsala wine
zuppa inglese trifle

DRINKS (BEVANDE)

acqua minerale mineral water
acqua naturale/frizzante still/sparkling water
acqua del rubinetto tap water
bicchiere glass
birra beer
bottiglia bottle
caffè coffee
cioccolato caldo hot chocolate
ghiaccio ice
granita iced drink, with coffee or fruit
latte milk
limonata lemonade
spremuta fresh fruit juice
succo concentrated fruit juice with sugar
tè tea
vino wine
vino rosso/bianco/rosato red/white/rose wine
vino secco/dolce dry/sweet wine
litro litre
mezzo half
quarto quarter
salute! cheers!

PUBLISHING INFORMATION

This fourth edition published February 2017 by **Rough Guides Ltd**
80 Strand, London WC2R 0RL
11, Community Centre, Panchsheel Park, New Delhi 110017, India
Distributed by Penguin Random House
Penguin Books Ltd, 80 Strand, London WC2R 0RL
Penguin Group (USA) 345 Hudson Street, NY 10014, USA
Penguin Group (Australia) 250 Camberwell Road, Camberwell, Victoria 3124, Australia
Penguin Group (NZ) 67 Apollo Drive, Mairangi Bay, Auckland 1310, New Zealand
Penguin Group (South Africa) Block D, Rosebank Office Park, 181 Jan Smuts Avenue, Parktown North, Gauteng, South Africa 2193
Rough Guides is represented in Canada by
DK Canada 320 Front Street West, Suite 1400, Toronto, Ontario M5V 3B6
Typeset in Minion and Din to an original design by Henry Iles and Dan May.
Printed and bound in South China

208pp includes index
A catalogue record for this book is available from the British Library
ISBN 978-0-24125-618-3

1 3 5 7 9 8 6 4 2

ROUGH GUIDES CREDITS

Editor: Neil McQuillian
Layout: Jessica Subramanian
Cartography: Katie Bennett
Picture editor: Phoebe Lowndes
Photographers: James McConnachie, Natascha Sturny
Proofreader: Jennifer Speake
Managing editor: Monica Woods
Production: Jimmy Lao
Cover photo research: Aude Vauconsant
Editorial assistant: Freya Godfrey
Senior DTP coordinator: Dan May
Publishing director: Georgina Dee

THE AUTHOR

Natasha Foges packed her bags and moved to Rome on a whim, and stayed for four years. Now based in London, she misses the food, the sun and the scooter rides, but escapes back to Rome as often as she can to revisit old haunts and overindulge on ice cream.

ACKNOWLEDGEMENTS

Natasha Foges would like to thank Neil McQuillian for a remarkably smooth edit, and Katie Bennett for her work on the maps; Lorenzo Zanasi for persevering with the Palatine; Richard, Chiara, Lesley and Antonio, essential companions on a Roman night out; and Will and Joe for keeping the home fires burning.

HELP US UPDATE

We've gone to a lot of effort to ensure that the fourth edition of the **Pocket Rough Guide Rome** is accurate and up-to-date. However, things change – places get "discovered", opening hours are notoriously fickle, restaurants and rooms raise prices or lower standards. If you feel we've got it wrong or left something out, we'd like to know, and if you can remember the address, the price, the hours, the phone number, so much the better.

Please send your comments with the subject line "**Pocket Rough Guide Rome Update**" to mail@roughguides.com. We'll credit all contributions and send a copy of the next edition (or any other Rough Guide if you prefer) for the very best emails.

Find travel information, read inspiring features and book your trip at roughguides.com.

PHOTO CREDITS

All photos © Rough Guides except the following:
(Key: t-top; c-centre; b-bottom; l-left; r-right)

1 Dreamstime.com: Luciano Mortula
2 Alamy Stock Photo: Paul Thompson
4 Alamy Stock Photo: Vito Arcomano
10 Mondo Arancina
11 SuperStock: Marco Scataglini
12–13 SuperStock: David Lorente
19 Metamorfosi
20 Alamy Stock Photo: Andy Parker
21 Boschetto Tre (b)
25 Getty Images: Gonzalo Azumendi (tr). **SuperStock:** Christian Handl (tl)
27 Alamy Stock Photo: Fine Art Images / Heritage Image Partnership Ltd (b); **Eye Ubiquitous** (tr)
38 Getty Images: Jean-Pierre Lescourret
43 Alamy Stock Photo: Vito Arcomano
45 Alamy Stock Photo: Susan Wright
48 Alamy Stock Photo: Andrea Magugliani
54 4Corners: SIME / Sandra Raccanello
59 Roscioli
65 Alamy Stock Photo: Gunter Kirsch
66 Dreamstime.com: Scaliger
75 AWL Images: Francesco Lacobelli
78 Alamy Stock Photo: Albert Knapp
81 Dreamstime.com: Lornet
83 Alamy Stock Photo: Vito Arcomano
86 SuperStock: Marco Cristofori
87 Gusto
90 Recafé
91 Stravinskij Bar
93 Alamy Stock Photo: Stuart Black
96 Alamy Stock Photo: Adam Eastland Art + Architecture
99 Alamy Stock Photo: AGTravel
101 Boschetto Tre
102 Nocci Dal 1974
105 Il Tiaso
108 Alamy Stock Photo: National Geographic Creative
111 Photoshot: Manousos Daskalogiannis
113 Alamy Stock Photo: Glyn Thomas
117 4Corners: SIME / Massimo Pignatelli
129 Alamy Stock Photo: imageBROKER
130 Alamy Stock Photo: Susan Wright
131 Ristorante Antico Arco
132 Glass Hostaria
135 Bridgeman Images
141 Alamy Stock Photo: Fabrizio Troiani
159 Alamy Stock Photo: Universal Images Group North America LLC / DeAgostini / DEA / S. VANNINI
161 Alamy Stock Photo: Art Directors / Jim Ringland

Front cover and spine: *Fiat 850 in Trastevere, Rome* **Robert Harding Picture Library:** Rainer Martini

Back cover: *Piazza Navona, Fontana dei Quattro Fiumi* **AWL Images:** Travel Pix Collection

Index

Maps are marked in **bold**.

A

B

C

I

J

K

L

M

N

O

P

Q

R

S

T

V

W

Z